THEATRE
as
HUMAN ACTION

THEATRE as HUMAN ACTION

An Introduction to Theatre Arts

THIRD EDITION

Thomas S. Hischak

ROWMAN & LITTLEFIELD
Lanham • Boulder • New York • London

Senior Acquisitions Editor: Stephen Ryan
Assistant Editor: Deni Remsberg
Production Editor: Jessica McCleary
Interior Designer: Susan Ramundo

Credits and acknowledgments for material borrowed from other sources, and reproduced with permission, appear on the appropriate page within the text.

Published by Rowman & Littlefield
An imprint of The Rowman & Littlefield Publishing Group, Inc.
4501 Forbes Boulevard, Suite 200, Lanham, Maryland 20706
www.rowman.com

6 Tinworth Street, London, SE11 5AL, United Kingdom

Copyright © 2019 by The Rowman & Littlefield Publishing Group, Inc.

All rights reserved. No part of this book may be reproduced in any form or by any electronic or mechanical means, including information storage and retrieval systems, without written permission from the publisher, except by a reviewer who may quote passages in a review.

British Library Cataloguing in Publication Information Available

Library of Congress Cataloging-in-Publication Data

Names: Hischak, Thomas S., author.
Title: Theatre as human action : an introduction to theatre arts / Thomas S. Hischak.
Description: Third edition. | Lanham : Rowman & Littlefield, [2019] | Includes bibliographical references and index.
Identifiers: LCCN 2018057207 (print) | LCCN 2018059215 (ebook) | ISBN 9781538126431 (electronic) | ISBN 9781538126417 (cloth : alk. paper) | ISBN 9781538126424 (paperback : alk. paper)
Subjects: LCSH: Drama. | Theater.
Classification: LCC PN1655 (ebook) | LCC PN1655 .H57 2019 (print) | DDC 792—dc23
LC record available at https://lccn.loc.gov/2018057207

∞™ The paper used in this publication meets the minimum requirements of American National Standard for Information Sciences—Permanence of Paper for Printed Library Materials, ANSI/NISO Z39.48-1992.

Printed in the United States of America

3 1327 00671 5486

Once again, for Brian O'Donnell, SJ

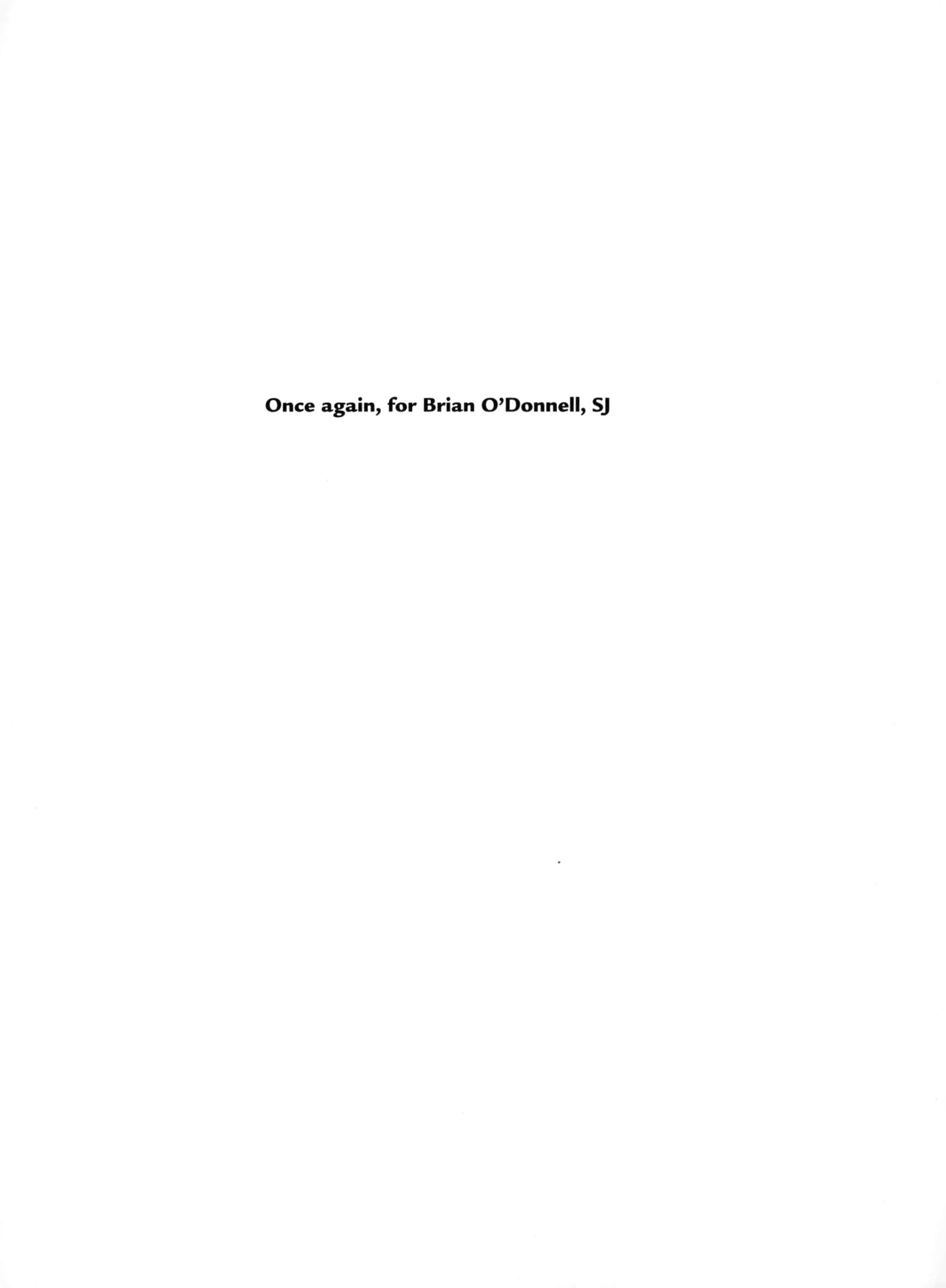

BRIEF CONTENTS

About the Author xv
Preface to the Third Edition xvii
Introduction xix

1 The Theatre 1
2 The Play 23
3 The Playwright 43
4 The Play Performers: The Actors 73
5 The Play Makers I: The Director and the Choreographer 93
6 The Play Makers II: The Producer 113
7 The Play Builders I: Theatre Architecture and Scenic Designers 121
8 The Play Builders II: The Other Designers 137
9 The Playgoers I: The Audience 157
10 The Playgoers II: The Critic 183

Parting Thoughts 191
Glossary 193
Websites 201
Film and Video Versions of the Plays 205
Index 209

CONTENTS

About the Author   xv
Preface to the Third Edition   xvii
Introduction   xix

1 The Theatre   1
Theatre vs. Drama   1
   What Is Theatre?   2
The Theatre Experience   5
   From Page to Stage   7
Theatre as Change   9
Theatre Conventions   10
   Place   11
   Time   11
   Acting   11
   The Mask   12
   Unique Conventions   13
Theatre Is Plural   14
Four Theatre Events   16
Topics for Group Discussion   20
Possible Research Projects   20
Further Reading   20

2 The Play   23
The Script   23
About Four Scripts   23
   Macbeth   24
   You Can't Take It with You   25
   A Raisin in the Sun   25
   Hamilton   26
The Elements of Drama   27
   Plot   28
   Character   28
   Theme   29
   Diction   30
   Music   30
   Spectacle   31
Types of Drama   32
Dramatic Structure   37
Topics for Group Discussion   39
Possible Research Projects   40
Further Reading   40

3 **The Playwright** 43
- The Blueprint 43
- Meet the Playwrights 44
- The Germinal Idea 46
- The Playwright's Process 48
  - Plot 53
  - Character 54
  - Revision and Rewriting 55
- Evaluating the Playwright's Work 55
  - Plot 56
  - Character 57
  - Diction 57
  - Theme 58
- The Business of Playwriting 58
- Looking at Twenty-One American and British Playwrights 60
- Topics for Group Discussion 71
- Possible Research Projects 71
- Further Reading 71

4 **The Play Performers: The Actors** 73
- Acting vs. Role-Playing 73
- Acting as an Art and a Craft 74
- A Brief History of Acting 75
  - Premodern Acting 76
  - Modern Acting 77
- Theories of Acting 79
- An Actor's Tools 80
- The Actor's Process 81
  - Analysis 81
  - Rehearsal 82
  - Sustaining a Performance 83
- The Business of Acting 84
  - Auditions 84
  - Professional Union 85
- Evaluating the Actor 87
- Topics for Group Discussion 90
- Possible Research Projects 90
- Further Reading 90

5 **The Play Makers I: The Director and the Choreographer** 93
- Behind the Scenes 93
- The Art of Directing 94
- Theatre Styles 96
  - Realism 96
  - Romanticism 97
  - Expressionism 97
  - Other *Isms* 98

CONTENTS • xi

    A Brief History of Directing   99
    The Directing Process   101
        Play Selection   101
        Analysis   102
        Casting   102
        Rehearsals   103
        Performance   105
        Musicals   106
    The Business of Directing   107
    Evaluating the Director and Choreographer   109
    Topics for Group Discussion   110
    Possible Research Projects   110
    Further Reading   111

6 The Play Makers II: The Producer   113
    What Is a Producer?   113
    The Business of Producing   115
    Topics for Group Discussion   118
    Possible Research Projects   118
    Further Reading   118

7 The Play Builders I: Theatre Architecture and Scenic Designers   121
    Theatre Architecture   121
        Proscenium Stage   122
        Thrust Stage   123
        Arena Stage   124
        Flexible Space   125
    Scenic Design   127
        Functions of Scenery   128
        Kinds of Scenery   129
    The Scenic Designer's Process   131
        Research   131
        Graphic Designs   132
        Implementation   134
    Topics for Group Discussion   134
    Possible Research Projects   134
    Further Reading   134

8 The Play Builders II: The Other Designers   137
    Costume Design   137
        Functions of Costume Design   137
    The Costume Designer's Process   139
    Lighting Design   141
    A Brief History of Theatre Lighting   142
    The Function and Elements of Theatre Lighting   142
        Intensity   144
        Distribution   144
        Color   144

xii • CONTENTS

    The Lighting Designer's Process   145
    Sound Design   146
        Acoustics   146
        Amplification   147
        Sound Effects   147
    Theatre Properties   148
    Makeup in the Theatre   148
    New Technology   151
    The Business of Theatre Design   153
    Evaluating Theatre Design   154
    Topics for Group Discussion   155
    Possible Research Projects   155
    Further Reading   155

9 The Playgoers I: The Audience   157

    Theatre Today   157
    Where Theatre Happens   159
        Broadway   159
        The Road   160
        Off Broadway   161
        Off-Off-Broadway   162
        Regional or Resident Theatre   163
        Theatregoing in Great Britain   165
        Summer Theatre   166
        Theatre Festivals   167
        Dinner Theatre   167
        Community Theatre   168
        Children's Theatre   168
        Educational Theatre   169
    Alternative Theatre   170
        Experimental Theatre   170
        Street and Guerrilla Theatre   171
        Performance Art   171
    Theatre of Diversity   172
        African American Theatre   172
        Latinx Theatre   173
        Asian American Theatre   174
        Native American Theatre   175
        Feminist Theatre   175
        Gay and Lesbian Theatre   176
    Foreign Influences   177
    Topics for Group Discussion   179
    Possible Research Projects   179
    Further Reading   179

10 The Playgoers II: The Critic   183
   Theatre Criticism   183
      Critics and Reviews   184
   The Student as Critic   186
   Topics for Group Discussion   190
   Possible Research Projects   190
   Further Reading   190

Parting Thoughts   191
Glossary   193
Websites   201
Film and Video Versions of the Plays   205
Index   209

ABOUT THE AUTHOR

Thomas S. Hischak is an internationally recognized author and teacher in the performing arts, and one of the foremost authorities on the American musical theatre. He is author of thirty-two nonfiction books about theatre, film, and popular music, notably *The Oxford Companion to the American Musical*, *The 100 Greatest American Plays*, *The Rodgers and Hammerstein Encyclopedia*, *Broadway Plays and Musicals*, *Through the Screen Door: What Happened to the Broadway Musical When It Went to Hollywood*, *The Tin Pan Alley Encyclopedia*, *Off-Broadway Musicals since 1919*, *Word Crazy: Broadway Lyricists*, *American Literature on Stage and Screen*, *1939: Hollywood's Greatest Year*, *Musicals in Film: A Guide to the Genre*, *Boy Loses Girl: Broadway Lyricists*, and *The Oxford Companion to American Theatre* (with Gerald Bordman).

He is also author of more than fifty published plays that are performed throughout the United States, Canada, Great Britain, and Australia. Hischak is a Fulbright scholar who has taught and directed in Greece, Lithuania, and Turkey.

From 1983 to 2015, he was professor of theatre at the State University of New York (SUNY) at Cortland, where he has received such honors as the 2004 SUNY Chancellor's Award for Excellence in Scholarship and Creative Activity and the 2010 SUNY Outstanding Achievement in Research Award. Four of his books have been cited as Outstanding Nonfiction Books by the American Library Association, and *The Oxford Companion to the American Theatre* was cited as an Outstanding Reference Work by the New York City Public Library in 2008. His playwriting awards include the Stanley Drama Award (New York City) for *Cold War Comedy* and the Julie Harris Playwriting Award (Beverly Hills, California) for *The Cardiff Giant*.

Hischak is currently on the adjunct faculty of Flagler College, where he teaches courses on theatre and film.

PREFACE TO THE THIRD EDITION

The task of introducing students to theatre is so much more complex and challenging than some of the other arts because the students' familiarity with the form either varies or is nonexistent. The purpose of this introductory textbook is to not only define, explain, and illustrate what theatre is, but also make theatre come alive for even the least-informed student. The hope is to present theatre as a living and changing art form that is inclusive rather than exclusive, accessible rather than elusive.

Those familiar with the two earlier editions of *Theatre as Human Action* will notice right away two major changes in this new edition: the addition of color photographs in the interior of the textbook and the change from *Rent* to *Hamilton* as the sample musical used throughout the book. More subtle changes include updated information on technical theatre; additional websites dealing with past and present theatre; a discussion of drama therapy; the inclusion of children's theatre; information on theatregoing in Great Britain today, as well as British playwrights; an updated and extended bibliography; and the use of more recent plays and musicals in the commentary and photographs.

What remains firmly in place is the basic premise of the textbook: Students need to have a frame of reference when learning about the basic elements of theatre. Constantly referring to plays and musicals that the student is not familiar with is not only frustrating, but also excludes them from the discussion. Theatregoing is an activity that requires no previous knowledge, not even the ability to read or write. Learning about theatre in a classroom should take the same open-minded approach. Since the instructor cannot (and should not) assume that every student is familiar with every play that comes up in the explanation and discussion of theatre, this textbook provides four frames of reference that both teacher and student can turn to.

THE PLAN OF THE BOOK

Four theatre scripts are introduced, described, and illustrated early on in the book:

- William Shakespeare's *Macbeth* as an example of tragedy, the classical style and structure, the use of poetry, and the endless possibilities the play offers for directors, actors, and designers.
- George S. Kaufman and Moss Hart's *You Can't Take It with You* as an example of a twentieth-century American comedy with a solid, well-made play structure and a work that still is widely produced and enjoyed.
- Lorraine Hansberry's *A Raisin in the Sun* as an example of a twentieth-century American drama, a landmark African American play, a work written by a woman, and a play with themes that are still relevant to modern audiences.
- Lin-Manuel Miranda's *Hamilton* as an example of the American musical theatre form, a twenty-first-century work that illustrates the diversity of contemporary theatre, and a historical piece with modern implications.

Once these four examples are presented in the textbook, it is hoped that the instructor will also show scenes from the four works that are available on video and online, further adding to students' initiation to these four theatre experiences. From that point onward, the textbook often refers back to the sample quartet, giving students a practical and effective frame of reference. Of course, many other plays and musicals are included in the commentary and illustrations because theatre is too diverse and complex to be confined to only four examples. But the foundation for understanding the writing, acting, directing, producing, designing, and criticizing of theatre rests on these four superior examples.

Theatre as Human Action is a continually evolving work that has been influenced by comments from both teachers and students. You are invited to add your comments, which will be useful in the preparation of future editions. The author can be contacted through his website: www.thomashischak.com.

ACKNOWLEDGMENTS

I would like to thank Elaina Wahl-Temple, Paul Denayer, Robert Glomboski, and Nikki Falaco for allowing me to use their creative work, and acknowledge the contribution of Stephen Ryan and Jessica McCleary at Rowman & Littlefield in making this third edition possible. I would also like to thank the different teachers and reviewers who kindly provided feedback on the first two editions and gave suggestions for this new edition. In particular, I acknowledge the useful comments from Justin Amellio (Indiana University South Bend), Steven Braddock (Niagara University), Amber Marisa Cook (Southeast Missouri University), Monica Cortés Viharo (University of Washington), Patricia Downey (University of South Dakota), and Laurel Whitsett (University of Texas at Arlington).

INTRODUCTION

Theatre is all around us, taking so many forms and assuming so many shapes, that it needs pointing out more than it requires an introduction. Theatre is the simplest kind of role playing we do every day, behaving and reacting differently to different people in our lives. Theatre is a small child pretending to be something he or she is not, be it a puppy or a superhero. Theatre is a group of students planning and performing a skit or play in a school. Theatre is also professionals preparing and presenting a highly polished piece of entertainment for a wide audience. All of these are forms of theatre.

Yet, the art of *theatre* involves so much more than what we see as an audience member or even as an amateur performer. Theatre is a combination of different arts, from writing and designing to performing and directing, and to be truly introduced to the theatre, all of its components must be explored. This book looks at the process of theatre, from the first idea a playwright has for a script through the preparation and rehearsals involving various kinds of artists to the final product presented before an audience. Theatre has been called the culmination of all the arts because it can involve literature, music, visual art, and dance. Theatre is so much more than what we may initially think.

In order to better explore the idea of the theatre, I have selected four plays that will be our frame of reference throughout the book. Thousands of plays and musicals have been written over the centuries, and for every concept presented in the following chapters, there are dozens of plays I could use as examples. But the chance of your being familiar with all or even half of these examples is not likely. Your theatre experience, whether it is very limited or very extensive, is bound to be quite different from mine and every other student in your class. So we need some common points of reference in order to make these ideas come alive.

Four very different plays have been chosen so that we can touch on different types, styles, and periods of theatre. There is also a good chance that you are familiar with these works from studying them in school, seeing them performed on the stage, or even just hearing about them. But even if they are new to you, they will be introduced and then explained throughout the book so that everyone will be able to use them as references. The plays are William Shakespeare's tragedy *Macbeth*, George S. Kaufman and Moss Hart's comedy *You Can't Take It with You*, Lorraine Hansberry's African American domestic melodrama *A Raisin in the Sun*, and Lin-Manuel Miranda's history musical *Hamilton*. If you have the chance to read (or listen to) these plays or view them onstage or on video, so much the better. (A list of video versions is given at the end of the book.) In any case, the plots and characters are explained in chapter 2 so that the subsequent use of them in this book will be useful to you. Within these four works are examples of all the areas that we wish to explore, from playwriting to production to criticism. They are the four pillars that the many aspects of theatre will rest on. Being solid and durable examples, they will guide us through the fascinating world known as the theatre.

1

THE THEATRE

THEATRE VS. DRAMA

As you read these words, this very night, hundreds of theatre events are taking place across America. Let us look at four of them.

In a midsized liberal arts college, the theatre department is presenting William Shakespeare's *Macbeth* in the campus performing arts center. The actors and crew are students at the college; the director and some other staff are members of the theatre faculty; and the audience is composed of students, faculty, and people from the community. At the same time, far away in a high school in another town, a production of the George S. Kaufman and Moss Hart comedy *You Can't Take It with You* is opening in the school auditorium. The cast and crew are high school students; the director is a teacher at the school; and the audience is filled with fellow students, members of the faculty, friends, family, and others from the community. Across the country in a major city, the region's resident theatre company is offering Lorraine Hansberry's *A Raisin in the Sun* as part of its five-play season in its two-theatre building. The professional

THE THEATRE EXPERIENCE No other play better captured the anxiety many Americans felt at the end of the twentieth century than Tony Kushner's 1993 epic drama *Angels in America*. It was a theatre experience potent in its time and has continued to move audiences, as with this 2018 Broadway production directed by Marianne Elliott. Pictured are AIDS-afflicted Prior Walter (Andrew Garfield) and Amanda Lawrence as the Angel who comes with portentous news about the future. *Sara Krulwich/New York Times/Redux Pictures*

actors, crew, director, and designers are members of the various theatre unions, and the audience consists of a wide cross section of the local population, from students to senior citizens. Finally, tonight on Broadway, Lin-Manuel Miranda's musical *Hamilton* is being performed at the Richard Rodgers Theatre, where it has been playing to sold-out houses since 2015. About 1,400 tourists and New Yorkers will crowd into the old theatre to see the prize-winning musical performed by a top-notch cast in a highly professional production.

These four situations are examples of theatre. They are much more than dramas; they are theatre events. The distinction is an important one. While *drama* refers to the script, *theatre* is an event. It is the presentation of the script performed on a stage by actors for an audience. Although *Macbeth* is studied and read in thousands of schools each year, it only becomes theatre when it comes alive on the stage. The CD of *Hamilton* is one of Broadway's more popular cast recordings, but *Hamilton* is not a piece of rap and hip-hop music to be downloaded and listened to; it is a musical drama meant to be performed in a theatre. The script, the literature of the stage, is only one of the factors in a theatre performance, albeit a very important one. But without all the other elements present, it is not a theatre event.

COLLEGE THEATRE The intimate Off-Broadway musical *The Spitfire Grill*, about some hopeful residents in a small, forgotten town, is the kind of theatre that often finds new life in college and university theatres. This production from Flagler College was directed by Kip Taisey with scenery and lighting by Paul Deneyer and costumes by Elaina Wahl-Temple. *Nikki Falaco*

What Is Theatre?

Consider this brief but thorough definition: *theatre is a reenactment of human action.* It is a *reenactment* because it is not really happening for the first time. Actors have

HIGH SCHOOL THEATRE Theatrical productions in junior and senior high schools cover a wide range of theatre today, from popular Broadway musicals to classic dramas. The lesser-known musical drama *Bonnie and Clyde* was staged by Jeff Dodd at St. Augustine (Florida) High School with Simone Glomboski and Chad Boyd playing the title characters. *Robert Glomboski*

rehearsed the play and are now pretending to be characters going through certain situations. The audience knows and understands this. They pretend along with the actors, letting the reenactment seem real. Theatre is *action* because something must happen during the event. A painting of a sunset, a poem about a lily, a concerto celebrating a river, and a dance about spring are all examples of the arts. But they need not have a plot or characters to be successful or fulfilling. Theatre needs action, and it must be *human* action. It is about people doing something, whether it is a quiet conversation between two characters, a duel between two rivals, or a vibrant song-and-dance number in a musical.

Theatre requires more factors than perhaps any of the other art forms. Four basic elements must be present for a theatre event to occur: *actors*, *script*, *audience*, and *place*. The actors are needed for the reenactment. They portray characters, deliver dialogue, and perform the actions of the play. The script is the blueprint they use, telling them what to say and do. But actors gathered together and performing without an audience watching them is not theatre. Unlike film and television, the audience must be in the same place as the actors. It need not be a formal indoor theatre (for a thousand years, theatre was always performed outdoors), but it must be a place in which performers and spectators are gathered together in order for the theatre event to happen. If you take away any one of these four factors, the result—a rehearsal, an improvisation, a play reading, a broadcast, a film—is not theatre, as we will be discussing it throughout this book.

REGIONAL THEATRE One does not have to travel to New York City to see professional theatre today. Many cities have a regional or resident theatre company that offers quality productions locally. This production of Lanford Wilson's comedy-drama *Talley's Folly* was presented at the Yale Repertory Company in New Haven, Connecticut, featuring Hal Linden and Joan Mackintosh as an unlikely pair of lovers. *Photofest*

The Word *Theatre*

The word *theatre* is used in so many ways in modern English that it can cause confusion. There are even two accepted spellings of the word, *theatre* and *theater*, which are often used interchangeably. (Many believe that the place, a theater building, should be spelled with an *er* while the art form should be *re*. We will consistently use the *theatre* spelling for all forms of the word in this book.) The word *theatre* comes from Latin and Greek words meaning "to view," yet over the centuries it came to mean both the place where a play is seen and the actual event of watching a play.

Today we talk about a movie theatre, an outdoor theatre, and a Broadway theatre, and we even use the expression "the Pacific theatre" to refer to the location of a war or other notable event. A theatre is a place that may take one of many different forms. Today most theatres are auditoriums or other indoor places that seat spectators in front of some kind of stage. But it is important to understand that in the past, the theatre event took place outdoors, in churches, marketplaces, coaching inns, palaces and country homes, and even on tennis courts. The important thing, according to our definition of *theatre*, is that the actors and the audience are brought together in one place. Regardless of what form that place takes, it is a theatre.

Theatre is also much more than a place. It is the whole experience of seeing a play performed. It is going to the place, watching the performance, responding to the live actors, and acknowledging them with laughter, applause, or other signs of recognition. We sometimes call this whole experience *theatregoing*, yet it is more than just going to the performance place. *Theatre* also refers to an art form, the dramatic arts. You can study theatre, you can practice it, you can evaluate it, even criticize it. Finally, *theatre* refers to a business or a profession. One can become a theatre director, a theatre critic, a theatre designer, or a theatre manager or perform any of the other jobs in the profession. When we refer to someone as being "in the theatre," much more is meant than his or her being in a theatre building. *Theatre* or *theater*, the word encompasses many ideas. Throughout this book we will explore all meanings of the word *theatre*, from the place to the ideas to the people.

THE THEATRE EXPERIENCE

The American playwright Thornton Wilder once wrote that theatre is a unique experience because it always takes place in the present tense. This does not mean a play is always set in the present. Whether it takes place in ancient Greece or in medieval England or contemporary America, the story unfolds *now*. In a novel the events are in the past tense; the hero "said" something and "did" something. In a play, the character Macbeth, for instance, "says" such and such and "does" certain things. It happens live in front of the audience and each time the play is performed the event is new. Theatre tells a story not by narrating a tale (although some plays have narrators) but by reenacting it. Characters speak in dialogue and perform certain actions. The audience observes, picks up information about past events, witnesses new events, watches the characters in action, and is hopefully involved with the play as it builds to a climax and all is unfolded. Because theatre takes place in the present tense, there is much more immediacy to watching a play than to reading a story in a book.

BROADWAY THEATRE While Broadway is the most known and celebrated theatre venue in the United States, it actually makes up a small portion of theatre activity in the nation. Yet, a long-running hit like *Wicked*, which has been playing to full houses on Broadway since 2003, is American theatre at its most radiant. *Photofest*

In fact, one does not have to know how to read at all to enjoy a play. Theatre has been called "literature for the illiterate" because of this. One cannot experience a piece of prose or poetry if one cannot read, unless the piece is read aloud. But theatre is not meant to be read, either to oneself or aloud; it is meant to be performed. The great dramas of the past and present can be enjoyed by anyone, regardless of background or education. Most of the audience in Elizabethan England was illiterate, yet *Macbeth* and other works by Shakespeare were very popular. And while those plays are much studied today, someone with no previous knowledge can see *Macbeth* and not only understand it but be enthralled by the reenactment. For thousands of years theatre was the only literature for the masses. Today, television, radio, movies, and the internet are the most common forms of entertainment. Yet none of them provides literature as such. Television and film scripts, as well as websites, are seldom published and rarely studied as literature; however, theatre continues to provide a rich literary heritage. Some people today might consider theatre a highbrow form of art, such as opera or classical music, but what has always made plays popular still makes them popular: live actors performing an intriguing story in an interesting way. The theatre experience has not changed.

Perhaps you have read plays for a class or your own enjoyment. There is a great deal of satisfaction that comes from reading plays, but one must remember that the script is only one-fourth of the theatre experience. Some people can visualize the action on the stage when reading a play, and there is something to be said for the way a play on the page can stimulate the reader's

THE THEATRE EVENT Audiences flock to the Epidaurus Festival in modern Greece, where classic plays are still performed much as they were 2,500 years ago. The same basic elements of theatre are still there: actors, audience, script, and place. *George Axendeer/Stockimo/Alamy Stock Photo*

MACBETH IN THE PRESENT TENSE The three witches torment Macbeth with a prophesy about the future in which Banquo's offspring will rule Scotland. This modern dress production by a theatre company in Lithuania may look different from a traditional staging, but it is still very much *Macbeth*. *Stanislovas Kairys/Alamy Stock Photo*

imagination. But as we will see in the chapter on the playwright, plays are not written to be read but to be produced. A play on the page can be exciting and moving, but it is not a theatre event.

From Page to Stage

Prose fiction tells a story; theatre *shows* a story. Here is an episode from *Macbeth* told as a piece of prose fiction. The narrator can describe events, relate dialogue, even give us the characters' thoughts. Notice how all of it is in the past tense. Here is what has happened up to this point in the story: Macbeth became king of Scotland by murdering old King Duncan. Although the crown was now his, he feared a prophecy that said the nobleman Banquo would be the father of future kings. So Macbeth hired some murderers to kill Banquo and his son Fleance when they approached the castle late one night to attend a banquet.

This is how a prose version of the episode might be written:

With the moon hidden away behind the thick clouds, the three murderers could barely see each other's face as they crouched near the hedge some fifty yards from the castle entrance. In order to surprise Banquo and the young boy, they carried no torch and spoke in low whispers so that they might hear anyone approaching. Those arriving at the castle on horseback usually dismounted a good distance from the entrance and had their servants bring the horses to the stables, leaving the visitors to walk the last section of road. This is where the murderers waited, their hands tightly grasping the knives hidden under their cloaks, though no one could possibly see them.

Suddenly the sounds of horses could be detected off in the distance. The three murderers strained to listen, only hearing faraway murmurs as the riders dismounted. Soon the horses were heard being led in the direction of the stables, and a voice commanded, "Give a light there, ho!" Was it Banquo? How was one to tell in this Godforsaken darkness! Yet all the other invited guests were already inside the castle. Everyone on the list had been accounted for except Banquo. This must be him. But was the boy with him?

The sound of footsteps approaching got louder, and as the two figures came over the hill, the murderers saw that one of them had a torch. It was a low-burning one but enough for them to make out a grown man and a boy, who carried the fire with an outstretched hand. One of the murderers grumbled, "A light, a light!" and seemed to curse this complication. The element of surprise was essential, but that torch could ruin everything. The murderers crouched lower behind the hedge, and one of them said "'Tis he," as the voices of the two travelers came closer.

"It will be rain tonight," the elder of the two arrivals said. It was clearly Banquo. The leader of the three murderers took this as his cue, leapt up, and shouted, "Let it come down!" With this the threesome attacked the two travelers with their knives outstretched. The boy dropped the torch in the confusion, and in the darkness only Banquo's shouting "O treachery!" and the fumbling of feet and arms could be heard.

"Fly, good Fleance, fly, fly, fly!" the father shouted as he vainly tried to fight off the three murderers, his sword drawn too late to protect him from the blows on all sides.

Banquo's words reminded the threesome that the king was adamant that the boy should die as well. Thinking the youth would be the easier target, they had neglected to concentrate on Fleance. One of the murderers headed to where the torch lay on the ground, raised it high, and searched all around for the boy. Banquo had fallen to the ground and was no longer fighting back. Failing to find the youth, the murderer returned to Banquo, who was breathing heavily, his face in the dirt.

"Thou mayest revenge, O slave!" he gasped and then was silent.

The three murderers, able to speak freely for the first time, erupted in argument.

"Who did strike out the light?"

"Was't not the way?"

"There's but one down; the son is fled."

"We have lost best half of our affair."

After searching the area once again with the fading torch and finding no evidence of the boy, the three murderers reunited near the hedge.

"Well, let's away," the leader said, "and say how much is done."

Then the three quietly turned toward the castle to report to the king.

Shakespeare's version is shorter and more compact. It gives few details, the script providing only the dialogue and major actions of the scene. The visual elements, such as the setting, the look of the characters, and the way the fight unfolds, are left up to those who produce the play. Shakespeare does not even suggest how the lines should be spoken. What he has given us is a blueprint for an exciting scene in the theatre. It is in some ways more difficult to read than the prose version, but remember that this scene was never intended to be read. Also, notice how the scene is now in the present tense.

3 MURDERER: Hark! I hear horses.
BANQUO *(within)***:** Give us a light there, ho!
2 MURDERER: Then 'tis he! The rest
That are within the note of expectation
Already are i' the court.
1 MURDERER: His horses go about.
3 MURDERER: Almost a mile; but he does usually,
So all men do, from hence to the palace gate
Make it their walk.
(Enter Banquo, and Fleance with a torch.)
2 MURDERER: A light, a light!
3 MURDERER: 'Tis he!

1 MURDERER: Stand to't.
BANQUO: It will rain tonight.
1 MURDERER: Let it come down! *(They set upon Banquo)*
BANQUO: O, treachery! Fly, good Fleance, fly, fly, fly!
Thou mayst revenge, O slave! *(Dies. Fleance escapes)*
3 MURDERER: Who did strike out the light?
1 MURDERER: Was't not the way?
3 MURDERER: There's but one down; the son is fled.
2 MURDERER: We have lost
Best half of our affair.
1 MURDERER: Well, let's away, and say how much is done. *(Exeunt)*

The Origins of Theatre

Where did theatre come from? When did it first appear? Was it invented, or did it develop over time? These questions have puzzled theatre scholars for centuries, and no satisfactory answers will ever be discovered. Because it is such an old art form, like dance and music, and goes back to a time before writing and other documentation, theatre cannot be clearly explained in terms of its origins. Yet there are various theories about how theatre came about, and such theories help us define the art form itself. Some critics believe that theatre was a natural progression from storytelling. In prehistoric societies, usually there were priests, shamans, tribal leaders, or other figures of authority who told stories aloud at some sort of gathering. To move from one person telling a story to a handful of actors showing a story is a logical step and might have been the manner in which theatre began. Other scholars argue that theatre grew out of ritual. A ritual is a ceremony of sorts that is planned, performed, and repeated so that the spectators or participants become familiar with its words and movements. We still have rituals today, such as the format of a sporting event or the celebration of a holiday such as Thanksgiving or the Fourth of July. While ritual is common to all peoples, the kinds of rituals a society embraces vary greatly. It is believed that rituals led to theatre since both involve performers, audience, and story and occur in a specified place. Most rituals are connected with religion, another possible origin of theatre, and most religions require the reenactment of an event from the past or an illustration of a belief. When this is done by performers before an audience, it is very close to theatre. A primitive tribe may act out the coming of spring as part of some kind of fertility rite, while more complex religions will have ceremonies that parallel or even dramatize events that are essential to their belief. The Roman Catholic Mass, for example, is a reenactment of the Last Supper, with the priest as a representation of Jesus and the congregation as the disciples. The Hebrew faith recalls and relives the Passover, with each family becoming a modern equivalent to the Jewish people in Egypt who survived their God's vengeance against Pharaoh and the Egyptians. Some religions are more "theatrical" than others, with elaborate ceremonies that seem like stage productions, while there can be simple rites that also echo the four elements of theatre. Whether theatre developed from storytelling, ritual, or religion, we know that the activity existed in various forms for hundreds of years before the first well-documented Western theatre productions in ancient Greece. Because theatre is such an instinctive human activity, its origins are both mysterious and obvious. When and how did humans first learn to wage war or discover love? Impossible to say. One might just as well ask, When did these activities not exist?

THEATRE AS CHANGE

Another unique aspect of theatre, as opposed to other literary and performing arts, is its ability to change. A Charles Dickens novel today is exactly as it was 150 years ago. A classic Hollywood film made in the 1930s has not changed over the years. A van Gogh painting in a museum never alters itself. All three of these art forms are frozen in time, maintaining the same properties over the years regardless if anyone is reading or observing them. But theatre cannot exist without changing. The script may be frozen (though each production might make alterations in the text), but the production is not. Classic plays from the past, such as *Macbeth*, have been produced in different ways over the centuries. A presentation in Shakespeare's outdoor Globe Theatre was done in contemporary costumes with teenage boys playing the female roles. The same play in the eighteenth century was done inside an elaborate theatre with ornate costumes and wigs that seemed to have little to do with the ancient Scottish setting of the play. *Macbeth* is presented today in many different ways, from a historically accurate piece to a romantic, poetic vehicle for actors to an avant-garde spectacle that deconstructs the play by turning it into a psychological study of evil. There is only one script but dozens of ways to perform that script.

Even modern plays go through such changes. Every new production of *A Raisin in the Sun*, *You Can't Take It with You*, and, eventually, *Hamilton* is different. This is obvious when one considers that the actors, the scenery, the costumes, and even the theatre spaces are different. Yet there are more subtle differences as well. The way that an actor interprets a role and the approach a director takes in presenting the play also change from production to production. No two productions of *A Raisin in the Sun* can be exactly alike, even if they each tried to duplicate the other. It is not in the nature of theatre to be set in stone. Even a touring company of a Broadway hit like *Hamilton*, which might use the same scenery, costumes, and direction as in New York, will not be able to replicate the original exactly. Two actors given the same assignment will end up with different results. Each new theatre space will alter the production. Even the different audiences will cause the production to vary.

If theatre changes from decade to decade and production to production, it also changes from night to night. Each reenactment of the same production will vary slightly. Live actors cannot duplicate themselves exactly night after night; they subtly change just as the audience does. Each performance is unique because of the dynamics between the live actors and a live audience. One influences the other each time a new combination is tried. One night the audience for *A Raisin in the Sun* may be quiet and reflective and greet certain scenes with a hushed reaction. The next night the spectators may be livelier, laughing at the humor in the script and reacting in a more vocal manner to the actors. On a third night the audience may be more aggressive, expressing anger and frustration at the plight of the characters and revealing a bitterness about the situation. Every time that the play is reenacted, the response can be different. This is one of the reasons why theatre is among the oldest and most durable of art forms: the experience is always changing, just as society and ideas change.

THEATRE CONVENTIONS

Although one does not need education or experience to appreciate a theatre production, there are unwritten rules and an unspoken agreement between the actors and the audience that are present in every theatre event. This ancient custom of accepting and believing things onstage is called a theatre *convention*. Different cultures have different conventions, but sometimes the unwritten rules are universal. For example, the very idea of the actor is a convention. A man comes onstage and says he is Alexander Hamilton. The audience knows that he is not really Hamilton but an actor portraying one of the Founding Fathers. When Hamilton dies in a duel, we know that the actor is pretending, but we accept the pretense all the same. Theatre conventions allow the theatre event to take place. Without being taught, the audience understands the concept of the reenactment. It is an instinctive aspect of human nature to understand pretending. A child pretends to be a dog, barking out loud and walking on all four "feet." No one had to teach the youth about pretending. Humans have always observed and imitated. The first and most important theatre convention is already in place.

Place

Other conventions are quickly picked up by the audience. When the curtain rises on the Chicago tenement apartment for a production of *A Raisin in the Sun*, we know it is not a real apartment but a stage setting. It might be in a realistic style or a suggested one, but the audience accepts the convention of scenery. When a character exits through a door saying that she is going into the bedroom, the audience pretends that there is another room offstage but knows that such a room probably does not exist. The convention of place allows a play to take place anywhere because the audience accepts the locale. A table and some chairs are used to denote a New York City pub where Hamilton and his friends meet in *Hamilton*. Yet, later, when that same table and one chair are brought back on stage, the scene becomes the study in Hamilton's house. Exterior scenes are difficult to re-create realistically onstage, but the convention of place allows theatregoers to travel to smoky battlefields, as in *Macbeth*. Sometimes a fence, a park bench, a campfire, or a tree is all that is needed to tell an audience that the location is outside.

THE CONVENTION OF ACTING The nature of theatre is such that audiences will accept an actor as anyone or anything onstage. The cast of the musical *Cats* (1982), which played on Broadway for eighteen years, had no trouble portraying "human action," even when they were not playing humans. *Cats* was directed by Trevor Nunn with sets and costumes by John Napier and makeup design by Candace Carell. *Photofest*

Time

The convention of time is less concrete but easily accepted as well. When the lights fade out or the curtain falls on a scene in *You Can't Take It with You*, we understand that the scene or act is over. If the lights or curtain rises a moment later and the characters are having breakfast, we believe that time has passed and that it is the next morning or one several days later. The dialogue in a play usually sets the time of the action, although lighting and sound effects can also indicate the passage of time. In *Macbeth*, two characters arriving at a castle at dawn talk about the strange sounds they heard during the previous night. Lena Younger, in *A Raisin in the Sun*, speaks of the morning light being the only time her little plant gets direct sunlight. These are among the many ways the convention of time can be utilized in the theatre.

Acting

There are also many acting conventions in theatre that audiences seem to understand without difficulty. Two people talking to each other on a street or in a room would normally face each other. But onstage, two actors in conversation may both face toward the audience or move away from each other or even position themselves so that one is behind the other, both facing the same direction. What seems like a ridiculous pose in real life might make an effective picture onstage. If, during a scene between a man and a woman, the actress moves closer to the audience and speaks her thoughts aloud before returning to the other actor, we accept that this comment was not heard by the male character. This convention is called an *aside*. It can be delivered directly to the audience to give information or commentary, or it can be used to speak to a certain character onstage without any of the other characters hearing. Since asides are delivered aloud and at a volume that allows the entire audience to hear, we know that the other actors must have heard it but the character did not. Yet we accept the convention all the same, knowing it is a pretense needed to tell the story. A similar convention is the *soliloquy*. An effective way for a character to express his thoughts is by speaking them aloud when alone onstage. Such soliloquies can be highly poetic, as in one of Macbeth's solo speeches, or more conversational, as in *Hamilton* when Alexander Hamilton's thoughts in lyrical form reveal his dreams for this new nation. When realism was introduced to the theatre in the late nineteenth century, soliloquies were often replaced by a *confidant*. This is a friend or companion to the main character who the hero talks to aloud, telling his or her thoughts. What was once a soliloquy became a conversation, with the confidant listening and occasionally adding comments or questions to the hero's speeches. Confidant characters go all the way back to the ancient Greek theatre. When it is important for a character's thoughts to be related to the audience, the convention of telling a confidant has always been a very useful theatre device. In *A Raisin in the Sun*, the mother, Lena, does not use soliloquy but speaks to her daughter-in-law Ruth, her confidant, about her worries about her son Walter.

There are many other acting conventions, from a stage whisper (which must be much louder than a real whisper) to a death scene (be it bloody and realistic or stylized and poetic). One actor can exit a scene, change costume, and reenter as a different character, and the audience accepts the convention as long as it is clear what is being done. A young female actress can play a character in the early scenes of a play and then be replaced by an older actress later in the play when that character has grown up. An actor can portray a lion onstage, and, regardless if one wears a detailed lion costume or just a fur headpiece and painted-on whiskers, the audience accepts the convention.

The Mask

Perhaps the most ancient acting convention in theatre is the *mask*. Although we use masks rarely in the modern theatre, the earliest theatre events were largely dependent on masks. In the ancient Greek theatre, one actor would play an old man, a beautiful queen, and a youthful shepherd all in the same play; each character was indicated by a different mask. Over the centuries the use of the mask would never completely disappear. The stylized commedia dell'arte players of Renaissance Italy, for example, used partial masks to indicate if the character was a lover, a clown, or an old man.

ANCIENT MASKS Actors wore masks in the ancient Greek theatre to establish the identity of a character. Today we expect to see the actor's face and expressions to understand the character. Yet, sometimes masks can be as expressive as the human face, as these colorful and stylized masks demonstrate. *Art Directors & TRIP/Alamy Stock Photo*

And masks are still used today on occasion. Children's theatre often relies on masks to portray animals and other nonhuman creatures. Very sophisticated masks can be found in *The Lion King* and other highly creative theatre productions that move away from literal realism. The symbol of the mask has long represented the art of theatre itself, and the contrasting masks of comedy and tragedy are still a common sight.

Unique Conventions

Some conventions do fade away, though. Since actresses were not seen on the stage for nearly a thousand years, female characters were portrayed by males. In Shakespeare's day, Lady Macbeth, the three Witches, and other women in that tragedy were played at the Globe Theatre by male apprentices. The audience easily believed this convention because they were not accustomed to having women appear onstage. Today the use of male actors for female roles is done on occasion, but it is often difficult for audiences to accept the convention seriously. Just as difficult is for an American audience to accept certain foreign conventions.

Customs in Western and Eastern theatre differ greatly at times, and each culture has to learn to understand the other's conventions. In many Asian countries, the use of dance is closely tied with acting. In a traditional Chinese play, for example, an actor may chant and perform a highly stylized dance step while moving across the stage. An Indian drama may call for a character to wear a huge, elaborate elephant mask to represent a god or a spirit. In the islands of Indonesia, cutout puppets are silhouetted onto a screen, as they represent human and animal characters. And in Japan, the unrealistic Kabuki actors (all male) wear expressive makeup and exaggerated wigs to play familiar character types. Because these conventions are centuries old and reflect cultural ideas found in Eastern art and literature, audiences readily accept these distinctive theatre conventions even after they have been exposed to Western realism in our theatre, movies, and television.

There are Western conventions that are just as puzzling to Easterners. Consider our modern musical theatre and its unusual conventions. In many Broadway musicals the characters may start with dialogue, then begin to sing lyrics and perhaps even break into dancing, each one growing out of the other even though none of it is at all realistic. Cowboys dance on the prairie in *Oklahoma!*, gangsters break into song in *Guys and Dolls*, and street

MODERN MASKS In contemporary theatre, masks are more likely to be used for nonhuman characters. The evil lion Scar in the Broadway production of *The Lion King* (1997) is revealed through a stylistic lion's mask, as well as through the actor's facial expressions. Julie Taymor designed the costumes and masks, and directed the Disney stage production. *Joan Marcus/Photofest; © Joan Marcus/Walt Disney Productions*

THEATRE IN INDIA Westerners must accept an entirely new set of theatre conventions to understand a Hindu theatre performance, from different approaches, to costume and makeup, to a stylized form of gesture and movement. This scene is from the dance drama *Kathakali*, which goes back to the sixteenth century. *Dennis Cox/Alamy Stock Photo*

gangs burst into ballet in *West Side Story*—yet the audience accepts it. In past decades, such a unique kind of Western theatre has found an audience in Asia, just as Eastern theatre techniques are being employed in the West. Throughout the world people are learning and understanding new theatre conventions. The human instinct to pretend and believe allows people to embrace new conventions, and the theatre continues on, changing as it always has.

THEATRE IS PLURAL

The final characteristic of theatre to be considered is its pluralism. Very little that occurs in the theatre is solitary; it usually takes place because of a group. This is true of those creating theatre and those watching it. Usually, one playwright writes the script; one director is in charge of the artistic vision; and one actor plays each role. But none of these individuals can complete the job without the other artists. The playwright must have certain individuals produce the script; a director needs actors and designers to fulfill his or her vision; actors need everyone, from the playwright (for the words) to the costume designer (for the clothes) in order to perform. This is why theatre is often referred to as a *collaborative* art form. A solo artist cannot present theatre unless he or she writes, directs, designs, produces, and performs a one-person play, a very rare occurrence at any time during the long history of theatre. Instead, creating theatre is a group experience. (In chapter 8, we will see how *performance artists* go against this group tradition and are true solo artists.)

THEATRE IN JAPAN The highly stylized Kabuki theatre of Japan makes few attempts to be realistic in telling its ancient stories. Instead, a colorful poetic form of performance is used that has its own theatrical conventions unique to Asian cultures. Depicted is a scene from a 2010 production of the classic Kabuki play *Yoshitsune and the Thousand Cherry Trees*. Photo © Laurie Lewis/Bridgeman Images

Some of the personnel are needed early in the process (e.g., the playwright), while others are not necessary until the production is nearing completion (e.g., the theatre manager). If one looks at theatre production as a process, one can more easily see how different members of the creative team are responsible for various steps in that process. The major personnel of a theatre event usually includes the

playwright, who writes the script, music, and lyrics and then submits the script to a
producer, who raises the money, secures a theatre space, and selects a
director, who hires (with the producer) the designers, casts the actors, and stages the play while the
designers create the sets, costumes, lights, and other technical aspects on paper, handing the designs over to the
technical director and his or her staff, who build and re-create the designs, while the
actors rehearse (with the director) and perform the characters in the play, and the
theatre manager runs the theatre space and its staff (box office, ushers, maintenance, etc.), and the
publicist advertises and promotes the production so that an
audience can gather and express reactions or
theatre critics can write reviews that may or may not encourage others to attend this theatre event.

While the above run-on sentence may be a gross simplification of the process, it gives one an idea about the collaborative nature of creating theatre. Many of these listed jobs are looked at in detail in subsequent chapters, but it is necessary to see each member of the team as part of one complex process.

Theatre is also pluralism because of its diversity. Theatre can be about anything, can be performed by very different kinds of people, and can be presented to any kind of audience. We have seen how literacy is not a necessary requirement for enjoying theatre, but also consider that theatre is not limited to any one culture, nationality, location, region, race, or philosophy. Since theatre has existed in different forms for different people for thousands of years, it must, by its nature, be pluralistic; that is, it cannot be confined to one narrow range of experience. Not all plays are for everyone, but the reverse is also true: for each person or kind of person, plays exist that are specifically for that person and others like him or her. During different times in the past, theatre was an elitist art form that was meant for and appreciated by only a small percentage of the people. Yet there have been other times when theatregoing was mass entertainment for all sections of a certain society. Today's theatre takes so many forms—from the glossy Broadway product to the Off-Off-Broadway experimental workshop to an amateur school performance—that its pluralism seems stronger than ever. Contemporary plays are about themes, subject matter, and character types that might have been unimaginable a half century ago. Theatre continues to be about everything and anything.

A third aspect of theatre as a plural experience has to do with the audience. To quote again from Thornton Wilder, "theatre is addressed to a group mind." One lone individual can appreciate and enjoy looking at a painting, listening to a piece of music, viewing a video of a film, reading a novel, or watching television. But it takes a group of spectators to watch a play. Theatre is meant to be experienced by a collection of individuals. The gathering of a group is essential to the theatre experience. The spectators must go to the place where the actors will act out the script. As a group, the audience reinforces each other's understanding and enjoyment of the play. An audience laughs together, may gasp together, sometimes collectively holds their breath at the same time, and applauds together. To do any of these by oneself in an empty auditorium would strike one as awkward and even intimidating. The group mind thinks together, reacts together, and then recognizes each other by hearing these reactions. Not everyone in the audience has the same feelings about a play. In fact, it is rare for each individual to have the exact same reaction, but as part of a theatre audience, an individual experiences the play collectively. He or she is part of the plural of theatre.

Being part of a collective means that attending a theatre event requires more from an audience member than watching television at home or a movie in a cineplex. In both of those cases, the actors are not present and the reactions from the spectators do not affect their performances. That is not true in the theatre, where the actors are always aware of the audience, can sense whether they are caught up in the performance, and can feel the unspoken communication that exists between performer and spectator. Consequently, one attends a theatre production with much more consideration for both the actors and one's fellow audience members. Some guidelines for viewing a play and the basic etiquette that live theatre deserves are discussed in the last chapter, but at this point it is worthwhile mentioning that one has to approach a theatre experience with an awareness of others that is perhaps unique in this modern technological age.

MACBETH Shakespeare's tragedy is among the plays given an approximate re-creation today at the replica of the Globe Theatre on the banks of the River Thames in London. The new Globe opened in 1997, and since then thousands of theatregoers have enjoyed classic plays in a historic environment. *Robert Stainforth/Alamy Stock Photo*

FOUR THEATRE EVENTS

At the beginning of this chapter, four contemporary theatre events were briefly described. Now that we have explored the basic elements of theatre—actors, script, place, audience—let us look at four theatre events from the past and see how each of these elements was present.

1. It is the summer of 1606 in London, England. Shakespeare's tragedy *Macbeth* has already been performed for King James in a private performance, but the play is now being presented for the public at the outdoor Globe Theatre. The octagon-shaped theatre, made out of timber, plaster, and thatch, is situated on the south bank of the River Thames because it is against the law for theatres to be built in the city limits for fear of fire and plague. The Globe holds about two thousand spectators, who have crossed the river by private boat or have walked over the London Bridge to get there. The audience ranges from educated aristocrats sitting in a gallery to illiterate common folk who stand on the ground in front of the stage. While some in the audience may be familiar with the historical figure of Macbeth, a Scottish king hundreds of years in the past, most are viewing the script with no previous knowledge or preparation. The actors for the afternoon presentation are professionals, a group of about fifteen men and a few teenage boys who will play the female roles. These actors know many roles and perform in several different plays during the warm months of the outdoor theatre season. Some of them are audience favorites, garnering applause and shouts of recognition on their first entrance. The actors speak the poetry quickly and enter and exit with few pauses, one scene ending as the next begins. They often talk directly to the audience, perhaps delivering a very lyrical passage to

the galleries and the coarser jokes to those standing at their feet. The story is filled with diabolical plots, murders, madness, and battles, and the action is continuous with no breaks or intermissions. The applause at the end is very vocal, even ribald perhaps, and the theatre event ends on a noisy and satisfying note.

YOU CAN'T TAKE IT WITH YOU The conservative Kirbys arrive at the Vanderhof household for a dinner party that will prove far from conventional in the original 1936 Broadway production of the Kaufman and Hart play, one of the most durable of all American comedies. Director: George S. Kaufman. *Photofest/Photographer: Vandamm Studio*

2. It is December 14, 1936, in New York City, and the audience is braving the cold to gather at the Booth Theatre, a 772-seat theatre on Shubert Alley in the so-called Theatre District. It is opening night for the new comedy *You Can't Take It with You* by George S. Kaufman and Moss Hart. The two playwrights had written a major comedy hit called *Once in a Lifetime* six years earlier and word from the out-of-town tryouts is that their new play is a winner. The audience, consisting of opening-night celebrities, avid theatregoers, critics from the many daily New York newspapers, curious socialites, and interested students in the balcony, take their seats in the plush theatre. When the curtain rises on the living room, dining room, and front hall of a middle-class home, the audience can tell from the architecture and the furniture onstage that this is a contemporary comedy in a very familiar setting. Yet once the wacky characters enter and the comic shenanigans begin, the spectators realize that this is no ordinary family. For three acts the audience is delighted with the unconventional but lovable Vanderhof family onstage and by the final curtain call most agree that *You Can't Take It with You* is a hit. The comedy was later praised by the critics and the play ran on

Broadway for nearly three years, followed by hundreds of productions in American theatres of all kinds. As recent as 2015, *You Can't Take It with You* was a hit again on Broadway.

A RAISIN IN THE SUN Broadway audiences in 1959 saw for the first time a real, nonstereotypic African American family on stage as they struggled with life and one another. The landmark play by Lorraine Hansberry was directed by Lloyd Richards and featured Claudia McNeil and Sidney Poitier as the mother and son who disagree on many things. *Photofest*

3. Twenty-three years later, a very different opening night on Broadway is taking place. It is the evening of March 11, 1959, and the place is the Ethel Barrymore Theatre on West Forty-Seventh Street. Lorraine Hansberry's *A Raisin in the Sun* is opening after months of trying to find an available New York theatre. New Yorkers are curious and skeptical about the opening because this is the first time a play by a woman "Negro" playwright has ever been presented on Broadway. In fact, only a handful of plays by African Americans have ever been seen in the Theatre District before. The audience is mostly white, but the producers have arranged for some prominent leaders in the black community to be present. There are also theatre critics, liberal theatregoers, friends and family of the mostly black cast, and again students up in the cheapest seats. When the curtain rises on the tenement apartment setting and the actors appear, the audience is hearing them speak in an African American way of speech that strikes some of them as strange and foreign. Many have seen black performers in musicals or comic sketches in revues, but now they are hearing a "Negro" family talk to each other in a realistic conversational way about their jobs, their frustrations, and their dreams. The featured actor in the drama, Sidney Poitier, has appeared in some films, but few of the other actors are familiar to the audience, though Claudia McNeil, as the grandmother, is so magnetic that soon she becomes well known.

Also in the cast to enjoy later fame are Ruby Dee, Diana Sands, Ivan Dixon, and Louis Gossett. The audience is attentive throughout the play, rarely expressing outrage or discomfort at the events taking place onstage. Yet everyone is deeply moved by the final, hopeful scene in which the family prepares for a new life together. The curtain call is a joyous triumph for Hansberry, the cast, and the development of African American theatre on Broadway. *A Raisin in the Sun* would later be made into a popular movie; receive hundreds of productions throughout the United States; and be seen on Broadway again in 2004 and 2014, the most recent revival starring Denzel Washington.

HAMILTON Early American history is retold with rap music and racial diversity in this popular musical. Lin-Manuel Miranda (center, on table) not only played Alexander Hamilton, but also wrote the book, music, and lyrics for the innovative musical. Director: Thomas Kail. *Sara Krulwich/New York Times/Redux*

4. The final theatre event we will look at takes place on February 17, 2015, in the Newman Theatre in Lower Manhattan. At the intimate Off-Broadway space run by the New York Public Theatre, the musical *Hamilton* is having its opening night performance. The innovative piece about one of America's Founding Fathers had received a workshop production at Vassar College the previous summer, and word is out that *Hamilton* is an electrifying experience. The theatre seats only 299 spectators, and it is full because interest in the musical has been growing, as word on the street is very enthusiastic. What the audience experiences that night is a sung-through musical about the life of Alexander Hamilton with a score that incorporates rap, hip-hop, rhythm and blues, pop, soul, and conventional musical theatre songs. The spectators also see famous white historical figures played by actors of different races. By the end of the evening, the audience rises to its feet with a sense of having experienced something new and exciting. By the next day, word is out that *Hamilton* is an exceptional theatre piece. The three-month Off-Broadway run quickly sells out, and in August the Public Theatre and other producers bring the musical uptown to Broadway, where it becomes a major critical and popular hit.

In none of the four events described has much information about the script been given. We will look at plots and other aspects of the scripts in the next chapter. These four re-created events are theatre events, not drama, which brings us back to where we started—looking at the difference between theatre and drama. These four memorable performances of theatre are one-time-only experiences. But then every theatre performance, in its own way, is such a unique experience. Yet even unique occasions need to be planned, rehearsed, and polished. In the succeeding chapters we will see how this planning, rehearsing, and polishing are done.

TOPICS FOR GROUP DISCUSSION

1. If theatre is human action, how does one explain the success of *Cats*, *The Lion King*, and other works that have no human characters?
2. The American musical play has perhaps more conventions than any other kind of Western theatre. List as many of the unwritten "rules" for watching a musical that you can think of.
3. Theatre has often used masks. Today in America we associate masks mostly with Halloween. In what ways is the celebration of Halloween like theatre?
4. Recall a play or musical that you have seen on stage and compare it to a movie version you have seen, pointing out the differences in the two viewing experiences.

POSSIBLE RESEARCH PROJECTS

1. Select a novel that you are very familiar with and decide what must be done to turn it into a play.
2. View a video on YouTube of an Asian theatre presentation (Kabuki, Noh, Peking Opera, Hindu, etc.) and list all the ways in which it differs from the Western theatre practices you are familiar with.

FURTHER READING

Arnold, Stephanie. *The Creative Spirit: An Introduction to Theatre.* New York: McGraw-Hill, 2014.
Artaud, Antonio. *The Theatre and Its Double.* New York: Grove, 1958.
Barranger, Milly S. *Theatre: A Way of Seeing.* Belmont, CA: Wadsworth, 2014.
Beckerman, Bernard. *Theatrical Presentation: Performer, Audience, and Act.* New York: Routledge, 1991.
Bentley, Eric. *The Life of the Drama.* New York: Atheneum, 1964.
Bojsza, Elizabeth, Jeanette Yew, and Catherine Cammarata. *Introduction to Theatre.* Dubuque, IA: Kendall Hunt Publishing, 2017.
Bordman, Gerald, and Thomas S. Hischak. *The Oxford Companion to American Theatre.* 3rd ed. New York: Oxford University Press, 2004.
Brook, Peter. *The Empty Space.* New York: Atheneum, 1968.
Cassady, Marsh. *An Introduction to the Art of Theatre.* Colorado Springs, CO: Meriwether Publishers, 2007.
Cohen, Robert. *Theatre: Brief Version.* New York: McGraw-Hill, 2013.
Downs, William Missouri, Lou Anne Wright, and Erik Ramsey. *The Art of Theatre.* Belmont, CA: Wadsworth, 2012.

Fergusson, Francis. *The Idea of a Theatre.* Princeton, NJ: Princeton University Press, 1987.
Gendrich, Cynthia M., and Stephen Archer. *Theatre: Its Art and Craft.* Lanham, MD: Rowman & Littlefield, 2017.
Henderson, Mary C. *Theatre in America.* New York: Harry N. Abrams, 1996.
Jones, Robert Edmond. *The Dramatic Imagination.* New York: Meredith, 1941/2004.
Kantor, Michael, and Laurence Maslon. *Broadway: The American Musical.* New York: Bulfinch, 2004.
Patterson, Jim A., and Patti P. Gillespie. *The Enjoyment of Theatre.* New York: Macmillan, 2010.
Schechner, Richard. *Public Domain: Essays on Theatre.* New York: Macmillan, 1969.
Smiley, Sam. *Theatre: The Human Art.* New York: Harper and Row, 1987.
Wilmeth, Don B., and Tice L. Miller. *Cambridge Guide to American Theatre.* New York: Cambridge University Press, 2007.
Wilson, Edwin. *The Theatre Experience.* New York: McGraw-Hill, 2014.

2

THE PLAY

THE SCRIPT

It is necessary to temporarily put aside the theatre event and devote one chapter to the script, the literary aspect of the theatre process. Having read and studied plays in school, most audience members are familiar with drama. It is written down, published, analyzed, and perhaps even read aloud in English classes. Yet, as we have seen, only when the play is produced does it become theatre. Because so much of the theatre process is temporary or poorly documented, it is often only the script that survives. Actors die; scenery and playhouses are destroyed; costumes deteriorate; and the memories of audience members fade and disappear. Reviews in a newspaper, old posters or programs, and even some photographs may be found to prove that a theatre event occurred, but they are only shreds of evidence and can be misleading. Even a video of a stage production fails to truly capture what the event was like. Only the script can keep a play alive and allow subsequent generations to rediscover the work, whether on the page or on the stage.

Scholars argue about the structure of Shakespeare's Globe Theatre, the style of acting used, and what the costumes might have been like. Yet Shakespeare's scripts survive, even if the copies are riddled with printing errors and have sections of dialogue missing. Because the script for *Macbeth* and other Elizabethan plays have very few stage directions and no production notes, it is the dialogue itself that scholars use to try to re-create what the original production must have been like. Later playwrights, such as Moss Hart or Lorraine Hansberry, give detailed directions in their scripts, and they are easier to visualize, even if we did not have photographs of the first productions. So the script becomes a primary tool in learning not only what a play is about but also what a past theatre event was like. And, of course, it is the script that is the basis for all future productions of the play. Drama is not theatre, we insist, yet it would be almost impossible to create theatre without drama.

ABOUT FOUR SCRIPTS

In case you are not familiar with our four model plays, the scripts are briefly synopsized here. If you are already familiar with them, then the following will help refresh your memory so that the references from the plays that are used throughout the book will be useful to you. These capsule synopses depict what happens in the drama as written in the script. It is necessary to understand the drama so that the production elements in producing these plays can be discussed effectively later in the book.

MACBETH In a 2016 London production at the Globe Theatre, Ray Fearon and Tara Fitzgerald played Macbeth and Lady Macbeth as regal monarchs far removed from the original Scottish setting. Directed by Iqbal Khan. *theatrepix/Alamy Stock Photo*

Macbeth

Ancient Scotland is ruled by King Duncan, a ruler selected by the powerful Scottish noblemen called *thanes*. The Thane of Glamis is Macbeth, and, with his friend Banquo, he has helped win a battle in favor of the king. Three witches meet the two men and greet them, predicting that Macbeth will be promoted to the Thane of Cawdor and eventually become king. To Banquo they prophesy that his offspring will become future kings. King Duncan rewards Macbeth for his valor by naming him the Thane of Cawdor. Recalling the witches' words, Macbeth starts thinking about the throne, and his wife, Lady Macbeth, begins to have ambitious thoughts as well. Duncan surprises the thanes by naming his son Malcolm as the next king, instead of letting them decide, and this prompts the Macbeths to take matters into their own hands. While Duncan is a guest in their castle, Lady Macbeth spurs her husband to murder the king in his sleep, and suspicion falls on the young Malcolm, who flees Scotland. Macbeth becomes king, but he is uneasy about the witches' prophecy concerning Banquo's offspring. The childless Macbeth hires three murderers to kill Banquo and his young son Fleance, but the youth escapes and Macbeth's paranoia increases, even seeing Banquo's ghost during a banquet in the castle. Macbeth seeks out the three witches to learn more, and they show him visions of future kings, all descended from Banquo. Unhappy with the way Macbeth is ruling Scotland, some of the thanes, led by Macduff, decide to oust the king, and they convince Malcolm to take the throne as intended by Duncan. As the thanes gather forces to wage a war against the king, Macbeth sends murderers to kill Macduff's wife and children. The news sends Lady Macbeth, ridden with guilt, to reenact the murder of Duncan while sleepwalking; then, she dies. Macduff takes his revenge on Macbeth and kills the king in battle, putting Malcolm on the throne and bringing temporary peace to Scotland.

You Can't Take It with You

The Vanderhofs are an offbeat family of New Yorkers who seem to exist outside the real world. Grandpa Martin Vanderhof gave up his uninteresting job years ago and now lives life as he wants. He likes to raise snakes, attend commencement exercises, and encourage others to enjoy life and not worry about money. As he points out, "You can't take it with you." His middle-aged daughter Penny is happy writing plays and painting portraits, neither of which she ever seems to finish. Her husband Paul Sycamore experiments with fireworks in the basement with Mr. DePinna, a gentleman who came to the house years ago to deliver ice and decided to stay. Penny and Paul's awkward daughter Essie practices for a career in ballet under the instruction of the temperamental Russian immigrant Boris Kolenkhov, and her husband Ed Carmichael likes to play the xylophone and print leaflets on his own printing press. When the "normal" daughter Alice falls in love with her boss, the rising young banking executive Tony Kirby, she is worried about what he and his straitlaced parents will think of her oddball family. Alice invites the Kirbys to dinner and everyone promises to behave themselves. But when Tony brings his parents to the Vanderhof home one day early for dinner, the household is in total chaos with ballet dancing, xylophone music, and fireworks. Although Penny tries to put together a last-minute dinner and insists that everyone play a parlor game, the evening is a disaster, climaxed by FBI agents bursting into the house and arresting everyone because Ed's printed leaflets are considered an antigovernment call for anarchy. The next day Grandpa puts everything in order, bringing Alice and Tony together and even convincing Mr. Kirby that there is more to life than money.

YOU CAN'T TAKE IT WITH YOU Jason Robards (far left), renowned for his dramatic roles onstage and on-screen, gave a delightfully lighthearted performance as Grandpa Vanderhof in the acclaimed 1983 Broadway revival of the popular Kaufman and Hart comedy. Also pictured are George Rose, Colleen Dewhurst, and (bowing) Elizabeth Wilson. Director: Ellis Rabb. *Photofest*

A Raisin in the Sun

In a crowded two-room tenement in Chicago in the 1950s live the Youngers, an African American family that consists of the recently widowed Lena Younger; her grown son Walter and his wife, Ruth; their young son Travis; and Lena's outspoken daughter, Beneatha.

A RAISIN IN THE SUN Popular film actor Denzel Washington (standing, second from left) played the ambitious Walter Lee in the 2014 Broadway revival of the classic drama by Lorraine Hansberry. Such challenging roles often draw actors from Hollywood to the stage. Director: David Cromer. *Sara Krulwich/New York Times/Redux*

Walter works as a chauffeur but has hopes of making something better out of himself someday, if he can just get a little capital. That money comes in the form of the late Mr. Younger's life insurance check for $10,000. Walter wants to invest in a liquor store, but his mother wants to use it for Beneatha's college education and the down payment on a decent house where they can escape the ghetto and live a better life. But Walter's frustration, the rocky marriage of Walter and Ruth, and the news that Ruth is pregnant and is considering an abortion convince Lena to give Walter $6,500 of the money to invest in his scheme. Walter is thrilled, and for the next week he is optimistic about the future. Lena buys the house in the suburbs, but it is in an all-white community, and, before they move in, the neighbors send a representative, Mr. Lindner, to the Younger apartment to offer to buy it back at a higher price. Walter is angered and throws Lindner out. Walter's friend Bobo arrives to say that one of their partners has run off with all the money, including Walter's $6,500. An embittered Walter sees all his dreams collapse, and he goes to Lindner to make a deal. Lena and Beneatha see it as selling out to the white man, and Walter, finally acting like the man he wants to be, tells Lindner they are moving into the new neighborhood. He refuses Lindner's offer, and the play ends as the family finishes packing and prepares to move to the new house.

> ### *Clybourne Park*
>
> Fifty-three years after *A Raisin in the Sun* opened on Broadway, a sequel of sorts opened on Broadway. *Clybourne Park* is a comedy-drama by Bruce Norris that takes two different viewpoints of Hansberry's famous play. Act 1 takes place in 1959 in the house that Lena Younger wishes to buy in the Clybourne Park section of Chicago. The white family selling their home is told by their real estate agent that a "Negro" family wants to purchase the house, leading to a heated discussion among neighbors and friends. Act 2 takes place in the same house in 2009 when the Clybourne Park neighborhood is being gentrified and young white couples are buying the midcentury-style homes in the now desirable part of Chicago. Lena's granddaughter, also named Lena, is trying to protect the neighborhood and her family heritage and gets into a fiery discussion with the white couple who wish to renovate the house out of recognition. *Clybourne Park* opened on Broadway in 2012 after regional and Off-Broadway productions and won several awards. The play is frequently produced, sometimes in repertory with *A Raisin in the Sun*.

Hamilton

In the Caribbean, the lowly born Alexander Hamilton rises from poverty and, in 1776, makes his way to New York City, where he befriends Aaron Burr, the Marquis de Lafayette, and other young revolutionaries who defy the snooty King George. Hamilton falls in love with and marries the monied Eliza Schuyler, although her elder sister, Angelica, also loves the ambitious and smart immigrant. Soon he works his way up to become George Washington's "right-hand man" but does not get to show off his military skills until the crucial Battle of Yorktown. The colonies gain their freedom just as both Hamilton and Burr's wives give birth, and both men are optimistic about their future. Hamilton is made secretary of the treasury; however, Burr is overlooked, adding to the rivalry between the former friends.

HAMILTON Not only are the historical details altered for dramatic effect in Lin-Manuel Miranda's musical *Hamilton*, the way the Founding Fathers are depicted is also unconventional and anachronistic. *Hamilton* is history filtered through a modern sensibility. Shown are the Marquis de LaFayettte (Daveed Diggs, left) and Alexander Hamilton (Lin-Manuel Miranda) from the original cast. *Photofest*

Hamilton's plans for a national bank are aggressively opposed by Virginians James Madison and Thomas Jefferson, but newly elected president George Washington is on Hamilton's side, and in a secret deal made with the two Southerners, Hamilton's financial plans are approved in exchange for the nation's new capital city being built on the Potomac River in Virginia. When Washington retires, Hamilton's enemies try to accuse him of stealing money from the government treasury, but Hamilton proves that the checks were his own money, blackmail payments made to cover up an affair he had with a married woman. Hamilton goes so far as to publish his guilt in the *Reynolds Pamphlet*, which destroys his political career. He retires from public life and is eventually forgiven by his wife, but tragedy strikes when their son, Philip, is killed in a duel. When Burr runs against Jefferson for U.S. president, Hamilton supports his longtime enemy Jefferson, contributing to Burr losing the election. Burr challenges Hamilton to a duel for slandering his name, and Hamilton accepts. But instead of aiming his pistol at Burr, Hamilton fires into the air, and Burr fatally shoots him in the chest. Eliza and Angelica spend the rest of their lives getting Hamilton's many essays published and spreading his ideas to future generations.

These thumbnail sketches can hardly begin to convey the complexity and many layers of character relationships that exist in the four plays. One needs not only more details of the story but fuller descriptions of the characters, samples of the dialogue, a sense of what the plays would look like, and an indication of the themes they contain. All noteworthy plays should contain these elements, each of which needs to be explained.

THE ELEMENTS OF DRAMA

We have seen that the four ingredients needed for a theatre event to happen are actors, script, audience, and a performance place. We will return to these throughout the book, looking at the various people who make these four things happen. Yet the script itself is made up of various elements, all of which are necessary to creating a play. These elements were first outlined over two millennia ago by the Greek philosopher Aristotle, who is also considered the first theatre scholar. With his insatiable appetite for discovering and studying everything around him, Aristotle looked at the theatre of his day and wrote a treatise called the *Poetics*, in which he analyzes what makes a play work onstage and which aspects of drama are the most essential. While today we may disagree with the order of importance that Aristotle poses, most do agree that he sums up the elements thoroughly and effectively. Not all of the *Poetics* survived, but we do have Aristotle's elements—in order of importance—for tragedy, one of the types of drama to be described later. He ranks the elements as plot, character, theme, diction, music, and spectacle.

Plot

The easiest element for audiences to understand is plot. What happens is of interest to everyone, and even the most philosophical play should have some sense of "What happens next?" Yet plot is more than just the story of the play. Plot includes how that story is told, what happens physically but also emotionally to the characters, and how the playwright unfolds the tale. Macbeth kills a king; that is story. Macbeth's guilt turns to neurosis as he suspects those around him; that is plot. While some modern plays may emphasize the other five elements over plot, it is still true that something happens in most plays. A character making a vital decision can be a major plot point, such as Lena in *A Raisin in the Sun*, who decides to buy a house in an all-white neighborhood. Or a plot may hinge on a coincidence, such as Alexander Hamilton befriending the young Aaron Burr when he arrives in New York City, not knowing their early friendship will lead to a deadly rivalry. In some plays the plot comes from the physical action, and the story has many twists and revelations, such as in *Macbeth*. But just as often the plot is more subtle and less physical, such as the character conflicts in *A Raisin in the Sun*. Some plays, such as the absurdist theatre pieces to be discussed later, make a point of having no story at all. Yet even in these actionless dramas that contain nonsensical activities, something happens. The very nature of putting actors onstage and having them speak and react off of each other means that some plotting will occur. The theatre in Aristotle's day was strong on plot, and it is understandable that he placed it first. What happens onstage, either physically or emotionally, is what drove Greek drama, and, in many cases, it still does today.

Character

Since theatre is human action, a play needs characters, just as a theatre event needs actors. Obviously a plot cannot take place without people, but characters in a play should be much more than human figures that are moved about by the story. From the very beginnings of theatre, audiences have expected characters onstage to hold one's interest, to capture not only our attention but our emotions as well. Whether we laugh at a hero, root for the heroine, or dislike the villain, the audience must somehow connect with the characters. Some plays demand that the characters be larger than life, such as the ambitious Macbeth or the extroverted King George III. Other characters fascinate us because of their quiet resolve and steady determination, such as Lena Younger. It is even possible for the characters in a play to be "normal," such as Alice and Tony in *You Can't Take It with You*, but still enthrall us with their sincere human qualities. While there are many satisfying plays that have only one-dimensional characters who are little more than types, most drama relies on fully developed characters with some depth to their portrayal. The many levels of emotion that Walter Younger has make his character much more fascinating than just an angry African American male, just as Alexander Hamilton's drive to be accepted as more than just an immigrant sometimes makes him obnoxious and obsessive. Even less explosive characters, such as the easy-going Grandpa in *You Can't Take It with You*, have layers to them, allowing actors to bring out the humanity in the people they are portraying.

Many modern plays seem to be about characters first and plot second, somewhat defying Aristotle's order of importance. Surely this can be said about *A Raisin in the Sun* and *You Can't Take It with You*. But in both cases the plotting is subtler than in, say, *Macbeth*, so it just may be a matter of degree. Regardless, in the best plays the audience should develop an *empathy* with some or all of the characters. Unlike sympathy, where one feels sorry for an unfortunate person, empathy in the theatre involves an emotional commitment on the theatregoer's part. One understands and shares feelings similar to those of the character, even if one does not directly identify oneself as being similar to that character. It is possible to have empathy for Macbeth and Lady Macbeth, not because one emotionally shares their murderous actions, but because it is possible to understand their ambition and, later, their guilt. Empathy is also a very personal emotion. One audience member may empathize with the Vanderhofs in *You Can't Take It with You* because of their unconventional but honest values, while another will have empathy for the young and reckless Alexander Hamilton, just as African Americans will find a special empathy for the Younger family. It is these kinds of connections with the characters that make for effective drama.

CHARACTER While the plot of David Auburn's drama *Proof* (2000) is indeed intriguing, it is the central character of Catherine who fascinates the audience. Mary-Louise Parker's stunning performance keeps us guessing whether Catherine is losing her mind, just as her famous mathematician father did. Director: Daniel Sullivan. *Joan Marcus/Photofest*; photographer: Joan Marcus

Theme

When one mentions the theme of a piece of literature, too many think in terms of a moral or a lesson that the work conveys. Great literature does not moralize, and truly effective plays cannot be summarized in the form of a lesson. Theme, according to Aristotle, is the primary idea behind a play. It is something that drives the plot and characters because it is an idea that is rich with complexity or dilemma. *Macbeth* is not a moral tale about what happens to overambitious people; instead, it is about the self-destructive power of ambition and how it can affect nations as well as people. The themes in *You Can't Take It with You*, *A Raisin in the Sun*, and *Hamilton* are more difficult to define. All three plays avoid overt villains and moralistic endings. One strongly feels for the Younger family and may be angered at the discrimination they face, yet Lorraine Hansberry's drama is so much more than an angry diatribe against racism. Lin-Manuel Miranda's *Hamilton* may reflect his own personal feelings about immigrants in the United States today, but he puts his ideas in the context of a story from history. Some plays have strong, thought-provoking themes, while others may be content with merely revealing the everyday human condition or exploring the foibles of human nature. One should judge a play not by the level of importance attached to its theme but rather by the way the theme still relates to its audience. A very old play such as *Macbeth* can still make an audience think and consider the dangerous appeal of ambition, just as the more recent *A Raisin in the Sun* can speak to us from a time before the civil rights movement. Audiences today are responding to the potent ideas of liberty and sacrifice in *Hamilton*. Timeless plays have timeless themes.

Diction

Diction is a deceiving term because one immediately thinks of vocal diction, the ability to speak clearly. Aristotle referred to much more than speaking aloud when he placed diction as his fourth most important element. In drama, diction is the language of the piece or the dialogue in the play and the manner in which it is presented. For centuries all drama was written in poetry, so Aristotle included the rhyme, rhythm, literary imagery, and even the beauty of the verse in his study. Although few nonmusical plays today use these poetic devices, all plays have diction. The way the Vanderhofs speak is very different from the African American flavor of the Youngers and the rhythmic cadences of the Founding Fathers in *Hamilton*. Some diction is realistic, as in *A Raisin in the Sun*, while other works employ a highly lyrical language, such as in *Hamilton* and other musicals. The playwright creates a form of spoken language for the dialogue, and, even though each character may have a distinct diction of his or her own, the overall effect must be of a cohesive kind of sound that runs through the whole play. Young and eager Beneatha in *A Raisin in the Sun* may speak quite differently from her old-fashioned mother, but both sound like African Americans living in Chicago in the 1950s. It takes both the playwright's words and the actors' vocal techniques to bring the diction of a play to life.

Music

When Aristotle listed music among his six elements, the chanting of verse and the dancing formations by the chorus in Greek tragedies were very common. Most plays were, in essence, a form of musical. Today we have a thriving musical theatre, and we consider music and dance as necessary components of such kinds of theatre. Yet music can be found in most plays, whether in the form of songs included in the text or even as background music that creates mood or establishes the atmosphere for a specific location. Consider the trumpeting sounds of battle in *Macbeth* or Essie's ballet dance music. Music is also present in every play in that the dialogue also presents patterns of sound that can have rhythm and cadence. Walter Younger's fervent, pulsating speeches when he is angry practically take on a rift sound even as Beneatha's rhythmic dialogue when talking of her African heritage seems to echo the tribal beating of that heritage. It is in the modern American musical where music predominates and, had Aristotle been able to see today's musicals, perhaps he would have placed music at the top of his list for some kinds of drama. Music certainly drives *Hamilton* and gives the work its diction for both the plot and the characters. Even more than most traditional musicals, where the music stops for dialogue scenes, *Hamilton* is "composed through," meaning all of the text is set to music, whether it is song lyrics or bits of prose set against the music in the background. Music becomes an extension of the people and the story, and even its themes are reflected in the uncompromising rap and hip-hop score.

SPECTACLE Andrew Lloyd Webber's musical extravaganza *The Phantom of the Opera* is Broadway's longest-running musical, entertaining new and repeat audiences since 1988. Such musicals place the spectacle aspect of drama much higher than Aristotle ever imagined. Sarah Brightman and Michael Crawford led the original cast, directed by Harold Prince, with sets and costumes by Maria Björnson. *Joan Marcus/Photofest; photographer: Joan Marcus*

Spectacle

Finally, Aristotle placed *spectacle* as one of the six elements, although he deemed it the least important. With so many "spectacular" productions on Broadway today, one might suspect that Aristotle could not imagine *The Phantom of the Opera* or *Wicked*. When he included spectacle, he meant all visual aspects of a play—primarily scenery, costumes (and masks), and dance. Since Greek plays mostly used the same outdoor stone structure as the scenery for all plays, there was very little that was spectacular to theatregoers. The cast did employ masks and costumes, and the chorus was involved in dance, but all of these components were minor compared to the other elements mentioned here. No wonder he put spectacle last.

Today, with elaborate scenery, lighting, makeup, and other visuals, spectacle becomes a major consideration in many productions. It is difficult to imagine a big Broadway musical that does not rely on spectacle. Yet most theatre is not on that level, and most plays do not rely heavily on spectacle. All theatre events are visual, even with the most modest sets and costumes. We still see a play rather than just hear it. So perhaps what Aristotle believed is still correct: spectacle adds richness and variety to a play, but rarely is it the essential element that makes theatregoing special. Any production of *Macbeth* must contend with costumes, armor, weapons, and some scenic depiction of the Scottish locales, though infrequently are these presented realistically. The Chicago household of the Younger family in *A Raisin in the Sun* must convey to the audience the social and economic situation of the characters. Yet the visuals for those two plays, as with *Hamilton* and *You Can't Take it with You*, are secondary. None of these four plays can be described as spectacular pieces, though some misguided productions have probably tried to turn them into such. Audiences traditionally like spectacle, and many modern theatre events have found popularity by offering impressive spectaculars, but the most effective and enduring dramas have always used spectacle sparingly.

One must keep in mind that Aristotle was a spokesman for Western theatre and his ideas apply more readily to plays in Europe and the Americas. It is important to understand that the arts in much of the rest of the world do not abide by this Western tradition. Just as we saw in the previous chapter that theatre conventions differ greatly between the East and the West, so too do the elements of drama. An Asian play may have plot, characters, theme, diction, music, and spectacle but they will not be presented in the same way as with a Western theatre performance. For example, spectacle is an extremely important element in the Kabuki theatre of Japan. The same cultural differences can be found in the types of drama to be discussed next.

TYPES OF DRAMA

Plays in ancient Greece generally fell into two categories: tragedy and comedy. The two genres were very distinct, with very little that was serious in the comedies and with rare comic relief in the tragedies. Yet over the ages the two types started to overlap, and today there are several classifications for drama, some terms showing this mixture (such as *tragicomedy*) while others being more specific (such as *musical comedy*). The major types of drama will be discussed next, but it is important to keep in mind that many modern plays are not purely one genre. In fact, some of the most effective scripts of the last one hundred years are rather difficult to classify.

Tragedy is one of the oldest types but one that is not so readily found in modern drama. In the *Poetics*, Aristotle defined a tragedy as a serious work with a hero who is great and good but has a flaw that brings down destruction on himself or herself. The hero, often referred to as the *protagonist*, is great, meaning that he or she is of noble rank, such as that of a king, so that his or her downfall affects many. He or she must have good qualities; otherwise, there is nothing tragic about punishing such a person. And most important, the central character must have a flaw, some error of judgment or personality fault that gets the best of the hero and causes the self-destruction. The Greeks called this flaw *hamartia*, a complex word that suggests a moral failing that the hero may or may not be aware of. Some people think of a death when they hear the word *tragedy*, and indeed we use the word outside of theatre to describe a horrible event in which many die. But onstage, tragedy does not require death as much as punishment. In Sophocles' play *Oedipus the King*, which Aristotle described as a "model" tragedy, the title character does not die, but he is punished severely: he is blinded by his own hand. All the same, since death is often considered the ultimate punishment, most tragedies do end with the hero dying. *Macbeth* might be termed a model tragedy as well. Macbeth is great (a powerful thane and later a king) and starts out good (he fights valiantly for his king), but his flaw (ambition) brings about his downfall and he is punished (killed by Macduff in battle).

Classic tragedies still appeal to audiences today, much as *Oedipus the King* and the early Greek tragedies moved audiences to experience the emotions "pity and fear" (as Aristotle described them). Yet it is very difficult for modern plays to easily fall into the category of tragedy, at least as it was defined by Aristotle. Modern heroes and heroines are rarely kings or powerful nobles but, more often, ordinary people. They may be good, have a flaw, and are punished because of it, but their fate rarely affects hundreds of other people. Arthur Miller's beloved drama *Death of a Salesman* has often been argued to be a modern tragedy. The central character, the struggling salesman Willy Loman, is a good man who wants what is best for his family; but his flaw, his misguided belief that popularity and phony confidence are enough to succeed in America, slowly destroys him and he commits suicide. Willy's fate doesn't affect the populace as a whole but, Miller and others argue, Willy represents thousands of misguided Americans and his fate is their fate. It is an argument that continues as playwrights and scholars try to apply the old definition of tragedy to new plays.

Comedy is the other oldest type of play, and it is a genre that is still written and produced today. One thinks of humor and laughter when the term *comedy* is used, yet, oddly enough, in some periods of theatre history, comedies were not all that funny. By strict definition (again Aristotle is the source most often used), comedy deals with social problems rather than political ones, and, despite the many complications of the plot and various flaws of the characters, the ending is a happy one. Both tragedy and comedy can have the same theme, such as jealousy, ambition, infidelity, revenge, and so on. It is the treatment of that theme that distinguishes the two genres. The tone is lighter in comedy, just as the characters may have exaggerated emotions, and the dialogue is usually sprightlier and nimbler than in serious drama.

COMEDY Playwright Neil Simon excelled at character comedy, and few comic characters are as beloved as the slob Oscar Madison (Walter Matthau, left) and his finicky housemate, Felix Ungar (Art Carney), as portrayed in the original Broadway production of *The Odd Couple* (1965). Director: Mike Nichols. *Photofest*

Some plays are funny because the story is comic, filled with complicated plots, broad character types, and plenty of physical action. This particular type of comedy is more specifically called a *farce.* Farce is sometimes considered low comedy because it appeals to less-exulted human instincts,

FARCE When an audience laughs more at what is happening than to whom it is happening, chances are the play is a farce. Plenty happens to everyone in Michael Frayn's *Noises Off* (1983), a gleeful backstage look at an English theatre troupe that is, ironically, performing a farce. Depicted is a scene from the original Broadway production directed by Michael Blakemore. *Photofest*

but farces are extremely difficult to write and are far from easy to produce. There is often a fine line between comedy and farce, and many plays move back and forth from one genre to the other, placing the two types side by side in the same plot. When the humor grows from witty lines, the personalities of the characters, and a satirical theme, one is in the realm of comedy; but when *what* the characters do is funnier than who they are or what they say, chances are that farce is at work. The two types are so closely interconnected that an actor or a director or designer can move a play from comedy to farce just by how a line is delivered, how a scene is staged, or what a costume looks like. Several scenes in *You Can't Take It with You*, for example, can be effectively played as farce or comedy.

Another specific type of comedy is *comedy of manners*, another genre not found today as readily as it was in the past. As the name implies, comedy of manners makes fun of the behavior and social conventions of a group of people. The most accomplished comedies of manners were written in eighteenth-century England, where playwrights such as William Congreve and Richard Sheridan spoofed the manners of their own age. The audience in the theatre laughed at the characters on-stage, who unmistakably resembled them. It is still possible to write such comedies today. Popular playwright Neil Simon often wrote about Jewish urban middle-class people, finding humor in their language and attitudes. Again, those plays are most popular with audiences who resemble such social types, even as they sometimes have a more universal appeal.

Finally, there is the form of comedy called *satire*, which also spoofs society but concerns itself with more than manners or trivialities. Satire usually takes on significant issues, themes such as politics, racism, the unequal distribution of wealth, women's rights, and other topics found in serious plays. Unlike other forms of comedy, satire has very specific targets and hopes to make audiences think differently about issues even as they are being entertained. Modern satires are hard to come by, and many quickly become outdated because they are so timely, but a well-written satire can be a very potent piece of theatre and can create more discussion and rethinking than even a tragedy.

Melodrama immediately conjures up images of exaggerated emotions, one-dimensional characters, and contrived plots. To say that something or someone is melodramatic today is not a compliment. But in theatre, a melodrama is any serious play that does not aspire to the heights of tragedy. In the nineteenth century, American melodramas were very popular, and many of the clichés associated with the term were created then: the mustached villain who wants to foreclose on the mortgage, the pure-hearted heroine tied to the railroad tracks, the daring hero with nothing but honesty in his heart, and so on.

Today old scripts from the past and new ones (usually described as "meller-dramas") filled with these qualities are played as comedies, and audiences laugh at what once was taken seriously. Because of this kind of association, producers and playwrights prefer to call their serious plays *dramas*. It is a vague and inaccurate term since all plays are, in essence, dramas. Whichever label is used, these are plays that are more serious than a comedy but not as classically tragic as a tragedy.

Melodramas can be incisive character studies with rich and poetic dialogue (such as *A Raisin in the Sun*), but they can also be thrilling murder mysteries or exciting adventures that make no attempt at thought-provoking theatre. The range for this kind of drama is vast, and no simple definition can hope to encompass the variety that is possible. It is usual for melodrama to have comic relief, and, over the past half century or so, it is not uncommon for comedies to have more than a touch of melodrama in them. When the two opposites get so close that they seem to balance

MELODRAMA Arthur Miller's melodramas all have strong themes and provoke an audience to consider conflicts that are not easily resolved. Willy Loman thinks he has figured out the way to a successful life in *Death of a Salesman* (1949), but it soon becomes clear that his values were misguided. Some argue that this is a modern form of tragedy. Pictured is the original Broadway production, featuring Lee J. Cobb (far right) as Willy. Director: Elia Kazan. *Photofest*

each other out, the term *tragicomedy* is used. This genre is the most difficult to define (and consequently playwrights rarely use it), but the mixture of comic and tragic elements is more common that one might suspect. There are moments of humor in *Hamilton*, for example, even though it is primarily a serious musical.

The *musical*, the only genre that is an American invention, is perhaps the most popular kind of drama today, but it is a relatively new development. Like most American innovations, the musical was made up of various kinds of European theatre: opera, operetta, melodrama, ballet, and other ingredients. Added to these were blues, jazz, and a distinctively American sound and a raucous kind of American comedy. These ingredients were first put together in the mid-1800s, and slowly there developed a kind of musical comedy that alternated between spoken dialogue, singing, and dancing. The plots for most early musical comedies were slight: boy meets girl in act 1, boy loses girl in act 2, then boy and girl get back together in act 3. With this model, producers were able to work in plenty of chorus numbers, duets, comic scenes, dance, and spectacle. From the start, spectacle played a major role in musicals and generally still does today.

The first musical to tackle serious themes was *Show Boat* (1927), a complex piece by songwriters Jerome Kern and Oscar Hammerstein that used music to deepen and further the plot, characters, and themes of the show. *Show Boat* was a landmark musical and one that can still be effectively presented onstage today. A later musical that created the format that most musical plays would follow was

MUSICAL The most popular form of theatre today in New York and London is the big musical, for example, *Les Misérables* (1987), which has thrilled audiences internationally. Originating in France, the epic musical was adapted into English and, directed by Trevor Nunn, opened in London in 1985, and on Broadway in 1987. *Photofest*

Oklahoma! (1943), in which the creative team of Richard Rodgers and Hammerstein fully integrated the score. This means that the songs and dances grew out of the characters' emotions and were an extension of the plot rather than a series of musical numbers that interrupted the story line. The American musical has grown much since *Oklahoma!* and composers, lyricists, and playwrights have explored new directions that the genre can take. *Hamilton* is a vibrant example of a musical that uses the foundations of past musicals then dares to experiment with new ways to tell its story. Just as *A Raisin in the Sun* cannot be labeled a typical melodrama, so too is *Hamilton* only one particular musical and cannot be called representative of the whole genre. But *Hamilton* contains the elements that have distinguished musicals from the start: story, songs, dance.

There is one final type of play, though it is usually combined with one of the genres already discussed. *Fantasy* is a general description for any play that creates its own reality. Whether it is comedy or tragedy or even a musical, a fantasy offers a world that has its own kind of logic, and the audience accepts fantastical elements as the norm. Children fly and fairies scheme in *Peter Pan*; angels come crashing through the ceiling in *Angels in America*; and animals talk in many children's plays. Fantasy can take many forms and be used for everything from escapist entertainment to painting a dark portrait of a future world. Some plays, such as *Macbeth*, use fantasy elements but might not be labeled fantasies as such. The witches seem to have supernatural powers and the audience is asked to accept unreal elements in the midst of a realistic tale. This is not so difficult to accept because of the "pretend" nature of live theatre. If we can believe that a modern actor is a medieval Scottish king, then we can accept witches disappearing into thin air. In a way, all theatre is a fantasy; the audience knows that nothing onstage is real but agrees to believe all the same.

> **From Play to Musical**
>
> In 1973, the play *A Raisin in the Sun* was turned Into a Broadway musical called *Raisin* with a book by Robert Nemiroff and Charlotte Zaltzberg, music by Judd Woldin, and lyrics by Robert Brittan. The musical was faithful to the original play, and most of the songs were extensions of the dialogue found in Hansberry's original script. The cast of characters remained the same, and much of the action was still in the Youngers's apartment on the South Side of Chicago in the 1950s. As successful as *Raisin* was (it ran 847 performances and won the Tony Award for Best Musical of the Season), it is seldom revived today. Some feel that it was unsatisfying as a musical, and others point out that little was gained by adding songs to the drama. As popular as musicals are today, it is still the play version of *A Raisin in the Sun* that is frequently revived in theatres across the country. Most musicals are based on successful plays, but in the case of *Raisin*, the transition from play to musical was a disappointing and, perhaps, unnecessary one.

DRAMATIC STRUCTURE

Not all plays are built the same. We say *built* rather than *written* because a play is a structure of sorts, and, though scholars may disagree on what form that structure takes, the piece must be built so that it holds up. In the nineteenth century there was much talk about the *well-made play*. This referred not to the quality of the playwriting but to the structure of the drama. Well-made plays were clearly and logically plotted, and every turn in the story was foreshadowed and explained. Today such a rigid structure is infrequently used. Over the centuries different structural styles have come in and gone out of fashion, but there are some basic elements of dramatic structure that seem to recur over and over and are still with us today. Regardless of the type of play being built, many of these elements are still present and are worth examining.

Inciting incident is a term not frequently used today, but it is still the best one for describing the impetus behind any plot. Before the action begins for the audience, even before the curtain rises, something has happened in the story that incites the plot line. This incident may have occurred many years earlier, such as the day Duncan was crowned king, before *Macbeth* begins, or more recently such as the death of Mr. Younger in *A Raisin in the Sun*. Of course, there is no way the audience can know about these incidents when the play begins, but some of the characters know about it, and it affects all of their subsequent actions. As the play unfolds, the audience learns of this and other past events, and it helps in making sense of either the story or the character's behavior. Determining the inciting incident is useful in understanding how the drama is structured and is a valuable tool for actors and the director as well as theatregoers.

Point of attack is an aggressive but accurate phrase to describe when the action begins. Few plays begin with a point of attack. Most modern plays introduce characters, set the scene, and even give information before getting around to starting the plot. Chitchat between the maid and the lady of the house is a clichéd example of "filler" used before the point of attack. Playwrights purposely used this kind of filler so that latecomers to the playhouse would not miss anything important. At some point before the play has progressed very far, a piece of information, an announcement, a letter, the arrival of a visitor, or some other device is used to telegraph to the audience that the plot has begun. Often this piece of information is the inciting incident, such as the revelation that Mr. Younger has died and a sizable life insurance check is expected. Other times it is a complication, such as Alice announcing that she wants to bring her boss, Tony, and his conservative parents to meet her screwball family. The point of attack must somehow grab the audience's attention and signify that something of interest is starting to happen. When the three witches hint to Macbeth and Banquo of their royal futures, both the characters and the audience are intrigued. The play has truly begun.

Exposition is any information about the past that is brought to the stage by the characters. News of a past inciting incident is an obvious example, but many plays need exposition throughout the drama, not just in the opening scene. Exposition can be revealed subtly through dialogue, as at the beginning of *A Raisin in the Sun*, or told point-blank to the audience, such as the revealing of the Vanderhofs's past lives when someone new enters the house in *You Can't Take It with You*. Writing exposition that is interesting and not too contrived is difficult, particularly in a realistic drama. Lorraine Hansberry handles exposition with skill throughout *A Raisin in the Sun* as we learn about the late Mr. Younger, Walter's failed investment, and the white neighborhood's resistance to an African American family moving in. Lin-Manuel Miranda takes a different approach, having Alexander Hamilton and other characters bluntly tell us about events that happen offstage, such as battles and political elections. Unlike a novel, where the narrator can easily tell us about past events and people, a play must handle such information carefully so that the drama is human action and not just talk about human action.

Foreshadowing onstage is hinting or blatantly telling the audience about something that will occur later in the story. It does not necessarily mean that the author gives away the ending, but the playwright does prepare the audience so that they can better understand some later plot developments. The witches in *Macbeth* are obvious devices for foreshadowing because they are prophets of sorts. They prophesy that "no man of woman born" can harm Macbeth. The king takes this as proof that he is invincible until he learns later in battle that Macduff was born outside his mother's womb because it was a cesarean delivery; he is indeed not born of woman. In most modern plays, foreshadowing is more quietly done. The Vanderhofs's fascination with firecrackers and printing leaflets prepares the audience for the raid by the FBI, just as discussion in the Younger household prepares the audience for Walter's loss of the money and the reaction that the white neighbors will have to black neighbors. Because *Hamilton* is history that may already be known to the audience, Miranda does not hide the ending. In the first scene, Aaron Burr introduces himself as the man who shot Alexander Hamilton. Foreshadowing is sometimes needed to clarify the story, but just as often it adds a richness to the drama by presenting ideas to the audience that add intrigue.

Complications are necessary in every play because without something going wrong for the characters, there is no conflict, and human action with no conflicts tends to be uninteresting. There are both comic and tragic complications in drama, and both are essential to good plotting. Alice loves her oddball family but is also ashamed to expose her fiancé to them. Macbeth plots to murder Banquo and his young son, but the boy escapes, and it looks like the prophecy will come true. Complications "thicken" the plot and propel the action forward. The conflicts may be subtle, such as Angelica's unspoken love for Alexander Hamilton, or outspoken, such as the fights between Walter and his wife, Ruth, concerning money and the raising of their child. While sometimes the conflict can exist between man and nature, it is usually the conflicts between people that are most potent onstage. The hero may battle a monster or an earthquake on-screen or in a book, but in the theatre it is human action that counts.

The *climax* of a play is when all the complications lead to the highest emotional moment of the story. In a comedy this may indeed be the funniest or most outrageous point of the play, while in tragedy and melodrama it can be the most moving or heartfelt moment. Some plays erupt into violence at the climax, such as the killing of Macbeth on the battlefield, while other works have a more restrained and even resigned kind of climax, such as the Younger family's decision to move into the white neighborhood despite the resistance that awaits them. A climax can inspire hope and optimism, such as Eliza and Angelica carrying on the ideas of the deceased Alexander Hamilton or the happy resolutions at the end of *You Can't Take It with You*. Of course, the highest emotional moment is sometimes a matter of personal choice, and what is most moving to one audience member may not be as effective to another. For example, modern audiences are sometimes more affected by Lady Macbeth's sleepwalking scene than Macbeth's death. Walter's explosive reaction when he discovers that he has been swindled out of his money is more emotionally charged than the less-dramatic ending of *A Raisin in the Sun*, and some theatregoers might accept that scene as the play's climax. Yet for each person watching a drama, the emotions should peak at some point so that the play is truly satisfying.

A play's *conclusion* suggests that some new order or sense of balance is reached after the climax. It does not imply that there must be a happy ending or even an ending at all. The conclusion was called the *denouement* in the old well-made plays and is often referred to today as the *resolution*. Yet many plays do not completely resolve themselves. Malcolm will take the throne at the end of *Macbeth*, but it is less clear what will happen to the surviving characters in our other three sample plays. What will happen to the Youngers when they move into their new house is problematic at best. Even if a play does not resolve itself, it does conclude, and some kind of settling of the dust occurs. We said earlier that most forms of comedy end happily for the hero and heroine and that tragedies end with some kind of punishment for the protagonist. Happy or tragic, a conclusion is essential for an audience to fully be satisfied with a play. Some dramas, such as the sociopolitical works by the German playwright Bertolt Brecht and the absurdist playwrights to be discussed in a later chapter, purposely deny the audience a satisfying conclusion. They know that a play that does not finish neatly is very disturbing to theatregoers, and that is their intent. But most playwrights find that a solid conclusion strengthens the impact of a play and its dramatic structure.

Much of the discussion so far has been about the literary aspects of theatre, and very little talk of production has been included. It is important to understand the literary side of the theatre event in order to appreciate the role of the playwright. He or she deals with the written word but, as we shall see in the next chapter, also must create a play with production in mind. The dramatic elements of a play, the types of plays, and the dramatic structure of plays are only important in terms of how they are presented on the stage. That is the playwright's challenge.

TOPICS FOR GROUP DISCUSSION

1. Choose three television series or miniseries currently popular and discuss how each might be classified: tragedy, comedy, farce, melodrama, or some mixture of these.
2. How much do you agree with Aristotle's ranking of the dramatic elements? Select two plays or films in which the order of importance might not follow the Greek philosopher's thesis.

3. Choose a film or play that the group has seen and see if the members of the group agree on what is the climax of the piece.
4. Discuss which scenes in *You Can't Take It with You* are farce and which are comedy.

POSSIBLE RESEARCH PROJECTS

1. Read or view Arthur Miller's *The Crucible* or *All My Sons* and make an argument why or why not the work can be considered a tragedy.
2. Read or view Tennessee Williams's *The Glass Menagerie* or *A Streetcar Named Desire* and rank the dramatic elements as presented in the play.
3. View the 1972 film musical *1776* and compare how some of the same historic events are depicted in it and *Hamilton*.
4. The unconventional Vanderhofs in *You Can't Take It with You* have inspired many other comic writers over the decades. Try to identify some films, television series, and even musicals that have used the premise of the "normal" person in an oddball family.
5. Read Bruce Norris's *Clybourne Park* and compare it to *A Raisin in the Sun* in terms of type of play, Aristotle's elements, and dramatic structure.

FURTHER READING

Beckerman, Bernard. *Dynamics of Drama: Theory and Method of Analysis.* New York: Drama Book Specialists, 1979.

Bentley, Eric. *The Life of the Drama.* New York: Atheneum, 1964.

———. *The Theory of the Modern Stage.* Baltimore: Penguin, 1968.

Bermel, Albert. *Farce: A History from Aristophanes to Woody Allen.* New York: Simon and Schuster, 1982.

Bloom, Ken, and Frank Vlastnik. *Broadway Musicals: The 101 Greatest Shows of All Time.* New York: Black Dog and Leventhal, 2010.

Bordman, Gerald, and Richard Norton. *American Musical Theatre: A Chronicle.* 4th ed. New York: Oxford University Press, 2010.

Butcher, S. H., trans. *Aristotle's Poetics.* New York: Hill and Wang, 1961.

Chernow, Ron. *Alexander Hamilton.* London: Penguin, 2005.

Corrigan, Robert W., ed. *Comedy: Meaning and Form.* San Francisco: Chandler, 1965.

———. *Tragedy: Vision and Form.* San Francisco: Chandler, 1965.

Dukore, Bernard, ed. *Dramatic Theory and Criticism: Greeks to Grotowski.* New York: Holt, Rinehart and Winston, 1974.

Else, Gerald F. *Aristotle's Poetics: The Argument.* Cambridge, MA: Harvard University Press, 1957.

Esslin, Martin. *An Anatomy of Drama.* New York: Hill and Wang, 1977.

Ganzl, Kurt. *The Encyclopedia of the Musical Theatre.* 2nd ed. New York: Schirmer Books, 2001.

Gassner, John, and Edward Quinn. *The Reader's Encyclopedia of World Drama.* Mineola, NY: Dover, 2002.

Green, Stanley. *Broadway Musicals Show by Show.* 7th ed. Milwaukee, WI: Applause Books, 2011.

Grode, Eric. *The Book of Broadway: The 150 Definitive Plays and Musicals.* Minneapolis, MN: Voyageur Press, 2015.

Hansberry, Lorraine. *A Raisin in the Sun* and *The Sign in Sidney Brustein's Window.* New York: Vintage, 1995.
Heilman, Robert G. *Tragedy and Melodrama: Versions of Experience.* Seattle: University of Washington Press, 1968.
Hischak, Thomas S. *100 Greatest American Plays.* Lanham, MD: Rowman & Littlefield, 2017.
———. *The Oxford Companion to the American Musical.* New York: Oxford University Press, 2008.
Kaufman, George S. *Three Plays by Kaufman and Hart.* New York: Grove, 1994.
Kaufman, George S., and Moss Hart. *You Can't Take It with You.* New York: Dramatists Play Service, 1998.
Kerr, Walter. *Tragedy and Comedy.* New York: Simon and Schuster, 1967.
Kott, Jan. *The Theatre of Essence.* Evanston, IL: Northwestern University Press, 1986.
Krasner, David. *American Drama 1945–2000: An Introduction.* Hoboken, NJ: Wiley-Blackwell, 2006.
Miranda, Lin-Manuel, and Jeremy McCarter. *Hamilton: The Revolution.* New York: Grand Central Publishing, 2016.
Saddik, Annette. *Contemporary American Drama.* Edinburgh: Edinburgh University Press, 2007.
Shakespeare, William. *Macbeth.* Folger Library ed. Edited by Louis B. Wright. New York: Washington Square, 1967.
Smith, James. *Melodrama.* London: Methuen, 1973.
Styan, J. L. *The Elements of Drama.* New York: Cambridge University Press, 1960.
———, ed. *Macbeth.* New York: Oxford University Press, 1990.
Szondi, Peter. *Theory of the Modern Drama.* Minneapolis: University of Minnesota Press, 1987.
Watt, Stephen. *American Drama: Colonial to Contemporary.* Farmington Hills, MI: Cengage, 2003.

3

THE PLAYWRIGHT

THE BLUEPRINT

The odd and archaic word *playwright* is the first clue to understanding the nature of writing for the theatre. The term *wright* is an old-fashioned expression for one who makes something. A shipwright builds ships; a wheelwright builds wheels; a playwright builds plays. Since novelists write books and poets write poems, doesn't the playwright write as well? He or she does, of course, but a playwright does more than write words. As we have seen, theatre involves much more than words on a page. In fact, those words on paper are only the blueprint for something that is yet to be built. An architect designs a house on paper; others use the blueprint to build it. The playwright works in the same manner. The script is not a finished product. It takes many people beyond the playwright to turn that piece of drama into a theatre event. We mention in the first chapter that reading a play is not a theatre event. It is worth repeating that when one reads a play, one is looking at a blueprint. No matter how vivid the reader's imagination, the script remains just one of the four aspects of creating live theatre.

Because the great plays in history have been published and studied throughout the centuries, we sometimes forget that the original authors of those works never intended for their scripts to be read. Plays are written to be produced. An architect would find little satisfaction is seeing his blueprints published in an architectural journal if none of his designs were actually built. So too, the playwright's art is only satisfactorily complete when the script is presented on a stage. William Shakespeare had many poems published in his day, but he never imagined that his *Macbeth* would appear in print. When his works were collected after his death and printed in the First Folio, it was a rare and practically unheard-of thing to do. Shakespeare wrote *Macbeth* to be presented onstage before a live audience, many of whom could not read his play even if they wanted to. George S. Kaufman and Moss Hart wanted *You Can't Take It with You* to be a hit on Broadway, not a book on a shelf. Lorraine Hansberry's *A Raisin in the Sun* could have been printed in an anthology of "Negro" plays in the 1950s, but the fact that it was the first play by an African American woman to be presented on Broadway is a much more amazing feat. Lin-Manuel Miranda's *Hamilton* has spawned a popular CD and many young people have downloaded certain songs from the show, but seeing the innovative musical on stage is the experience that the author originally intended and still his primary intent.

Consider the unusual and frustrating position of the playwright. He or she can begin the process of theatre yet is unable to complete it. The playwright works on the script, usually alone and without any guarantee that it will be produced, then ends up with only a blueprint. A novelist has a manuscript to sell, an artist has a painting to show, and a composer has a piano concerto to perform. The playwright has no such finished product. All that can be hoped is that others will be willing to finance, direct, act, produce, and promote the script. In fact, the playwright need not be present during the casting, rehearsing, and performing of a play. While a

WILLIAM SHAKESPEARE No one knows for certain what the great Elizabethan playwright looked like, although this portrait, which hangs in the National Portrait Gallery in London, is attributed to artist John Taylor and believed to be a good likeness of Shakespeare near the end of his theatre career. *Bridgeman Images*

new play will require the input of the playwright throughout the preparation for opening night, most plays produced today do not need the author of the words to be present. William Shakespeare, George S. Kaufman, Moss Hart, and Lorraine Hansberry are no longer alive, but their plays are. The blueprints they have left behind are the starting points for hundreds of theatre events each year. The playwright is essential in starting the theatre process, but no one is more unnecessary on opening night. All the same, the buildings they design still stand because they were made so well. No wonder they are called *playwrights*.

MEET THE PLAYWRIGHTS

William Shakespeare (1564–1616) is still the most produced playwright in the Western world, and no one has been studied and written about more than the "Bard of Avon." Ironically, we know less about his life than we do about most other playwrights, even those who lived earlier than Shakespeare.

The facts are few and far between: he was born in the English village of Stratford-upon-Avon to the son of a glove maker; he married at the age of eighteen and had three children; his name shows up in London in 1592 as an actor, poet, and playwright; he is credited with writing thirty-seven plays, 154 sonnets, and a handful of long poems; he retired to Stratford in 1611 and died there in 1616. Surrounding these facts are theories, legends, guesswork, and fiction about the details. Over the centuries, doubts have been raised over whether Shakespeare actually wrote the works attributed to him. But the important thing has always been the plays themselves. No one wrote finer tragedies, comedies, histories, farces, and romances (those tragicomedies that mix the two types) in the history of the English language. Among the most produced of his plays today are *Romeo and Juliet*, *A Midsummer Night's Dream*, *Macbeth*, *Hamlet*, *The Taming of the Shrew*, *Twelfth Night*, *King Lear*, *As You Like It*, *Richard III*, *The Comedy of Errors*, and *The Tempest*. It is also essential to remember that Shakespeare was a man of the professional theatre of his time. He wrote his plays with certain theatres, actors, and audiences in mind, and he always wrote plays to be produced, not to be read. (His poems, on the other hand, were published in his lifetime and actually got more critical attention than did his plays.) Shakespeare understood the theatre: he knew what would play on the stage, and he had an amazingly good ear for what sounded best in a theatre. It is for these reasons that his works are still produced all over the world and are not just sitting on library shelves.

George S. Kaufman and **Moss Hart** were two of the most successful writers and directors in the American theatre from the 1920s through the 1950s. The senior member Kaufman (1889–1961) was born in Pittsburgh and served on the staffs of newspapers in Washington, D.C., and New York before joining with Marc Connelly to write his first successful comedy, *Dulcy* (1921), followed by such collaborations as *Merton of the Movies* (1922) and *Beggar on Horseback* (1924). Throughout his career, Kaufman was known as the "Great Collaborator" because all but one of his works were written with others. With Edna Ferber, he penned *The Royal Family* (1927), *Dinner at Eight* (1932), and *Stage Door* (1936). With Morrie Ryskind he wrote the musical librettos for *Animal Crackers* (1928), *Strike Up the Band* (1930), and *Of Thee I Sing* (1931). But it was with Hart that Kaufman wrote his most interesting and popular comedies. Moss Hart (1904–1961) was born into a poor Jewish family in New York City where he fell in love with the theatre. His first two plays failed, but success came when he collaborated with Kaufman on the Hollywood spoof *Once in a Lifetime* (1930). The team's other works include *Merrily We Roll Along* (1934), *You Can't Take It with You* (1936), *The Man Who Came to Dinner* (1939), *George Washington Slept Here* (1940), as well as the musical *I'd Rather Be Right* (1937). Kaufman's other works with other collaborators include *The Cocoanuts* (1925), *June Moon* (1929), *The Band Wagon* (1931), *The Late George Apley* (1944), *The Solid Gold Cadillac* (1953), and *Silk Stockings* (1955). With others or alone, Hart wrote the books or sketches for the musicals *Face the Music* (1932), *As Thousands Cheer* (1933), and *Lady in the Dark* (1941), as well as the comedy *Light Up the Sky* (1948). Both men also worked in Hollywood, Kaufman contributing to such films as *A Night at the Opera* (1935), *A Day at the Races* (1937), and *Nothing Sacred* (1937), and Hart writing or cowriting *Gentleman's Agreement* (1947), *Hans Christian Andersen* (1952), *A Star Is Born* (1954), and *Prince of Players* (1955). Both Kaufman and Hart were much-sought-after directors as well. Besides staging many of his own plays, Kaufman directed such hits as *The Front Page* (1928), *My Sister Eileen* (1940), and *Guys and Dolls* (1950). Hart staged such successes as *Junior Miss* (1941), *Dear Ruth* (1944), *My Fair Lady* (1956), and *Camelot* (1960).

GEORGE S. KAUFMAN and **MOSS HART** Although George S. Kaufman (right) was an established playwright before he teamed up with Moss Hart, the younger playwright was able to inspire Kaufman to write some of his best work when they collaborated, coming up with two of the finest American comedies: *You Can't Take It with You* (1936) and *The Man Who Came to Dinner* (1939). *Photofest*

Lorraine Hansberry (1930–1965) was born in Chicago's South Side, where, although she was raised in a middle-class family, she was well aware of the life of African Americans living in the substandard tenement apartments around her. Hansberry's father was an early civil rights activist, and she met several prominent black leaders and artists growing up. When her father tried to move the family to a restricted white neighborhood in Chicago, pickets and protests greeted them; the case went to court; and the Hansberrys were evicted. She studied art and theatre at the University of Wisconsin, the University of Guadalajara in Mexico, and Roosevelt University. In 1950 Hansberry moved to New York to pursue her writing career, paying the bills by working as a typist and saleswoman. She completed *A Raisin in the Sun* in 1957, and a producer wanted to present it on Broadway, but no theatre was available. So the production toured to Philadelphia, New Haven, and Chicago, getting such an enthusiastic response that it finally arrived on Broadway in 1959, running two years and winning the New York Drama Critics Circle Award. The play was filmed with success in 1961, but Hansberry's next play, *The Sign in Sidney Brustein's Window* (1964), was not popular. Her untimely death from cancer at the age of thirty-four ended one of the most

LORRAINE HANSBERRY Because she died at the age of thirty-four, the full potential of this talented African American playwright was never realized. Her collected writings were turned into a theatre piece after her death, and it is titled, appropriately, *To Be Young, Gifted, and Black*. *Photofest*

promising careers in the American theatre. Hansberry's husband, Robert Nemiroff, also a respected writer, completed her unfinished play *Les Blancs* in 1970 and compiled a program of her works called *To Be Young, Gifted, and Black*, which has often been produced.

Lin-Manuel Miranda (b. 1980) was born in New York City into a family of Puerto Rican, Mexican, and African American descent. His mother, Luz Towns, was a clinical psychologist and his father, Luis A. Miranda Jr., a political consultant for the Democratic Party. Miranda wrote poetry as a child and, as a student at Wesleyan University, cofounded Freestyle Love Supreme, a comedy group that used hip-hop and rap in its performances. While still a college student, Miranda wrote his first draft of *In the Heights*, a musical about a Latinx neighborhood in New York City's Washington Heights, and used rap, salsa, and various kinds of other music in the songs, several of which were in Spanish. As a student, Miranda also acted in college productions and directed some as well. A reworked version of *In the Heights* opened Off Broadway in 2007, with a revised book by Quiara Alegria Hudes; Miranda provided the music and lyrics, and played the central character of Usnavi. The production was a critical and popular success, so it moved to Broadway in 2008, where it won Tony Awards for Best Musical and for Miranda's score. He also wrote the songs for the Broadway musical *Bring It On* (2012) and the Off-Broadway musical *21 Chump Street* (2014), even as he acted on stage, on television, and in the movies. For the hit musical *Hamilton* (2015), he wrote the book, music, and lyrics, and played the title role. Miranda continues to write and perform in various forms of media, and a prominent career seems inevitable.

THE GERMINAL IDEA

While there have been a handful of occasions in which a producer or a star came up with an idea for a play and hired someone to write it, most plays start with the playwright. But where does the playwright start? Like all creative writers, playwrights need a seed or a simple image that will serve as the departure point for developing a piece of writing. This beginning notion can be described as a *germinal idea*. Just as a seed germinates and grows, so too does the playwright's idea for the script. The germinal idea can be something as simple as a quick glimpse of a person.

Many years ago playwright Garson Kanin went backstage after a show to visit some friends, and he saw a beautiful blonde chorus girl sitting in the dressing room reading a book by the philosopher Nietzsche. The image of a supposedly "dumb blonde" devouring German philosophy struck Kanin as unusual and intriguing. That germinal idea led to Kanin's celebrated comedy *Born Yesterday* about a not-so-dumb gangster's gal who grows into a new person when she is exposed to learning. Kanin's quick view of the chorine was not enough to provide plot, dialogue, and all the elements that Aristotle listed—Kanin had to develop all those on his own—but seeing that blonde was a starting point.

Germinal ideas can come from anywhere. A newspaper story, a rumor overheard, a historical event, a local legend, family gossip, and other items can inspire a plot idea. An unusual or vibrant character is also a common departure point for playwrights. Many of Tennessee Williams's dramas began with a unique and theatrical character based on someone he knew in real life, such as his funny, irritating mother, later portrayed as Amanda in *The Glass Menagerie*.

A place can provide a germinal idea as well. Lanford Wilson was so struck by the faded grandeur of a decaying hotel in downtown Baltimore that he used it as the setting for his popular play *The Hot L Baltimore*, about various lowlifes living in a crumbling hotel about to be razed. Some playwrights find their germinal ideas in Aristotle's element of theme. One may want to write about an important issue, such as capital punishment or the AIDS epidemic, and the topic becomes the starting point. Regardless of whether the germinal idea is one of plot, character, place, or theme, the playwright will eventually have to cover them all if he or she is to write a coherent and satisfying play.

Many plays (and almost all musicals) are based on previous works of art. If a novel, for example, is adapted into a play, the original book might be considered the germinal idea for the project. Yet often the playwright still needs to find an original notion in determining just how to put this story on the stage. Perhaps one character in the novel might be turned into a narrator who will address the audience directly. Or perhaps one scene or episode from the book is to become the focal point of the play. How the playwright chooses to approach a dramatization of a previous work requires its own germinal idea. We know that *Hamilton* is based on a biography by historian Ron Chernow, but Lin-Manuel Miranda had to make bold decisions and come up with new ideas to turn the story of this Founding Father into a musical that resonates with today's audience.

Determining which germinal idea a playwright started with is not easy. In fact, in a well-rounded play, the original inspiration is probably hidden in the finished product. Did Lorraine Hansberry know a strong, maternal character like Lena Younger, who inspired her to write *A Raisin in the Sun*? Or did she start with the memory

THE GLASS MENAGERIE Tennessee Williams did not need to look outside of his own family for the germinal idea for his famous 1945 "memory play." In this 1983 Broadway revival, Williams's alter ego, Tom, was played by Bruce Davison (left). Jessica Tandy portrayed his mother, Amanda, and Amanda Plummer (in background) played his troubled sister, Laura. John Heard was the "gentleman caller" Jim, and the production was directed by John Dexter. *Photofest*

of when her family tried to move into a white neighborhood, and use that as her plot idea? Unless the playwright chooses to explain the origins of a work in an introduction or interview, it is not known, and it is not important to know in order to understand and appreciate the play. What is important is to realize that plays are not born out of a playwright's head fully formed and fleshed out. They start out as ideas that must grow and develop to become a finished product. It is a process that all playwrights must go through in writing a play.

Where Did Shakespeare Get the Idea for *Macbeth*?

We know so little about Shakespeare's life, and even less about his working methods, that it seems unlikely to come to any understanding of what gave him the germinal idea for *Macbeth*. Yet scholars have studied Shakespeare more than any other writer and have come up with possible answers. A popular book by Raphael Holinshed called *Chronicles of England, Scotland, and Ireland* (1587) tells about a Scottish king named Macbeth, who defeated King Duncan in battle and ruled Scotland with wisdom for seventeen years. There was another tale in Holinshed of a murderer named Donwald, who was egged on by his wife to kill King Duff. And a pageant at the time by Matthew Gwinne featured three witches who foretold the royal lineage of Banquo. There were also older books about Scotland that Shakespeare may have been familiar with. As with all of his plays based on history, Shakespeare altered facts and created events to please his audiences. In the case of *Macbeth*, it seems he was also interested in pleasing his king. James I, then the monarch in England, was descended from the Scottish line of Banquo. While some legends say that Banquo assisted Macbeth in overthrowing King Duncan, Shakespeare's version has Banquo blameless and Macbeth as the villain, though a vivid and fully dimensional villain. It is thought that *Macbeth* was first written for a 1606 court performance in which James I and the visiting King Christian IV of Denmark were in attendance. (*Macbeth* is one of Shakespeare's shortest plays; it is known that King James did not like long plays.) James would have been pleased to see his great ancestor Banquo portrayed as a wise and conscientious warrior whose son survives to begin a long line of noble kings. Also, James was interested in witchcraft and even wrote a book called *Demonology* in 1597. No doubt the three witches in *Macbeth* are also there to appeal to the king. So we can begin to imagine the process that Shakespeare went through in writing *Macbeth*. He took an old story from a history book, rearranged facts, and added elements to humor his monarch. Yet Shakespeare also created one of the theatre's most intriguing tragic characters, a good man driven to evil by overwhelming ambition. The playwright may have started with a given plot and a historical character, but he then went on to develop the elements of diction, theme, and spectacle, resulting in one of the theatre's most popular tragic plays.

THE PLAYWRIGHT'S PROCESS

Regardless of which of Aristotle's elements a playwright starts with, all must be tackled before a play is complete. There must be a story of some sort; there must be characters to enact it; they must speak in dialogue; there should be a rhythm or sense of music in the telling; some spectacle (even slight) must be involved; and, finally, the play must be about something (the theme). Of all these, perhaps the greatest challenge is dialogue. A novelist may explain how a character feels or describe what action takes place, but a playwright must do it all with dialogue. Stage directions, descriptions of the set and costumes, notes about the characters, and other information given by the playwright are useful and enlightening, but none of them are as necessary as dialogue. The text of *Macbeth* has no character notes, no set descriptions, and only the barest of stage directions. Everything is dialogue, and, in the case of Shakespeare, that is more than sufficient; it is all in the words. It may seem like a rather sketchy blueprint to leave behind, but those words have inspired actors, directors, and designers for centuries.

Stage dialogue has changed over time as much as theatre itself. The ancient Greek plays had formal but poetic dialogue that could be chanted as well as spoken. In the Middle Ages many of the plays were written in singsong rhymed couplets that remind modern audiences of nursery rhymes. Shakespeare and the Elizabethan playwrights wrote dialogue in blank verse with rich poetic imagery. The French and English plays of the seventeenth and eighteenth centuries were often filled with elaborate wordiness that satirized upper-class speech patterns. Melodramas in the nineteenth century used an inflated kind of prose that was as artificial as it was grandiose. Realistic and conversational dialogue as we know it today was not heard on the stage until the late 1800s. Musical theatre would develop a form of dialogue of its own, moving back and forth from spoken prose to sung lyrics. Even in modern times dialogue varies greatly. Some playwrights, such as Eugene O'Neill and David Mamet, are known for their gritty, realistic "street" dialogue while others, such as Tennessee Williams and August Wilson, excel at poetic talk with rhythmic patterns. But one thing still remains essential to all dialogue: it must sound right. Audiences will be hearing the words, not reading them, so a successful script must have some kind of speakability. Stage dialogue has to be clear and conversational, yet it must also be intriguing and more interesting than everyday talk. You can read a novel, but you have to hear a play.

Let us look at some brief samples of dialogue from our four plays. Shakespeare uses a simple, chant-like form of verse for the three witches, rhyming in an almost childlike way. Here are the opening lines of the play.

1 WITCH: When shall we three meet again
In thunder, lightning, or in rain?
2 WITCH: When the hurlyburly's done,
When the battle's lost and won.
3 WITCH: That will be ere the set of sun.
1 WITCH: Where the place?
2 WITCH: Upon the heath.
3 WITCH: There to meet with Macbeth.
1 WITCH: I come, Graymalkin!
2 WITCH: Paddock calls!
3 WITCH: Anon!
ALL THREE: Fair is foul and foul is fair.
Hover through the fog and filthy air.

For the character of Macbeth, the playwright turns to a form of blank verse that does not require rhyme or singsong but explores ideas with rich imagery. Here are Macbeth's pessimistic comments when he hears that his wife has died:

MACBETH: She should have died hereafter;
There would have been a time for such a word.
Tomorrow, and tomorrow, and tomorrow
Creeps in this petty pace from day to day
To the last syllable of recorded time;
And all our yesterdays have lighted fools
The way to dusty death. Out, out, brief candle!
Life's but a walking shadow, a poor player,
That struts and frets his hour upon the stage
And then is heard no more. It is a tale
Told by an idiot, full of sound and fury,
Signifying nothing.

The dialogue in *You Can't Take It with You* makes no attempt to be poetic. It is written in succinct prose that is conversational but livelier and more playful than ordinary talk. Because the piece is a comedy (and at times a farce), the dialogue often moves swiftly with the robust cadence that suggests the high energy of the Vanderhof clan.

> **PENNY:** Do you have to make candy today, Essie? It's such a hot day.
> **ESSIE:** Well, I got all those new orders. Ed went out and got a bunch of new orders.
> **PENNY:** My, if this keeps on I suppose you'll be opening up a store.
> **ESSIE:** That's what Ed was saying last night but I said No I want to be a dancer.
> **PENNY:** The only trouble with dancing is, it takes so long. You've been studying such a long time.
> **ESSIE:** Only eight years. After all, mother, you've been writing plays for eight years. We started about the same time, didn't we?
> **PENNY:** Yes, but you shouldn't count my first two years, because I was learning to type. *(RHEBA enters from kitchen)*
> **RHEBA:** I think the candy's hardening now, Miss Essie.
> **ESSIE:** Oh, thanks, Rheba. I'll bring some in, mother—I want you to try it.
> **RHEBA:** Finish the second act, Mrs. Sycamore?
> **PENNY:** Oh, no, Rheba. I've just got Cynthia entering the monastery.
> **RHEBA:** Monastery? How'd she get there? She was at the El Morocco, wasn't she?
> **PENNY:** Well, she gets tired of the El Morocco and there's this monastery, so she goes there.
> **RHEBA:** Do they let her in?
> **PENNY:** Yes, I made it Visitors' Day, so of course anybody can come.
> **RHEBA:** Oh.
> **PENNY:** She arrives on Visitors' Day, and—just stays.
> **RHEBA:** All night?
> **PENNY:** Oh, yes. She stays six years.
> **RHEBA:** Six years? My, I bet she busts that monastery wide open.

Even when *You Can't Take It with You* gets a little philosophical, there is still a casual, homegrown tone to the dialogue.

> **GRANDPA:** What do you think you get your indigestion from? Happiness? No, sir. You get it because most of your time is spent doing things you don't want to do.
> **MR. KIRBY:** I don't do anything I don't want to do.
> **GRANDPA:** Yes, you do. You said last night that at the end of a week in Wall Street you're pretty near crazy. Why do you keep on doing it?
> **MR. KIRBY:** Why do I keep on—why, that's my business. A man can't give up his business.
> **GRANDPA:** Why not? You've got all the money you need. You can't take it with you.

Although the dialogue in Lorraine Hansberry's *A Raisin in the Sun* is also conversational, it is often more poetic. Mrs. Younger wishes to be optimistic but when she looks back, she can only recall hardship.

RUTH: Yes, life can be a barrel of disappointments, sometimes.
MAMA: Honey, Big Walter would come in here some nights and slump down on that couch there and just look at the rug, and look at me and look at the rug and then back at me—and I'd know he was down then . . . really down. And then, Lord, when I lost that baby—little Claude—I almost thought I was going to lose Big Walter too. Oh, that man grieved hisself! He was one man to love his children . . . God knows there was plenty wrong with Walter Younger—hardheaded, mean, kind of wild with women—plenty wrong with him. But he sure loved his children. Always wanted them to have something—be something. That's where Brother gets all these notions, I reckon. Big Walter used to say, he'd get right wet in the eyes sometimes, lean his head back with the water standing in his eyes and say, "Seem like God don't see fit to give the black man nothing but dreams—but He did give us children to make them dreams seem worthwhile." He could talk like that, don't you know.
RUTH: Yes, he sure could. He was a good man, Mr. Younger.
MAMA: Yes, a fine man—just couldn't never catch up with his dreams, that's all.

The African American form of speech and the point of view of segregated Americans are quite different from the speech and attitudes in *You Can't Take It with You*. Walter Younger is filled with bitterness and pessimism. Listen to the way he expresses himself when he learns that Willy Harris has run away with all of Walter's share of the money.

WALTER: Talking 'bout life, Mama. You all always telling me to see life like it is. Well—I laid in there on my back today . . . and I figured it out. Life just like it is. Who gets and who don't get. Mama, you know it's all divided up. Life is. Sure enough. Between the takers and the "tooken." I've figured it out finally. Yeah. Some of us always getting "tooken." People like Willy Harris, they don't never get "tooken." And you know why the rest of us do? 'Cause we all mixed up. Mixed up bad. We get to looking 'round for the right and the wrong; and we worry about it and cry about it and stay up nights trying to figure out 'bout the wrong and the right of things all the time . . . and all the time, man, them takers is out there operating, just taking and taking. Willy Harris? Shoot—Willy Harris don't even count. He don't even count in the big scheme of things. But I'll say one thing for old Willy Harris . . . he's taught me something. He's taught me to keep my eye on what counts in this world. Yeah (*shouts*)—thanks, Willie!

The dialogue in *Hamilton*, which is sung by solo voices or in unison by a chorus that remains on stage for most of the musical, captures a completely different sound. Although many different kinds of music are used in the score, the character of Hamilton usually expresses himself in a rap pattern. Early in the first act he introduces himself to some young revolutionaries (and the audience) with a fast-talking verbal barrage.

HAMILTON: I am not throwing away my shot!
I am not throwing away my shot!
Hey yo, I am just like my country,
I'm young, scrappy, and hungry,

and I'm not throwing away my shot!
I'm 'a get a scholarship to King's College.
I prob'ly shouldn't brag, but dag, I amaze and astonish.
The problem is I got a lot of brains but no polish.
I gotta holler just to be heard.
With every word, I drop knowledge!
I'm a diamond in the rough, a shiny piece of coal
tryin' to reach my goal. My power of speech:
unimpeachable.
Only nineteen but my mind is older.
These New York City Streets get colder, I shoulder
ev'ry burden, ev'ry disadvantage
I have learned to manage. I don't have a gun to brandish,
I walk these streets famished.
The plan is to fan this spark into a flame.
But damn, it's getting dark, so let me spell out my name . . .

The character's thoughts in *Hamilton* are often echoed by the ensemble, just as the chorus did in the ancient Greek theatre. Instead of a rapid pattern, the lyric for Eliza as she describes how she fell in love with Alexander Hamilton flows easily and with a dreamy quality.

ELIZA AND WOMEN: Helpless!
Look into your eyes, and the sky's the limit I'm helpless!
Down for the count, and I'm drownin' in 'em.
ELIZA: I have never been the type to try and grab the spotlight.
We were at a revel with some rebels on a hot night,
laughin' at my sister as she's dazzling the room
then you walked in and my heart went
"Boom!"
Tryin' to catch your eye from the side of the ballroom,
ev'rybody's dancin' and the band's to volume.
ELIZA AND WOMEN: Grind to the rhythm as we wine and dine.
ELIZA: Grab my sister and whisper, "Yo this one's mine"
WOMEN: Oooh
ELIZA: My sister made her way across the room to you.
WOMEN: Oooh
ELIZA: And I got nervous thinking,
"What's she gonna do?"
WOMEN: Oooh
ELIZA: She grabbed you by the arm,
I'm thinkin' "I'm through"
WOMEN: Oooh
ELIZA: Then you look back at me and suddenly I'm
ELIZA AND WOMAN: Helpless!

As different as the dialogue is in these four plays, each has the quality of good playwriting. The characters are expressing themselves in an exciting way, using different forms of diction to reach the audience and reveal what the play is about.

Having completed a script, most playwrights want to hear it read. Such a reading might range from an informal group of friends who gather and read the script aloud to a staged reading done in a theatre in which actors have prepared and rehearsed with a director. Not only does a reading give a playwright a chance to hear his or her words spoken by others, but it also tells possible producers much more about the script than if they had merely read it on the page. Even musicals are first presented as readings, with the actors speaking the dialogue and singing the songs. If a script is like a blueprint for a building, then a reading is similar to a three-dimensional scale model of a building. The words have risen off the page and are heading toward becoming a theatre event. Of course, readings will show one very little about the play's physical actions, the set changes, the costume problems, and other production aspects, but a reading tells one almost everything about the dialogue, a key to any play's success.

Plot

In the theatre, plot is very different from that found in prose fiction. Since a play shows a story more than it tells a story, the playwright must carefully decide which episodes in a tale can be dramatized and which can be talked about in dialogue. Choosing the most dynamic moments in a story to re-create onstage is one of the playwright's most important tasks. Lin-Manuel Miranda decided not to show the early years of Alexander Hamilton in the Caribbean, the death of his mother, and his struggle to earn passage to the United States. These events are quickly told to the audience, and then the focus is on Hamilton's getting involved with the young revolutionaries in New York. Shakespeare chose to show Macbeth when he gets the idea of becoming king, his efforts to murder the current king and secure the throne, and then his later disintegration and fall. In each case, the playwright had to highlight the parts of the story that were the most stageworthy.

PLOT Although Arthur Miller's drama *The Crucible* (1953) is based on events that occurred in Salem, Massachusetts, in 1692, the story was relevant because of the anticommunist "witch hunts" of the 1950s. Today, Miller's strong plot is still engrossing, as demonstrated by the 2002 Broadway revival directed by Richard Eyre. Pictured, left to right, are Liam Neeson, Brian Murray, Laura Linney, and Jack Willis. *Joan Marcus/Photofest; photographer: Joan Marcus*

Plots in the theatre have to be more practical than in the other narrative arts. Limited scenery and a small number of actors usually mean that a playwright has to compress the action of the story into key scenes that can be done onstage. One must also be practical about the details as well. Does an actor have enough time to make an important costume change and still be onstage at the beginning of the next scene? Will the changing of scenery cause the story line to drag or lose impact? Can the physical action demanded by the script be done onstage effectively? Is the play written so that actors can play more than one role in a large cast and not confuse the audience? Shakespeare was aware of all of these points. He knew that the actors at the Globe Theatre had to enter the acting area and exit it as well, there being no front curtain or blackouts. So in all of his plays he made sure that no character onstage at the end of a scene was included in the very beginning of the next scene. He also knew that the theatre company at the Globe was limited to about a dozen adult actors and three or four boys to play female roles. So he worked out his plot so that actors could be doubled. King Duncan and Macduff, for example, never appear onstage together so that both characters could possibly be played by one actor. Shakespeare also realized that it was impossible to present an entire battle onstage, so he chose key moments in the fighting to dramatize in *Macbeth*. These scenes are short and require no scenery so as not to interrupt the mounting excitement as the battle and the play come to a close.

Just as a playwright must hear dialogue to tell if the play sounds right, so too must the play be presented onstage for one to determine whether the plot works effectively. This quality of stageability is sometimes difficult to spot in the script but becomes more evident during rehearsals. The action of the play cannot take a backseat to the characters and dialogue. What happens physically on the stage has great impact, and the playwright must not forget this. From obvious moments of theatricality, such as the fight between Macbeth and Macduff, to the quieter moments of plot, such as the arrival of the insurance check in *A Raisin in the Sun*, the script must have action.

Character

We have seen that the element of character has provided the germinal idea for many plays. Since theatre is about human action, characterization is essential. Creating characters that are three-dimensional, have consistency and yet can surprise us, and can change or grow during the course of the play will determine how an audience embraces a theatre event. Story can interest an audience and dialogue can intrigue them, but only through character can an audience have real empathy with a play. It is important to engage the audience with characters whom they can get involved with, even if they do not personally like them. Mrs. Younger is a warm, noble character who evokes both empathy and sympathy in an audience. Macbeth, on the other hand, usually gets little sympathy from the audience, but they can empathize with this ambitious man all the same. Grandpa in *You Can't Take It with You* is easy to like, and the audience quickly bonds with him because his philosophy of life is so direct and simple. Alexander Hamilton, on the other hand, is a complex character whose goals are more complicated and personality is sometimes abrasive and off-putting. Yet the audience sticks with Hamilton and even accepts his faults because there is much to admire in the man.

Revision and Rewriting

As a playwright once noted, "Plays are not written; they are rewritten." All writers revise and polish their work before it is completed, but playwrights rewrite more and longer than do other authors. After a reading of a new play, a playwright will go back to the script and use what he or she has learned from hearing it aloud. One speech is too long and repetitive; another is too short and unclear. One scene is too wordy and slows down the progress of the story; another scene is so brief that it confuses the audience. A whole character may not be coming across as intended, and much of his dialogue has to be rewritten. Words or phrases that looked fine on the page are sometimes hard to understand when spoken or are difficult to pronounce. These kinds of changes do not stop once the play is chosen for production and is cast. Revisions in a new play will continue throughout rehearsals, with the playwright sometimes rewriting to suit the talents or deficiencies of an actor or, at other times, filling out a speech in order to cover a scenery or costume change. The reasons for revision may be artistic or practical, but they are needed all the same. The collaboration between a playwright and the theatre company when working on a new, untried script is both thrilling and frustrating. Other people are asking the architect to change the blueprint a little here and a little there. Sometimes the result is a stronger, better building; sometimes the structure collapses. When the Russian playwright Anton Chekhov first saw his play *The Sea Gull* performed in Saint Petersburg in 1896, the audience laughed and booed it off the stage. Yet when the same script was later presented in Moscow by a different company, it was a success. The blueprint had not changed, but the production was a very different one and the new builders made the play work.

There are times when the playwright's process does not end even with opening night. Changes have been known to be made weeks and months after a play has opened on Broadway. Musicals have sometimes dropped a song or dance number, replacing it with another. The touring version or a later revival of a play or musical may be altered from the original production, and sometimes the scripts issued for school productions differ from what was done by professionals. The blueprint is sometimes altered by each new set of builders. That is why theatre is a living art form. A theatre event changes each time it is re-created, and playwrights, who write the blueprint for that event, realize this. The novelist or the painter completes the book or painting, and both pieces of work remain as they left them; a play keeps adjusting and shifting focus long after the playwright is gone.

EVALUATING THE PLAYWRIGHT'S WORK

We have seen that the blueprint (the script) and the building (the production) are not the same, but it is possible to look critically at a script and make decisions about its quality without seeing it staged. Some plays read better than others, but all must be read with an eye on how they might be produced. Some dramas, like Eugene O'Neill's works, have very detailed stage directions, character descriptions, and scenery and costume notes. Reading such a script may at times seem like reading a novel with everything explained and described. Other scripts, such as those by Shakespeare, supply only the words and the barest of stage directions; visualizing the play as you read it takes much more imagination. In either case, we must always keep in mind that plays are not written to be read.

How Are Musicals Written?

Because a musical play consists of much more than dialogue and stage directions, the writing process differs somewhat. Three kinds of playwrights are needed to create the script for a musical: the *librettist*, or book writer, who pens the prose dialogue; a *lyricist*, who writes the words to the songs; and the *composer*, who creates the music. These three jobs may be done by three different people; one playwright might write the book and lyrics, and another the music; or one person may do all three, as in the case of Lin-Manuel Miranda and *Hamilton*.

Regardless of the number of people involved, in the modern theatre all three jobs must be coordinated so that the dialogue moves into singing without a jarring inconsistency or an awkward transition. Characters are established not only in the dialogue but also in the words they sing and the music they sing the words to. Ever since the landmark musical *Oklahoma!* in 1943, most musicals integrate the songs with the story and the characters, and all are held together by the same theme and tone of voice.

Someone once asked the celebrated composer-lyricist Stephen Sondheim which came first, the music or the lyrics, and he replied, "The book." Plot and character are still the threads that hold a musical together, even if it has little story, such as *A Chorus Line*, or none at all, as in *Cats*. Musicals may be full of singing and dancing, but they are still about human action (even if those human aspects come in the shape of animals or spirits). Once the librettist has outlined the story and major characters, the songs and dances are incorporated into it. Sometimes a song will replace a dialogue scene, or a dance can be used to substitute for exposition or characterization. In *Hamilton*, the songs are the dialogue. *Hamilton* is considered a *sung-through* musical—that is, one that tells almost all of its story through song. When dialogue is used, it is either sung or spoken over the music so that the rhythmic pattern is never broken. While this technique was first used in opera, modern musicals usually retain a musical theatre kind of presentation, even in sung-through musicals.

Even more than in a play, a musical requires a great deal of collaboration. Three different people may be creating a blueprint, which is then built by a director, a choreographer, a musical director, a team of designers, and a cast of performers. In many ways the musical play is the ultimate theatre experience because it involves all of Aristotle's elements to the fullest. Spectacle and music are an integral part of the whole, becoming as important as plot, character, diction, and theme.

WRITING MUSICALS Added to the usual challenges of writing plot, character, and dialogue is the integration of songs when a musical is created. Hugh Wheeler wrote the "book" for the musical thriller *Sweeney Todd, the Demon Barber of Fleet Street* (1979), and Stephen Sondheim provided the music and lyrics. The fact that one man's work blends seamlessly with the other's is a tribute to great musical theatre writing. Angela Lansbury and Len Cariou were the original singing murderers Mrs. Lovett and Sweeney Todd, respectively, on Broadway. Director: Harold Prince. *Photofest*

Plot

The best way to evaluate a script is to consider it in terms of Aristotle's dramatic elements—in particular, plot, character, and diction. The plot must engage the audience, whether it is elaborate and taking place during a span of many years, as in *Macbeth* and *Hamilton*, or focused on a small group of people during a short period of time, as in *A Raisin in the Sun* and *You Can't Take It with You*. Some plays may have audience members sitting on the edge of their seats wondering what will happen next, while other scripts may be more about the characters than what is happening to them. Still, a plot is the thread that holds the play together, the "human action" in our definition of theatre. You can ask yourself if the plot was logical, clear, concise, and if it built up to a climax; but there are plays that defy logic, are purposely unclear, are sprawling rather than concise, and take a circular path rather than a traditional one that leads up to a climax. Event follows event in a chronological, historical pattern in *Macbeth* and *Hamilton*, but the story in *A Raisin in the Sun* and *You Can't Take It with You* is more casual, occurring in a traditional, consequential manner. All four plays have solid and effective plots but not for the same reasons. Yet, in each case, we want to see what happens next because our interest in the human action is engaged.

Character

To evaluate the playwright's handling of characters, one can ask about their consistency and their growth. A character should seem to be consistent with what the playwright has provided, yet there should be the possibility for change. Macbeth, for instance, is first presented as a good warrior and a loyal subject to the king. So when his ambition prods him to bloody deeds, he is at first hesitant, then remorseful, and finally paranoid about his actions. Had Macbeth gone from noble subject to bloodthirsty murderer with no logical progression, the character might be considered inconsistent. Walter Younger's discontent at the beginning of *A Raisin in the Sun* logically leads to his desperate attempt to make it big by trusting Willie Harris with all his money. It is consistent with his character and therefore believable. Consistency does not mean that a character stays the same throughout the whole play. Fully dimensional characters grow, develop, and change during the course of the plot. Lady Macbeth may seem a cold and unemotional queen who has none of her husband's doubts and regrets. Yet the last time we see her in the play, in the famous sleepwalking scene, her fears and remorse so long held inside come spilling out. She has gone from an icy murderess to a pathetic victim of her own cruelty. Villains who never waver in their villainy are no more interesting than heroes who are steadfastly predictable in their goodness. When the major figures in a play behave consistently and still manage to grow or change, that is expert playwriting.

Diction

As you can see from the samples of dialogue from our four scripts, the words used in a play vary greatly. Mrs. Younger cannot and should not express herself with the same kind of language that Lady Macbeth uses. The hyped-up revolutionaries in *Hamilton* do not communicate with one another with the same kind of dialogue that the Vanderhofs use. The time and place of the play may dictate the kind of dialogue used, but more often the language is determined by the individual characters. Ruth and Beneatha may both be African American women living in a Chicago tenement in the 1950s, but their language is not the same. Ruth is direct, to the point, a bit cynical, and somewhat weary in her dialogue. Beneatha is a bit younger, more educated, more aggressive, and even a little poetic in her speech. A sign of weak playwriting is when all the characters in a play seem to sound alike. This kind of dialogue probably has the ideas and speech pattern of the playwright rather than those of the characters, and, consequently, the lines could be assigned to any person onstage. In a well-written play, each character speaks for oneself and only that character would say that line in that situation.

Theme

Not all plays are about something momentous or important, but they all have a theme. One must not judge a script by how much one agrees or sympathizes with the playwright's theme or ideas. It is the expression of those ideas that makes for great drama. While it is difficult to evaluate a playwright's theme without getting judgmental and moralistic, it is possible to evaluate how the writer handles the chosen theme. Lorraine Hansberry does not let *A Raisin in the Sun* wallow in bitterness or preachiness, yet few works are as potent about the closed-in situation that African Americans found themselves in before the civil rights movement. The greatest plays are those that take on an important issue and turn the theme into human action that enlightens an audience.

THE BUSINESS OF PLAYWRITING

Playwriting is a profession as well as an art form, so it is worthwhile knowing a little about the business of writing for the theatre. As a playwright once stated, it is next to impossible to make a living writing plays, but once in a while it is possible to make a killing in the theatre. This means that writing plays is not as lucrative as other jobs, but if a play or musical finds great success, then the playwright's rewards are considerable. Just as a script comes to life in a production, so too the payment that a playwright receives comes after the work is produced. Very rarely is a playwright paid to go and write a play. It is usually the other way around: producers are only interested in plays that are already written. Unlike movies or television, one is never paid for a concept or an idea for a play. Only the expression of that idea, written out in standard play format, is bought. In the theatre you will rarely encounter a credit such as "original story concept by" as you do in other media. It is also unusual today to see more than one playwright listed for a production unless it is a musical with a separate composer, lyricist, and book writer. But in the past, playwriting teams, such as Kaufman and Hart, were often found on Broadway. Such teamwork is rare in nonmusicals today. Although theatre is a collaborative art form, most plays are written by one person working alone.

Let us follow the process that a playwright might go through in getting his or her play produced on Broadway—not so common an occurrence these days but worth looking at all the same. After the playwright feels that the script is ready, he or she will send it to a producer. The various aspects of producing will be looked at in a later chapter, but it can be pointed out here that the producer's first step is to find a *property*—that is, a play or musical to be presented on a stage. Like other writers, playwrights might use an agent to submit the script for them, especially if they are well established and this is not their first professional production. If the producer wants to present the script, he or she will take an *option* on the play. This is an amount of money paid to a playwright to secure exclusive rights to produce the script. The producer usually has one year to raise the necessary money for the production, and during that time the playwright cannot give the play to any other producer. If, at the end of the year, the producer has not raised the necessary money, a new option might be secured; otherwise, the rights revert back to the playwright, who can look elsewhere for a producer. If the money is raised, the producer can then make

THEME An outstanding example of thought-provoking melodrama with a riveting theme is John Patrick Shanley's *Doubt* (2005), in which Sister Aloysius (Cherry Jones) suspects the parish priest, Fr. Flynn (Brian F. O'Byrne), of inappropriate behavior with a young male student. Director: Doug Hughes. *Joan Marcus/Photofest; photographer: Joan Marcus*

a contract with the playwright about the *royalty*. The royalty system is how a playwright is paid. It is a fee for each performance, the amount depending on the level of the theatre production. A high school or college might pay about $75 per performance for a production of *A Raisin in the Sun*. A Broadway production might pay ten times that, with the playwright sometimes even getting a percentage of ticket sales. The royalty is not the same thing as paying for scripts for a play. Although a playwright usually gets 10 percent of the price of a script, the royalty is based solely on the performance of that script. Because *You Can't Take It with You* is one of the most-often produced of all-American comedies, the hundreds of performances each year by various groups add up to a sizable amount for the estates of Kaufman and Hart. Even when a playwright is deceased, a royalty still has to be paid. The only plays that are royalty free are those written before the international copyright took effect, about 1900. Shakespeare was paid no royalty in his day; he was paid a flat fee by the theatre company, and it presented *Macbeth* as often as it wanted. Today there is no royalty for *Macbeth*. Unlike the other three plays we have looked at, *Macbeth* is considered *public domain*, a written work that has no copyright and is not owned by any author or publisher.

In order to ensure that the contract between the producer and the playwright is equitable, the *Dramatists Guild* will approve it before it is signed. The Dramatists Guild is the professional organization for playwrights and acts something like a labor union. Members include those who write plays as well as those who compose music for the theatre, write lyrics for theatre songs, and write the "book" for musicals. The Guild will not only approve the contract but will act as intermediary if a problem should arise between the playwright and the producer during the rehearsal process. The Guild will also see that the playwright gets some of the income derived from script sales, future royalties, movie sales, cast albums, and other *subsidiary rights*. These rights include income that comes after a play or musical has opened, and we will look at them more carefully in the chapter on the producer.

Once contracts are signed and the play is in rehearsal, the playwright will remain with the producer and production team, making the kind of revisions that we discussed earlier. After the play starts being performed, the author's royalties begin. Should the play have a long run, the royalties will mount up week after week. Should the play quickly close, the royalties stop when the performances do. It is possible for a playwright to spend a year writing a play and another year waiting for the producer to raise the money and another six months for the production to come together, only

The Pulitzer Prize

While there are many theatre awards and prizes (some of which will be discussed later), the most prestigious award for playwrights is the Pulitzer Prize for drama. As the word *drama* suggests, the award is given to a script, not a production, so the award honors the author. The Pulitzer Prize awards were founded by newspaper tycoon Joseph Pulitzer in 1917 and are given in several categories in the arts each year by a committee at Columbia University in New York City. A Pulitzer winner in drama must be an original American play that "shall best represent the educational value and power of the stage in raising the standards of good morals and good manners." Over the years the opinions of the committee have become less conservative, and many daring and "amoral" plays have won the award. Pulitzer Prize–winning plays used to all come from Broadway, but over the years works from other New York and even regional theatres have won. From 1918 until 1932, only nonmusical plays were honored, but, in 1933, the musical satire *Of Thee I Sing* won the award, and other musicals have won since then. Most of the playwrights discussed in the next section won Pulitzer Prizes in drama, as well as George S. Kaufman and Moss Hart for *You Can't Take It with You* and Lin-Manuel Miranda for *Hamilton*.

to see the play close in a week. All the playwright would earn would be the option money and one week of royalties. As previously noted, it is not easy making a living as a playwright.

But one should not ignore the benefits of the playwright's career. Unlike a novel that is a bestseller for a year or two and then fades away, a popular play continues to live. After the Broadway production might come a touring production, then presentations in regional theatre and schools. Even though the playwright's work is done, the script can sometimes continue to bring in money for the author for twenty or thirty years or more. And there is the satisfaction of having one's work reborn with each new production, knowing that throughout the country they are building new structures based on one's blueprints.

LOOKING AT TWENTY-ONE AMERICAN AND BRITISH PLAYWRIGHTS

Of the hundreds of playwrights who have written oft-produced scripts over the years, let us look at a twenty-one American and British writers among those from the past and those currently working in the theatre. All of these playwrights have had books or articles written about their work and are often studied, but let us look at them as produced playwrights who are still very much a part of the American and British theatre.

George Bernard Shaw (1856–1950), arguably the most famous and most controversial English dramatist of the twentieth century, was born in Ireland and had several literary careers during his long career. He is most remembered for his plays which, while usually comedies, dealt with such weighty issues as poverty, prostitution, religious hypocrisy, profiteering, and socialism. Shaw also excelled in writing delightful satires that poked fun at love, patriotism, feminism, philosophy, and literature itself. Among his most often produced plays on both sides of the Atlantic are: *Mrs. Warren's Profession* (1893), in which prostitution is shown as a business grown from poverty; *Arms and the Man* (1894), which mocks blind heroism and celebrates the practical man; *Candida* (1897), in which a foolish young poet falls in love with a married woman; *Caesar and Cleopatra* (1901), a whimsical retelling of ancient history; *Man and Superman* (1901), about the battle of the sexes; *Major Barbara* (1905), which debates the moral question of making money from war; *The Doctor's Dilemma* (1906), involving the decision over who gets a special cure and who dies; *Pygmalion* (1912), the popular satire on the class structure in which a speech professor passes off an ignorant flower girl as a lady; *Androcles and the Lion* (1912), a children's fable told with a wry sense of humor; and *Saint Joan* (1923) with Joan of Arc presented as a philosophical tower of strength. Shaw's plays are wordy and sometimes take the tone of a debate but the characters are lively and fascinating. and they still hold the stage effectively.

Eugene O'Neill (1888–1953) was America's first world-class playwright and, in the opinion of many, our greatest writer of plays. Surely no other American experimented as much as O'Neill did, writing realistic dramas, expressionistic plays, trilogies and cycles of plays, and even psychodramas in which the characters reveal their thoughts unheard by the other characters. O'Neill was the son of a celebrated actor, the dashing James O'Neill, who found success in romanticized costume dramas on Broadway. Eugene had no interest in that kind of theatre, so when he started writing scripts, they were done by "little" theatres that experimented with new forms. By 1920, O'Neill's dramas were seen on Broadway, and many of them

EUGENE O'NEILL O'Neill's plays are challenging, with demanding roles for actors and complex scenes for directors. Such is the case with *The Iceman Cometh* (1946) and the large and diverse cast of disillusioned characters who escape the real world at Harry Hope's seedy bar. Shown is a scene from the acclaimed 2018 Broadway revival directed by George C. Wolfe. *Sara Krulwich/New York Times/Redux*

were popular, even though they were long and usually had a tragic point of view. In fact, O'Neill's work is sometimes in the mold of the great tragedies of the past. Of the dozens of full-length plays that he wrote, those most produced today include *A Moon for the Misbegotten* (1957), about two mismatched lovers who reach an understanding during a night of drinking and confession; *Desire under the Elms* (1924), in which a farm boy falls in love with his stepmother with tragic results; *Ah, Wilderness!* (1933), O'Neill's only comedy and a nostalgic view of a New England family and a teenager who is coming of age; *The Iceman Cometh* (1946), about a group of failed men and women who find temporary hope in a mesmerizing salesman; and *Long Day's Journey into Night* (1956), an autobiographical drama about the O'Neill family, four individuals tormented by their lost dreams and painful present. These and other plays are revived periodically on Broadway, in regional theatres, and throughout the world. No other playwright has explored the dark side of America with such passion and insight as O'Neill.

Oscar Hammerstein (1895–1960) is perhaps the single most important figure in the American musical theatre, even though he never wrote a note of music. His ideas, his books for musicals, and his lyrics did more than any other writer did to make the musical into a recognized art form. Hammerstein came from a theatrical family of producers and managers, but he wanted to write for the musical theatre, making the stories more believable and the lyrics more honest and revealing. After contributing to many light musicals and operettas, he and composer Jerome Kern collaborated on *Show Boat* (1927), an epic tale about life along the Mississippi River that is generally considered the first musical play. For the first time a musical went

OSCAR HAMMERSTEIN As the librettist and lyricist for such landmark musicals as *Show Boat* (1927) and *Oklahoma!* (1943), Hammerstein must be considered one of America's best playwrights and not just a Broadway songwriter. The 1994 long-running revival of *Show Boat* on Broadway, directed by Harold Prince, proved that after seven decades the first "musical play" was still potent theatre. Scenic design by Eugene Lee. *Photofest*

far beyond the usual musical comedy fare and showed that a musical could be as rich and enlightening as a serious drama. Hammerstein perfected the model even further with composer Richard Rodgers and *Oklahoma!* (1943), the first musical in which character, plot, story, and score were all integrated into a unified whole. That musical, and other Rodgers and Hammerstein hits, such as *Carousel* (1945), *South Pacific* (1949), *The King and I* (1951), and *The Sound of Music* (1959), became the standard by which musical plays were judged for many years. Hammerstein is still produced across America, and his musicals with Rodgers are still very popular in Europe as well.

Thornton Wilder (1897–1975) was famous as both a novelist and a playwright, creating award-winning classics in each field. He was born in Madison, Wisconsin, and grew up living there and in such exotic places as Hong Kong and Chefoo, China, because his father was a diplomat. Wilder was educated at Oberlin College and Yale University and later taught at the University of Chicago. His first book, *The Cabala*, was published in 1926, and he would go on to write several other novels over the next five decades, the most famous one being *The Bridge of San Luis Rey* (1927). He started writing innovative one-act plays in the 1930s, several of which are still frequently produced. His experimentation with unconventional storytelling, abstract playing space, and character-narrators would come together in *Our Town* (1938), an expressionistic view of life as seen through a group of characters in a small New England town. Of his other plays, the two most celebrated are *The Skin of Our Teeth* (1942), a satirical look at the history of humankind that follows a family through both prehistoric and contemporary times, and *The Matchmaker* (1955), a charming farce about a group of Yonkers citizens who have a day of adventure in New York City. *The Matchmaker* later served as the basis for the popular musical *Hello, Dolly!*

(1964). Wilder's plays and novels are all so different from each other that it is difficult to pinpoint a particular style or theme in his work, but they all share a vivid and theatrical sense of experimentation that keeps them as fresh and effective on the stage today as when they were first written.

Noel Coward (1899–1973) was a British stage, film, and television performer, as well as a playwright, songwriter, and director—a multitalented artist whose very name conjures up images of sophisticated and witty theatre. Ironically, Coward was born into poverty and went on the variety stage as a boy to help feed his family. His disturbing drama *The Vortex* (1924) brought him his first recognition, although it was atypical of his later work. Many of Coward's plays are clever comedies with sparkling dialogue, but he also wrote some fine melodramas, as well as musicals. Coward's most popular comedies include *Hay Fever* (1925), about an eccentric family who drives their weekend guests to distraction; *Private Lives* (1930), in which a formerly married couple is reunited, only to find that they still love and loathe one another; *Design for Living* (1933), about a trio of bohemians who casually fall in and out of love with one another; *Present Laughter* (1939), about an aging matinee idol driven crazy by the many who adore him; and *Blithe Spirit* (1941), a farce fantasy in which a married writer is caught in an awkward situation when a medium brings his first wife back from the dead. Perhaps his most acclaimed drama is *Cavalcade* (1931), an epic chronicle of two families that takes place during a period of forty years, and among his popular musicals are *This Year of Grace* (1927), *Bitter Sweet* (1928), *Words and Music* (1932), *Conversation Piece* (1933), and the repertory of short plays and musicals *Tonight at 8:30* (1935). Coward also wrote and/or acted in many films, and late in his career, he performed in nightclubs and on television with great success.

THORNTON WILDER The 1938 drama *Our Town* is still one of the most produced nonmusical plays in the United States. So much has changed in America in the past eight decades, yet Wilder's play still speaks to us about how precious life is. Paul Newman (center) played the stage manager who marries Emily (Maggie Lacey) and George (Ben Fox) in this 2002 Broadway revival of *Our Town* directed by James Naughton. *Showtime/Photofest; © Showtime*

Lillian Hellman (1905–1984) was far from the first major woman playwright in America (there were successful female writers for the stage going back to the 1840s), but her plays in the 1930s and 1940s were tough, honest dramas that played so well onstage that the gender of the author became irrelevant. Hellman's work often concerns moral choices and the power that deception has to destroy us all. Her most performed dramas are *The Children's Hour* (1934), in which a vindictive child uses the fear of lesbianism to revenge herself on two teachers; *The Little Foxes* (1939), where a greedy family in the South bargain each other into unhappiness; *Watch on the Rhine* (1941), in which the rise of Nazism in Europe affects an American family in Washington; and *Toys in the Attic* (1960), about a weak man destroyed by his loving but suffocating sisters.

Tennessee Williams (1911–1983) was perhaps America's most poetic playwright. Although he did not write his plays in verse, Williams's characters speak in a flowing, revealing kind of poetry that makes them unforgettable. He came to fame with his autobiographical drama *The Glass Menagerie* (1945), about a young man who seeks to leave his domineering mother and reclusive sister. Among Williams's beloved dramas are *A Streetcar Named Desire* (1947), in which a faded Southern belle is destroyed by the real world in the form of her ruthless brother-in-law; *Summer and Smoke* (1948), concerning a delicate small-town woman who is both attracted and repulsed by sex; *Cat on a Hot Tin Roof* (1955), about a wealthy Mississippi family filled with lies and greed; and *Night of the Iguana* (1961), in which a defrocked minister is forced to face himself because of two very different women. Williams's plays are often about a fragile, sensitive, even damaged person who must confront the cold, realistic world around him or her. Williams himself led a sad and tortured life; he was born in Mississippi and raised in St. Louis, the setting for *The Glass Menagerie*. He was a homosexual in an era that convinced him that he was a freak of nature, and, like many of his characters, he felt he was on the outside of society. Yet his characters seem to glow with humanity, and their eccentricities make them bigger than life and keep his plays as potent as ever.

Arthur Miller (1915–2005) is one of America's most durable playwrights, having had a long career in the theatre (over sixty years) and writing a handful of classic plays that are always being produced. Miller was born in New York to a family that was devastated by the Depression, and many of his plays are about families thrown into turmoil by the mistakes they have made. His first success was *All My Sons* (1947), concerning a father so bent on success for his sons that he commits a crime that he lets others pay for. Miller's most famous play is *Death of a Salesman* (1949), about a traveling salesman who has spent his life making sure that he and his sons were popular and well liked but realizes too late that they have all missed the key to true success. Other oft-produced Miller dramas include *The Crucible* (1953), which uses the infamous witch trials in Salem, Massachusetts, in 1692 to illustrate the havoc in the 1950s with the fear of communists in American society; *A View from the Bridge* (1955), about a working-class family whose hidden sins are revealed when some relatives who are illegal immigrants move in with them; and *After the Fall* (1964), an autobiographical drama based on Miller's marriage to the movie star Marilyn Monroe. If Tennessee Williams is the American master of the poetic drama, Miller excels at the terse, thought-provoking problem play with readily identifiable characters.

Peter Shaffer (1926–2016) was an English playwright whose number of works were limited but several of his plays were very successful in London and New York. Shaffer first found recognition with the domestic drama *Five Finger Exercise* (1958), followed by the comedy double-bill *The Private Ear* and *The Public Eye* (1962), the stylistic historic drama *The Royal Hunt of the Sun* (1964), and a second double bill, *Black Comedy* and *White Lies* (1965). His drama *Equus* (1973) was about a psychiatrist who, in curing a disturbed teenage boy of his unhealthy worship of horses, discovers the lack of passion in his own life. It was an international hit which was followed by the equally successful *Amadeus* (1979) about the Italian composer Salieri who is so jealous of the musical gift God has bestowed on the obnoxious youth Mozart that he sets out to destroy him. Much lighter in tone is the comedy *Lettice and Lovage* (1987), about an overimaginative tour guide. Interestingly, most of Shaffer's full-length works have a similar theme: A so-called normal character becomes obsessed with a wildly abnormal person.

Neil Simon (1927–2018) was one of America's most commercially successful playwrights, writing many hit plays over a long period of time. Simon began his writing career in early television, where he developed his talent for sparkling comic dialogue and amusing characters that are as delightful as they are familiar. He was considered primarily a comic writer because of his early successes *Barefoot in the Park* (1963), in which a young married couple discover their differences, and *The Odd Couple* (1965), about a mismatched pair of divorced men trying to live in the same apartment. Simon's later plays moved into more serious ground, though rarely

PETER SHAFFER Inspired by rumors that Italian composer Antonio Salieri was responsible for the early death of Wolfgang Amadeus Mozart, Shaffer wrote the engrossing drama *Amadeus* (1979), told from the aged Salieri's point of view. In this 2014 production at the Chichester Festival in England, Rupert Everett, as Salieri, tries to seduce Mozart's wife, Constanze (Jessie Buckley). Director: Jonathan Church. *Geraint Lewis/Alamy Stock Photo*

did he totally abandon humor in his works. His seriocomic plays include *Chapter Two* (1977), concerning a widower who tries to make a second marriage work; the autobiographical trilogy *Brighton Beach Memoirs* (1983); *Biloxi Blues* (1985); *Broadway Bound* (1986), about Simon's youth in Brooklyn, his time in the army, and his early days in television; and *Lost in Yonkers* (1991), in which two young boys are cared for during the Depression by their cold and hardened grandmother. Simon was basically an autobiographical playwright, most of his works based on some aspect of his own life.

Edward Albee (1928–2016) was an experimental playwright who moved in and out of favor for five decades but wrote a handful of plays that have never gone out of fashion. Albee found success with some absurdist one-act plays, such as *The Zoo Story* (1959), *The Sandbox* (1960), and *The American Dream* (1961), all tragicomic views of modern life. His first full-length play, *Who's Afraid of Virginia Woolf?* (1962), remains one of the most devastating of all American dramas, a funny, terrifying look at a middle-aged couple who survive on the thin line between reality and fantasy. *A Delicate Balance* (1966) explores the fearful secrets that exist in marriage; *Three Tall Women* (1994) examines three aspects of the same woman, each part of her existing in a different time; and *The Goat, or Who Is Sylvia?* (2002) looks at a marriage when it is confronted by a bizarre case of infidelity. Albee's plays are difficult, puzzling, entertaining, and often worth the effort to try to understand them.

Stephen Sondheim (b. 1930) does not write plays but has proved to be one of our most brilliant playwrights because of the music and lyrics he has written for the musical theatre. The well-educated New Yorker was a friend and protégé of Oscar Hammerstein, from whom

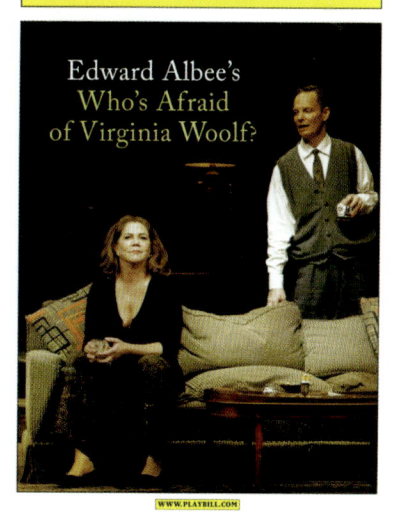

EDWARD ALBEE Few American plays found both the comedy and the tragedy in marriage as did Albee's first full-length work, *Who's Afraid of Virginia Woolf?* (1962). A middle-aged couple, played in the 2005 Broadway revival by Kathleen Turner and Bill Irwin, and a young couple experience an evening of "fun and games" that no audience can ever forget. Director: Anthony Page. *Photofest*

STEPHEN SONDHEIM The musicals scored by Sondheim have been described as "adult," not because of salacious subject matter, but because they often deal with mature and complicated relationships. The affair between nineteenth-century actress Desiree (Glynis Johns) and married lawyer Frederick (Len Cariou) in *A Little Night Music* (1973) is a good example. Director: Harold Prince. *Photofest*

he learned about writing musicals. In many ways, Sondheim continues the innovative writing for the stage that Hammerstein initiated in the 1920s. His first Broadway credits were as the lyricist for the hit musicals *West Side Story* (1957) and *Gypsy* (1959). Starting with the farcical *A Funny Thing Happened on the Way to the Forum* (1962), Sondheim wrote both music and lyrics for a series of bold and groundbreaking musicals that were as accomplished as they were unlike each other. Only a handful of his works have been commercial hits, but no one has provided more adventurous musicals than Sondheim. Among his many notable works are *Company* (1970), a complex psychological look at a New Yorker who both craves and fears marriage; *Follies* (1971), in which regrets and mistakes of the past come back to haunt four people at a theatrical reunion; *A Little Night Music* (1973), a sophisticated and adult operetta about the romantic foibles of high society in nineteenth-century Sweden; *Sweeney Todd, the Demon Barber of Fleet Street* (1979), a dark musical melodrama about a serial killer in Victorian London; *Sunday in the Park with George* (1984), in which the characters in a famous painting are brought to life in the past and the present; *Into the Woods* (1987), where various fairy tales take on more complex ideas when examined as moral choices; and *Assassins* (1991), which views America through the eyes of those who have killed or sought to kill U.S. presidents.

Alan Bennett (b. 1934) is a British actor-turned-writer who has had a busy career in the theatre, film, radio, and television. As a student at Oxford University, he cowrote and performed in a satirical revue titled *Beyond the Fringe* (1960) with fellow students Jonathan Miller, Peter Cook, and Dudley Moore. The comedy was a hit at the Edinburgh Festival, then in London, and then on Broadway in 1962. The four friends then parted ways, and each went on to notable careers, Bennett concentrating on writing, with some occasional returns to acting. After the success of his academic comedy *Forty Years On* (1968) and the sex farce *Habeas Corpus* (1973), he had an international hit with the historical drama *The Madness of King George III* (1991). His other plays of note include *Talking Heads* (1992), a series of poignant, funny, and sometimes disturbing monologues; *The Lady in the Van* (1999), about an eccentric old woman who lives in her vehicle on the playwright's property; *The History Boys* (2004), in which a group of gifted students prepares for Oxford and Cambridge with the help of their unconventional teacher; and *The Habit of Art* (2009), about a troupe of actors rehearsing a play about poet W. H. Auden and composer Benjamin Britten. Bennett has recorded dozens of audio books, both of his own works and literary classics.

Tom Stoppard (b. 1937) is a literary descendant of George Bernard Shaw in that his plays are mostly comedies but deal with diverse and sometimes weighty subjects, ranging from moral philosophy to rock and roll. Stoppard burst on the British theatrical scene with his play *Rosencrantz and Guildenstern Are Dead* (1966), which mixes pseudo-Elizabethan theatrics with satiric absurdism. While it was a success in both London and New York, and has received hundreds of productions throughout the years, many of Stoppard's subsequent plays are more awarded and admired than widely popular. Among his most renowned works are *Jumpers* (1972), in which a morals philosopher tangles with a murder, a crazy wife, and a troupe of acrobats; *Travesties* (1974), a semihistorical romp in which Lenin, James Joyce, and the modern art movement collide in Switzerland during World War I; *The Real Thing* (1982), a funny yet sobering look at the state of matrimony; *Arcadia* (1993), telling two stories, one in the early nineteenth century and the other today, both tales set in the same room; *The Invention of Love* (1997), an exploration into the mind of poet A. E. Houseman; *The Coast of Utopia* (2002), a complex trilogy about the philosophical seeds of communism in the nineteenth century; *Rock 'n' Roll* (2006), about political (and musical) repression in Czechoslovakia under the Communist-controlled government; and *The Hard Problem* (2015), in which various characters involved in a "think tank" try to define the nature of true "goodness." Stoppard's plays are known for their brilliant wordplay, dazzling characters, and mind-bending ideas. He has also written for television, the movies, and British radio.

Caryl Churchill (b. 1938) is a potent and controversial British playwright whose plays on feminism and sexual power take many different forms. Churchill began her writing career in 1958, but she did not receive widespread recognition until her drama *Light Shining in Buckinghamshire* (1976), which was set during the English civil war. She found success on both sides of the Atlantic with her gender-bending comedy *Cloud Nine* (1979), in which the sexual mores of Victorian England and modern London were explored with a feminist point of view. Churchill's other

TOM STOPPARD The characters of Hamlet's school-days friends Guildenstern (Joshua McGuire, left) and Rosencrantz (Daniel Radcliffe) are minor roles in Shakespeare's tragedy *Hamlet*, but Stoppard puts them center stage in the cunning comedy-drama *Rosencrantz and Guildenstern Are Dead* (1966). This 2017 production at the Old Vic in London was directed by David Leveaux. *Geraint Lewis/Alamy Stock Photo*

SAM SHEPARD The tragicomic *True West* is the most often produced of Shepard's plays. In the 2000 Broadway revival, John C. Riley (standing) and Philip Seymour Hoffman played two antagonistic brothers who start to take on one another's personalities. During the Broadway run, the two actors alternated playing each brother. Director: Matthew Warchus. *Joan Marcus/Photofest; photographer: Joan Marcus*

AUGUST WILSON Like *A Raisin in the Sun*, *Fences* (1987) is set in the 1950s, when African Americans were denied many opportunities for a better life. Troy Maxson (Lenny Henry) was once a promising baseball player in the "Negro leagues" but now is a garbage collector in Philadelphia. His son Cory (Ashley Zhangazha) is being wooed by colleges with a football scholarship, but Troy plans to dash his son's dreams before the white man does it for him. This 2013 London production was directed by Paulette Randall. *Geraint Lewis/Alamy Stock Photo*

prominent plays are *Top Girls* (1982), in which famous ladies from history converse with modern, successful businesswomen; *Serious Money* (1987), a satire written in rhymed couplets about the British stock market; *Mad Forest* (1990), a sometimes surrealistic drama about the Romanian Revolution of 1989; *The Skriker* (1994), a fantasy about a fairy who, speaking in English and its own original language, is obsessed with two teenage mothers; and *Love and Information* (2012), a series of scenes and vignettes that involve more than one hundred characters who are nameless and without specified gender. Churchill is as known for her inventive and experimental use of language as she is for her bold and adventurous themes.

Sam Shepard (1943–2017) managed to become popular despite the fact that his plays are dark and pessimistic. Shepard wrote about rural America as a decaying landscape where dreams are lost and the past is filled with the sins of one's ancestors. His drama *Buried Child* (1978) best typifies this theme, with a dead infant buried on the farm and dug up for the climactic ending. Strangely enough, there is plenty of humor in Shepard's plays, and the scripts provide vibrant vehicles for actors. Among Shepard's most produced works are *True West* (1980), in which two very different brothers start to exchange personalities while writing a movie script; *Fool for Love* (1983), about a possibly incestuous love-hate relationship between two volatile siblings; and *A Lie of the Mind* (1985), in which two oddball families cross paths when the abusive son of one marries the daughter of the other. Shepard was also a recognized film actor and sometime director.

August Wilson (1945–2005) is the most commercially and critically successful African American playwright in the history of the American theatre. Raised in Pittsburgh, where he dropped out of school, Wilson started writing poetry and then plays, keeping a poetic flavor in his dialogue. He wrote about African Americans in various decades throughout the twentieth century, but no matter what the time frame, his characters are ablaze with passion, dreams, and often self-destructive power. His first success was *Ma Rainey's Black Bottom* (1984), about a 1920s blues singer who is both an aggressor and a victim. This was followed by a series of dramas that were all well received, making Wilson the most awarded African American playwright on record. His other works include *Fences* (1987), about a former "Negro league" baseball player who tries to suffocate his son's dreams of glory before society does it for him; *Joe Turner's Come and Gone* (1988), set in a Pittsburgh tenement where a stranger comes looking for his runaway wife; *The Piano Lesson* (1990), in which an old piano that has been in the family for generations becomes both a source of pride and a ghost of past wrongs; *Seven Guitars* (1996), concerning the events leading up to the murder of a promising blues singer; *King Hedley II* (1999), in which an ex-con tries to start over again during the so-called prosperous Reagan era; *Jitney* (2000), about a group of gypsy-cab drivers whose personal problems start to overlap; *Gem of the Ocean* (2004), which centers on an aged ex-slave with mystical powers; and *Radio Golf* (2007), in which a rising politician is confronted by the past.

Marsha Norman (b. 1947) is a playwright equally proficient and successful as the author of intimate dramas and large-scale musicals. She was born in Louisville, Kentucky, and worked there as a journalist in Louisville and then as a grammar school instructor and a teacher for special needs children in a state hospital. Inspired by a troubled teenager, she wrote her first play, *Getting Out*, about that girl and her situation. The play was first presented by the Actors Theatre of Louisville and then Off Broadway in 1979, followed by many regional productions over the years. Norman moved to New York City to continue her playwriting career, but many of her subsequent plays were done first at the Actors Theatre of Louisville. Norman won the Pulitzer Prize for *'night, Mother* (1983) and her other plays include *Circus Valentine* (1979), *Traveler in the Dark* (1984), *Sarah and Abraham* (1987), *Last Dance* (2003), and *The Master Butchers Singing Club* (2010). She has found even wider success writing the books for Broadway musicals, including *The Secret Garden* (1991), *The Red Shoes* (1993), *The Color Purple* (2005), and *The Bridges of Madison County* (2014). Norman has also written for television, and she teaches at the Juilliard School in Manhattan.

David Mamet (b. 1947) is known for his crackling dialogue filled with four-letter words and repetitions, which at times give it the feel of a rap song. Mamet's works were first produced in Chicago, the setting for some of his plays, and he found fame with his *Sexual Perversity in Chicago* (1975), an antiromantic look at two couples in failed relationships. Mamet's characters (crooks, salesmen, Hollywood producers, college professors, and so on) rarely have many redeeming characteristics, but their high-flying speech and dynamic personalities often make them fascinating. His frequently produced plays include *American Buffalo* (1977), about three thieves hoping to steal a valuable coin from a millionaire's collection; *Glengarry Glen Ross* (1984), dealing with cutthroat salesmen selling worthless Florida real estate; and *Oleanna* (1992), about possible sexual harassment between a professor and his female student. Mamet also writes and directs for the screen and has carried some of his theatre traits into his movie projects.

Wendy Wasserstein (1950–2006) was perhaps the best of the many women playwrights working in the American theatre at the end of the twentieth century. Her point of view is not feminist as much as her subject matter and characters are enlightening on women's issues. She was also concerned with her Jewish heritage, and some of her plays are about the conflict between a modern lifestyle and an ancient tradition of living the Hebrew faith. Despite such weighty issues, all of Wasserstein's plays are comedies, and her humor is as incisive as her observations. Born and raised in a wealthy Jewish family and educated at the best schools,

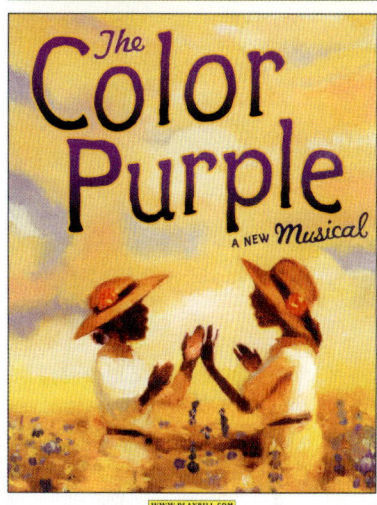

MARSHA NORMAN Such powerful dramas as *Getting Out* and *'night, Mother* proved Norman to be one of the finest playwrights of her day. Yet she has been equally adept at writing the scripts for musicals, such as her expert stage adaptation of Alice Walker's 1982 novel *The Color Purple* into a popular musical in 2005. *Photofest*

Wasserstein infuses her characters with bright intellects and knowing dialogue. Her first success was *Uncommon Women and Others* (1977), about the various goings-on at a girls' boarding school. Her other notable comedies include *Isn't It Romantic* (1981), about two women trying to break away from family and find lasting love in the modern city; *The Heidi Chronicles* (1989), which follows a smart but unsure art historian from her days in prep school through various relationships to the age of AIDS; *The Sisters Rosensweig* (1993), concerning three siblings who have risen up in the world but are still uncomfortable about their commonplace origins and Jewish roots; *An American Daughter* (1997), about a progressive doctor who is confronted with political hypocrisy; and *Third* (2005), in which a liberal college professor has her ideas shaken by a conservative student. Wasserstein also wrote some screenplays for Hollywood.

Paula Vogel (b. 1951) is a powerful writer of controversial plays about very serious subjects, yet there is often an offbeat sense of humor present as well. She was born in Washington, D.C., the daughter of an advertising executive, and educated at Catholic University, Bryn Mawr College, and Cornell University. Vogel was noticed in New York City with her first produced play, *The Baltimore Waltz* (1992), an allegory about the AIDS epidemic. Her most awarded play is *How I Learned to Drive* (1997), about a teenager who is sexually abused by her uncle. Vogel's other works include *And Baby Makes Seven* (1993), *Desdemona—A Play about a Handkerchief* (1993), *Hot 'n' Throbbing* (1994), *The Mineola Twins* (1999), *The Long Christmas Ride Home*, (2003), *Don Juan Comes Home from Iraq* (2014), and *Indecent* (2017). She has taught playwriting at Brown University, where she founded the Brown/Trinity Repertory Consortium, and at Yale University.

PAULA VOGEL Provocative subject matter can be found in all of Vogel's plays, and the fascinating drama *Indecent* (2015) is no exception. In 1906, a Yiddish theatre troupe puts on the play *The God of Vengeance* about a lesbian relationship and tours Europe but is met with antagonism when it is performed in New York City in 1923. *Indecent* was produced at a handful of regional theatres and Off Broadway before arriving on Broadway in 2017. Director: Rebecca Taichman. *Sara Krulwich/ New York Times/Redux*

These twenty-one playwrights cannot even begin to illustrate the number and diversity of American and British writers for the theatre. There are also many Hispanic, Asian, gay and lesbian, sociopolitical, and disabled playwrights who help make the theatre so rich and vital. They all share in common the challenges and rewards of writing plays and musicals. They are the theatre's architects, and the blueprints they provide are the foundations for thousands of theatre events each year.

TOPICS FOR GROUP DISCUSSION

1. Pick a play that you are very familiar with and try to determine what might have been the playwright's germinal idea.
2. What do you imagine to be the differences between writing a play and writing a screenplay?
3. How much freedom should modern directors and actors have in changing the "blueprint" of a play hundreds of years old?

POSSIBLE RESEARCH PROJECTS

1. View the 1938 movie version of *You Can't Take It with You* and describe the many changes the screenwriters made to the original stage "blueprint."
2. Read or view August Wilson's *Fences*, a melodrama about an African American family living in a big city in the 1950s, and compare it to Lorraine Hansberry's *A Raisin in the Sun*, which has a similar setting.
3. Research the life of Alexander Hamilton and point out the changes Lin-Manuel Miranda made to history for the sake of dramatic action in *Hamilton*.

FURTHER READING

Bach, Steven. *Dazzler: The Life and Times of Moss Hart.* New York: Knopf, 2001.
Bigsby, Christopher. *Contemporary American Playwrights.* New York: Cambridge University Press, 2000.
Brown, Jared. *Moss Hart: A Prince of the Theatre.* New York: Back Stage Books, 2006.
Carter, Steven R. *Hansberry's Drama: Commitment and Complexity.* Champaign: Meridian/University of Illinois Press, 1991.
Cheney, Anne. *Lorraine Hansberry.* Boston: Twayne, 1984.
Chernow, Ron. *Alexander Hamilton.* London: Penguin, 2005.
Cohen, Alan, and Steven L. Rosenhaus. *Writing Musical Theatre.* London: Palgrave Macmillan, 2006.
Cohen, Edward M. *Working on a New Play.* New York: Prentice Hall, 1988.
Cole, Toby. *Playwrights on Playwrights.* Lanham, MD: Cooper Square Press, 2012.
Egri, Lajos. *The Art of Dramatic Writing.* New York: Touchstone, 1972.
Frankel, Aaron. *Writing the Broadway Musical.* New York: Drama Book Specialists, 2009.
Goldstein, Malcolm. *George S. Kaufman: His Life, His Theatre.* New York: Oxford University Press, 1979.
Grebanier, Bernard. *Playwriting: How to Write for the Theatre.* New York: Thomas Y. Crowell, 1961.
Guernsey, Otis, Jr., ed. *Playwrights, Lyricists, Composers on Theatre.* New York: Dodd, Mead, 1974.

Hansberry, Lorraine. *A Raisin in the Sun* and *The Sign in Sidney Brustein's Window*. New York: Vintage, 1995.

———. *To Be Young, Gifted, and Black*. Adapted by Howard Nemiroff. Englewood Cliffs, NJ: Prentice Hall, 1969.

Hart, Moss. *Act One: An Autobiography*. New York: Random House/St. Martin's Griffin, 1959/2014.

Hischak, Thomas S. *Boy Loses Girl: Broadway's Librettists*. Lanham, MD: Scarecrow, 2002.

———. *Word Crazy: Broadway Lyricists from Cohan to Sondheim*. New York: Praeger, 1991.

Jester, Caroline, and Caridad Svich. *Fifty Playwrights on Their Craft*. London: Methuen Drama, 2018.

Kerr, Walter. *How Not to Write a Play*. New York: Simon and Schuster, 1955.

Kline, Peter. *The Theatre Student: Playwriting*. New York: Richard Rosen, 1970.

Kolin, Philip C., and Colby H. Kullman. *Speaking on Stage: Interviews with Contemporary American Playwrights*. Tuscaloosa: University of Alabama Press, 1996.

Lawson, John Howard. *Theory and Technique of Playwriting*. New York: Drama Book Specialists, 1967/2018.

Marranca, Bonnie. *American Playwrights: A Critical Survey*. New York: Drama Book Specialists, 1981.

McKissack, Pat. *Young, Black, and Determined: A Biography of Lorraine Hansberry*. New York: Holiday House, 1998.

Meredith, Scott. *George S. Kaufman and His Friends*. New York: Doubleday, 1974.

Miranda, Lin-Manuel, and Jeremy McCarter. *Hamilton: The Revolution*. New York: Grand Central Publishing, 2016.

Patterson, Lindsay. *Black Theatre: A Twentieth-Century Collection of the Work of Its Best Playwrights*. New York: Dodd, Mead, 1971.

Rose, Philip. *You Can't Do That on Broadway! A Raisin in the Sun and Other Theatrical Improbabilities*. New York: Limelight, 2001.

Rowe, Kenneth Thorpe. *Write That Play*. New York: Funk and Wagnalls, 1939/1968.

Savran, David. *The Playwright's Voice: American Dramatists on Memory, Writing, and the Politics of Culture*. New York: Theatre Communications Group, 1999.

Sinnott, Susan. *Lorraine Hansberry: Award-Winning Playwright and Civil Rights Activist*. Newburyport, MA: Conari, 1999.

Smiley, Sam. *Playwriting: The Structure of Action*. Englewood Cliffs, NJ: Prentice Hall, 1971.

Teichmann, Howard. *George S. Kaufman: An Intimate Portrait*. New York: Atheneum, 1972.

Wolf, Carol. *Playwriting: The Merciless Craft*. CreateSpace, 2016.

Woolford, Julian. *How Musicals Work: And How to Write Your Own*. London: Nick Hern Books, 2013.

4

THE PLAY PERFORMERS: THE ACTORS

ACTING VS. ROLE-PLAYING

Kristen Jones lives in an apartment in a midsize American city. On a Thursday morning she is spoon-feeding her ten-month-old daughter, who sits in a high chair in the kitchen. Kristen coos and laughs and communicates with her baby in silly and endearing ways. Kristen is playing the role of a mother. The phone rings, and it is Kristen's late-middle-aged mother. She is calling long distance to say that she wishes Kristen would change her mind and come home for Thanksgiving. Kristen listens sympathetically and converses with the older woman, trying to explain why she and the family cannot travel at the moment. Kristen is playing the role of a grown daughter. That afternoon Kristen's best friend, Melissa, stops by the apartment to tell her all about a party she is planning for the Saturday after Thanksgiving. The two women talk comfortably together, laughing and sharing complaints about relatives. Kristen is playing the role of a best friend. After the baby's nap, mother and daughter go down the street to the bank, where they wait in a long line only to be told that she cannot cash her tax-refund check because it needs her husband's signature as well as hers. Kristen complains, but it does no good. She is playing the role of the frustrated customer. When her husband, Mike, comes home at five o'clock, Kristen tells him about her day, and he relates what his day was like, each accepting the support and understanding of the other. Kristen is now playing the role of a wife.

Because Kristen really is a mother, a daughter, a friend, a customer, and a wife, she is not acting. Yet her role-playing demands that she adjust her tone of voice, her choice of words, her level of intimacy, and even her point of view each time she switches from one role to another. She uses different tactics, has different goals, and employs different forms of communication depending on which role she is playing. We all do it. There is nothing deceiving or dishonest about role-playing. Modern life is so complex and a person's interaction with different people so complicated that we all role-play. But are we acting? Before we try to answer that questions, let us look at the rest of Kristen's day.

At six thirty that night, she leaves the apartment and drives to a performing arts center where a professional theatre company is presenting *Macbeth*. Kristen is cast in the role of Lady Macbeth, a Scottish queen of early British legend. Kristen puts aside her other roles as she applies her makeup, arranges her hair in an unusual style, and puts on the costume of a Scottish noblewoman. Entering the stage for her first scene, Kristen has gone beyond role-playing. She is not really a queen or a Scottish woman or a citizen of a long-ago era. She is acting. Perhaps there are aspects of her real life that surface during her performance. After all, she is a married woman (like Lady Macbeth); she loves her husband (though perhaps in a very different way than Lady Macbeth does); and as an actress, she can use her imagination to try to become this vibrant character. But Kristen is acting, not role-playing.

THE COMPLETE ACTOR There are only a handful of actors today who are equally talented and successful in both musicals and dramas. One of them is Audra McDonald, who has been praised and awarded for her Broadway performances in everything from *Ragtime* (1998) to *A Raisin in the Sun* (2004). She is seen here in one of her most demanding roles, the tragic title character in Michael John LaChiusa's musical drama *Marie Christine* (1999). Director: Graciela Daniele. *Joan Marcus/Photofest; photographer: Joan Marcus*

We often use the word *acting* as meaning behavior, as in "Stop acting up" or "Why are you acting so moody?" But in theatre, acting is pretending to be someone or something we are not. Actors do not merely shift roles as we do in everyday life; actors create specific roles that may have little to do with their everyday role-playing. Acting is closer to pretend than to behavior. All children know how to pretend to be something or someone different than what they are. Even before we are old enough to understand our own identity, we mimic and copy and pretend to be something we see and are fascinated with. A toddler "playing horsey" is not role-playing; he is acting. Psychologists refer to this innate capability in humans to pretend as the *mimic instinct*. All people in all cultures have this desire and talent for imitating things and other people. In the first chapter we saw how the convention of acting is basic to theatregoing. Because we all have the capability to pretend, we accept actors onstage pretending to be someone we know they are not. We "believe" in their love scenes, fight scenes, and death scenes even though we know they are not real. This suspension of belief on the audience's part allows actors to perform. It is an unwritten but clearly understood agreement between actor and audience, and without it there can be no theatre event.

ACTING AS AN ART AND A CRAFT

No job in the theatre has such a direct link with the audience as the actor's. Theatregoers hear the playwright's words, see the designers' handiwork, and perhaps even sense the director's touch, but it is the actor that we see and hear directly. It is the most familiar of all the elements of theatre and the one area that even the least experienced theatregoer forms an opinion about. Acting is also the oldest of the theatre elements, predating scripts and theatre buildings and later jobs such as designers and directors. An actor performing before spectators is the most basic of theatre events. Because we see actors on television and movies all the time, acting in the theatre is one area that audiences most understand. This sometimes misleads people to think that acting is easy, that anyone with enough willpower can do it effectively. In fact, when asked what was most impressive about Kristen's performance as Lady Macbeth, many spectators would say it was her memorization of all that Shakespearean verse. Memorization is part of the actor's task, but it is hardly what makes acting difficult. It would be comparable to saying the most challenging aspect of sewing is threading the needle. Memorizing, like threading a needle, is a necessary first step but far from the real challenges of acting.

Let us consider acting both an art and a craft. The craft is like many other crafts: you learn it; you practice it over and over; and eventually you get the techniques down. Actors learn how to move onstage, how to use their voices, when and when not to breathe, and other techniques. Quite frankly, almost anyone can be taught these elements of craft, but, by themselves, they will not make one an actor. The art of acting is much less concrete and difficult to master. It is a combination of thinking, imagination, reacting, and experience. We will go into the details of these later, but it is worth pointing out here that it is an art form that is extremely difficult to be objective about. Although it is easy for anyone to have an opinion about an actor's performance, it is far from easy to reach a consensus on acting. Kristen's performance as Lady Macbeth may move one audience member to tears; another may be left cold by her acting; and a third spectator might deem the performance gimmicky and melodramatic. The problem with the art of acting is not that there are three different opinions but that all three might be correct.

Acting is such a subjective activity that it is impossible for it to be judged objectively, whether by spectators and critics or by directors and other actors. We bring so many prejudices with us into the theatre that no two audience members see the exact same thing in an actor's performance. One theatregoer might find the actor playing Aaron Burr in *Hamilton* haughty, a snob, and an opportunist with no backbone. Another audience member might sympathize with Burr as the capable, intelligent man who always seems to be overlooked and is eventually driven to take revenge on the man who kept him from becoming president. Much of their opinions are formed by the way each views the character. We all fall into the trap of confusing the actor with the character and blaming the shortcomings of the performance on the faults in the character. We are also prejudiced by what we consider "good" acting. One spectator might say the actor playing Grandpa Vanderhof in *You Can't Take It with You* is dull and monotonous while another finds him subtle and wryly charming. The broad performance of the actor playing King George III in *Hamilton* will strike some as deliciously satirical, others as overblown and clichéd. Some audience members are impressed with volatile and hyperkinetic acting while others think more highly of quiet, realistic performances. Like all the arts, there are many sides to acting and many ways to view those sides. Even though we cannot pin down the art of acting and evaluate it objectively, we can look at its history, theories, and techniques in order to better understand it.

ENSEMBLE ACTING When a small group of actors with roles equal in size and challenges work together so effectively, it is called ensemble acting. Such was the case with the 1976 Off-Broadway revival of Eugene O'Neill's autobiographical drama *Long Day's Journey into Night* directed by Jason Robards. The haunted Tyrone family was played by, left to right, Zoe Caldwell, Kevin Conway, Robards, and Michael Moriarty. *Photofest*

A BRIEF HISTORY OF ACTING

The history of theatre tells us much about actors over the centuries: who they were, how they were revered and idolized at times, and how they were scorned and looked down upon at other times. For most of theatre history, actors were male. During some periods they were hidden behind masks or elaborate makeup. We have statues, woodcuts, paintings, and (later) photographs and even recordings of actors. We know all about the actors, but we do not know very much about acting in the past. What did the actors sound like? How did they move onstage? What gestures or facial expressions were employed? How broad or how subtle were they? These remain a mystery to us. We know that stage acting in past centuries was probably very different from modern acting. In fact, we suspect that modern audiences would laugh or wince if they saw a tragedy performed as it was in times long past. Yet audiences then were very moved by actors and often commented on how effective they were. Perhaps the theatregoer's idea of effective pretending has changed with time. What will future audiences think one hundred years from now when they look at our movies and our idea of powerful acting?

The First Actor?

In 534 BC, a play contest was held in Athens, the first documented theatre event in Greece. The winner of the competition was Thespis, who wrote and performed the leading role in a tragedy that is now lost. Here is how legend says the performance came about: Theatre events up to this time consisted of a chorus of performers who chanted, danced, and recited poetry as a means of telling a story; but on that fateful day, Thespis stepped forward from the chorus and, as a specific character, addressed the audience and the chorus. He had no other characters to act with, but he made a personality come alive, and the possibilities thereafter were endless. So, according to legend, Thespis was the first actor. Unlike chorus members, who were storytellers, Thespis was an actor in the full sense of the word. Today we still refer to actors as *thespians*, though it is considered an archaic term. Nonetheless, the actor as we define it today dates back to Thespis.

Premodern Acting

Acting must have been on a grand scale during the days of Thespis and other ancient Greek actors. Plays were presented in huge outdoor amphitheatres, and the actor's voice had to carry through the mask he wore to the last rows high up on a hill. It is likely that the performers had to use a broad gesture of the arms if any movement was to be detected by all the spectators. Yet these must not have been shouting and declamatory announcers, for the Greeks were moved, as Aristotle writes, to "fear and pity." In the Middle Ages the actors were members of the clergy who performed religious dramas in churches. Later medieval plays were enacted by amateurs, members of various trade guilds, who performed stories from the Bible on outdoor temporary stages for certain holy days. During the Elizabethan era when Shakespeare's works were first produced, the actors were professional men with boy apprentices playing the female roles. While we might view a male youth playing Lady Macbeth today with suspicion, it did not keep the English theatregoers of the time from being caught up in the action. From the Greek, medieval, and Elizabethan scripts, we can tell that actors often interacted with the audience and frequently addressed the spectators directly, even in very serious works. By the seventeenth-century neoclassic period in France, actresses started appearing on the stage more and more, and audiences learned to accept women in women's roles. In the eighteenth century, famous actors and their acting companies dominated the stages of Europe. There is some evidence that the acting style was becoming more lifelike or, as we would say today, realistic. Prose became as popular as poetry onstage, so dialogue moved closer to conversation rather than declamatory verse. Yet there is much to suggest that gestures and mannerisms were still very broad and that actors (and audiences) prized vocal prowess over other aspects of acting.

Very few acting schools or acting books seem to have existed until the 1700s. Actors learned their craft from other actors, either as apprentices or through

CHORUS Before there were individual actors, there was only a chorus of actors. Today a chorus is mostly found in musicals, as in a singing or dancing chorus. But in the Greek theatre the chorus members were links between the audience and the story. In this modern Greek production of Euripides' tragedy *The Bacchae*, the chorus is still important. This 2012 London production was directed by Peter Hall. *Photo © Tristram Kenton/Bridgeman Images*

experience playing small parts in theatre companies. Although scholars had been writing about acting theoretically since the Roman Empire, these were not instructional or how-to books but rather treatises on the art of performance. The most famous and thought-provoking of these kinds of commentaries was *The Paradox of the Actor* (1773), by the French encyclopedist Denis Diderot. He suggested that in performance the portrayal of a character merges and feeds off of the personality of the actor. The paradox is that an actor playing Macbeth uses his own voice and body but must try to imagine the thought process and emotions of a murderous Scottish king. Diderot was a very methodical person and thought acting could be categorized and turned into an objective system in one's head. Modern theory does not agree with this, but Diderot was accurate when he wrote of the dilemma of acting. In the next century, acting books by another Frenchman, Francois Delsarte, aimed to teach student performers how to act by physicalizing all emotions. In his illustrated books, Delsarte showed how specific poses or facial attitudes would convey the appropriate message to the audience. For example, both hands on the cheeks and the mouth open would be the effective pose for the emotion of horror, while clutching one's breast would designate grief. As silly as these books appear to modern actors, many performers subscribed to Delsarte's methods in the 1800s, and, as clichéd as they appear today, audiences reacted to the emotions as he predicted.

Modern Acting

Acting, as we are familiar with it today, can be traced to the work of the Russian director-actor Konstantin Stanislavsky and the "system" he first developed in the 1890s. In a series of books, Stanislavsky presented some bold and original ideas about acting, most of which actors today take for granted. He said that an actor learns one's art not by watching other actors but by observing real life. If one is to play an old man onstage, one does not copy how other actors have played such elderly characters, nor does one use hunched-over postures and crackle-voiced diction to "play" old. Instead, the actor should go out and observe real people, observe elderly citizens on the streets and in public places, and look at the variety of behavior that such an age presents. Above all else, Stanislavsky wanted his actors to be truthful, and he felt that only through observation could truth be captured onstage.

Another one of his concepts was that of the *magic if.* An actor should use his or her "emotion memory" to recall feelings experienced in one's past. Actors should ask themselves how they would personally react if put in the position of the character. Recalling the death of a loved one, for example, should lead an actor to discover the emotions necessary to portray grief truthfully onstage. All of this requires that an actor concentrate when performing, and only through deep concentration can the paradox of the actor be solved.

Finally, Stanislavsky demanded that his actors find the *spine* of the characters they portray. The spine is the goal or objective that the character has deep inside that drives everything he or she says and does. Since this spine is rarely discussed in exposition or dialogue, it is the actor's task to search it out and experiment with it in rehearsals.

Stanislavsky's actors were asked to keep detailed journals about their characters, doing both factual and emotional research into the makeup of the person being portrayed. Even the smallest role in a Stanislavsky production was approached this way. The actress playing the maid would imagine what the maid earned; how she lived; where she came from; and her attitudes about, and relationships with, all of the other characters in the household.

Word of Stanislavsky's system soon spread across the Western world, and it was debated, discussed, and eventually embraced by most theatre companies. In the United States, the system was later translated and interpreted by Lee Strasberg and other acting coaches, and it was called the *Method*. With a great deal of emphasis put on emotional memory, the "Method actors" (as they were labeled) placed the actor's emotional connection to the characters and the situation above all else. Techniques such as clear diction and appropriate volume were considered secondary, resulting in some dynamic acting but sometimes sloppy or incomprehensible theatrics. Some actors who learned the Method at the Actors Studio in New York went on to fame and helped create an American style of acting. Actors such as Marlon Brando, Joanne Woodward, James Dean, Paul Newman, and Jane Fonda made the Method world famous when their performances were captured on film. The tradition is carried on today with such prominent actors as Al Pacino, Meryl Streep, and Robert De Niro. But as dazzling as these performers often are, the Method has been misused or misinterpreted by lesser actors, and the result can be self-absorbed and gratuitous acting onstage and on-screen. Most actors today are not, strictly speaking, Method actors, but all of them use some aspects of Strasberg's ideas,

EXTERIOR ACTING Laurence Olivier created his characters from the outside in, first determining the look and sound of the person before exploring the interior mental state. He is pictured here playing Romeo opposite Vivien Leigh's Juliet in a stage production seen in London and then New York in 1940. *Moviestore Collection Ltd/Alamy Stock Photo*

as well as much of what Stanislavsky presented over a hundred years ago. The modern actor is faced with a variety of theories about acting, and each acting school or acting class in a college or university will differ somewhat from another. The paradox of the actor continues on.

THEORIES OF ACTING

Because acting is such a subjective art, there is no agreement as to the best way to teach acting. In fact, many believe that acting is not an art that can be taught. Others say that you can teach the craft of acting but not the art. While there is no general agreement, there is no shortage of different theories of acting. The field can be narrowed down to two approaches: the internal and the external. Many theories are variations of either or both, so these two polar opposite schools of thought ought to give a fair survey of the theories that continue to exist.

The *external approach* says that an actor develops a character from the outside in. The character's physical attributes are decided on, then the way the character would wear clothes or use props. The actor will search for a voice for the character, choosing a dialect perhaps or a vocal quality that will best convey the person. After the exterior is refined, the actor then delves into the psyche of the character. Motivation for one's actions, mental processes, and emotional ingredients are then added. The lines in the script are considered gospel truth, and everything must somehow spring from the text in some way. Finally, rehearsals are used to polish the externals so that the internal will come naturally. Some very famous actors have used this approach and given sterling performances. The renowned British actor Laurence Olivier, for example, could not grasp his character until he had decided on the makeup to be used and the vocal tones he would employ. In both classical and contemporary roles, Olivier was a strong believer in the script, arguing that the playwright's words were the ultimate truth of the character.

The *internal approach*, as you might suspect, works in the opposite way. The actor first studies the motivation and objectives of the character. The script is necessary, but the real truth is to be found between the lines of the text. Such an actor cannot be concerned with movement onstage and the way to speak the lines until the internal truth of the character is discovered. The actor might even paraphrase the dialogue at first or improvise scenes not in the script in order to get at this internal truth. Rehearsal time is a period of experimentation for this kind of performer, and only late in the preparation process will the character's words and actions be solidified into a polished product. The Method actors already listed are good examples of performers who use the internal approach with success. Both of these theories of acting "work" onstage, though an actor who is extreme in either is sometimes more difficult to work with than is ideal. An extreme internalist will upset rehearsals by wandering about the stage when other performers are trying to solidify the stage

INTERIOR ACTING Marlon Brando epitomized the American method actor, who created his character psychologically from within. His greatest stage role was the brutish Stanley Kowalski, who destroys his sister-in-law, Blanche (Jessica Tandy), in Tennessee Williams's *A Streetcar Named Desire* (1947). *Photofest*

movements. Also, actors who have memorized the script as written are frustrated when the internal actor is speaking whatever his emotions prompt him to say. On the other hand, an extreme externalist can be just as disruptive in rehearsals. The actor might fuss about prop and costume details when others are trying to tell the plot and develop the characters. The externalist may also be so concerned with accents and vocal tricks that the other actors have trouble communicating onstage with so many external gimmicks. But these are extreme cases, and it is surprising how often actors with different approaches work so well together in rehearsals and performances.

AN ACTOR'S TOOLS

Regardless of which approach an actor uses, all performers use the same tools. The script gives them the lines and characters; the director guides them through the rehearsal process. But an actor's tools are more individualized. Most of the time an actor must use the tools that he or she already has. One's body, for example, is uniquely one's own, and, aside from cosmetic tricks and artificial aids such as padding or a bald wig, it is the body with which the actor is stuck. While in one's mind an actor feels that she is perfect to play the feisty, young college student Beneatha in *A Raisin in the Sun*, that person's imagination will be little help if she is fifty years old. A young actor can sometimes play a character older than himself; indeed, in educational theatre that is the only kind of actor available. But in professional theatre an older actor will be cast in the part, and all of the training and theoretical approaches will not allow the young actor to be cast far beyond his or her age. Another tool that is relatively inflexible is the actor's voice. Vocal training can improve an actor's speaking and singing voice, but each of us has a specific vocal quality that is very difficult to disguise. Some actors are expert in creating different voices, changing their pitch, resonance, and articulation for each role they play, but most performers are forced to make do with the vocal cords they are given. An actor with a thin, squeaky voice is unlikely to play Macbeth, just as an actress with a breathy, husky voice is not likely to be cast as the sweet ingenue Alice in *You Can't Take It with You*. All true actors work on perfecting the tools of voice and body, but, being physiological tools, they are limited.

Such cannot be said for the psychological tools that actors may possess. While it is not necessary to have a high IQ or an impressive GPA to be a thinking actor, one must have a sense of inquiry, a curiosity about human behavior, and a strong imagination to excel at acting. A physically attractive performer with a beautiful flowing voice but without any of these mental processes may find a certain amount of success, but it is unlikely that such a person will ever be a proficient actor. It is the actor's psyche that allows him or her to create vivid characters and to let them come to life though use of the voice and the body. The actor's most valuable tool is this mental ability. Without it, no theory or approach to acting will work. Some believe that highly emotional people make better actors than do emotionally stable ones. There have certainly been many examples of both kinds of human beings who have triumphed on the stage, but emotions close to the surface are no better than emotions hidden deep inside. It is the way the actor uses these very personal feelings in bringing truth to the character that matters. Audiences cannot tell if the actress playing Ruth Younger in *A Raisin in the Sun* is personally as bitter and distraught as her character is in the story. They do not need to know. The actress brings Ruth alive, and that is what really counts.

THE ACTOR'S PROCESS

Whether an actor is using the internal approach, the external approach, or a variation of either, some generalities can be said about the process that the performer goes through during rehearsals and performances. Before actors are cast in a part, they are involved in an ongoing process to refine individual skills and polish their craft. Even after they start to make a living in the theatre, most professional actors continue to study breathing techniques and take classes in acting, dance, voice, and physical exercise in order to keep the tools they have in prime condition. The preparation for acting is never fully completed, and each new role is not just a new job but another experiment or a chance to explore the art form. Just as an athlete does not stop training and practice once the season has started, actors realize that they also must "keep in shape" physically and mentally in order to do the best they can onstage.

Analysis

Once an actor is cast in a role, a more specific kind of preparation starts. Even before rehearsals start, the actor reads the script and starts thinking about the character to be portrayed. Actors read scripts differently from others in and outside of the business. The comic cliché is that performers read only their own lines, counting them and trying to determine if the role is large enough to warrant one's attention. In reality a professional actor reads the plot and ideas in a script for what it tells him or her about a character and what makes that character tick. Not only the character's lines but what other characters say about the role in question is the first clue as to what drives the character. Later in rehearsals these ideas will be discussed with the director and other actors, but this preliminary study or analysis allows the actor to get familiar with the character. The actor starts to view all of the events in the script in terms of how they affect the role to be played.

For example, the actress playing Lena Younger in *A Raisin in the Sun* must look at the anticipated life insurance check as a gift from God and a way to a better life; she views her troubled son Walter with compassion, worry, and love. The actor playing Walter, on the other hand, sees the check as his one-and-only opportunity to make something out of himself, to become a man in a society that sees him merely as a "boy"; he looks at his mother, Lena, as being old-fashioned with small dreams that are conservative and pathetic. Even actors in minor roles must look at the entire play as it relates to their placement in it. The actor playing the income tax man Henderson in *You Can't Take It with You* has only one scene in the first act. If someone asked that actor what *You Can't Take It with You* is about, he would be right in saying that it is about a government clerk who goes to the Vanderhof house to determine why Grandpa has not paid his taxes. That might be a narrow description of Kaufman and Hart's vibrant comedy but to Henderson (and the actor playing him), that is indeed what it is about.

CHARACTER ANALYSIS One of the most enigmatic characters in world theatre is the fascinating title role in Henrik Ibsen's classic drama *Hedda Gabler* (1891), a restless wife who strives for the power denied to women in her time. Distinguished American actress Eva Le Gallienne captured the many facets of Hedda in a 1948 Broadway production by the American Repertory Theatre. *Photofest*

Rehearsal

Once rehearsals start, the actor continues to explore and learn about the character, but he or she now does so as part of a group. The director guides, suggests, and maybe even insists on ways to play the character, just as other actors and the way they interpret their characters will affect this learning and exploration process. Throughout the rehearsals the actor must do the things that are necessary to the craft of acting, such as memorizing lines, movements, and cues. Everyone understands about the memorization of lines, but the use of a *cue* is less known. A cue is anything that signals an actor to speak or to move. It can be a phrase or word spoken by another actor, or it can be a piece of movement or the use of an external element, such as a knock at the door or a telephone ringing. Just as important as what the character says, the actor must know when to speak, when to interrupt another actor-character, and when to pause in a speech. For this one needs to understand and use cues effectively. Sometimes cues are obvious.

> **HE:** Where are you going?
> **SHE:** Out. Away from you. Good-bye!

When the actress hears the word *going*, she knows it is her cue to speak. Since his line is a question, her line is easy to memorize because it follows logically: the idea for her line is set up in his line. But sometimes the idea for a line is not so obvious.

> **HE:** What is the matter with you? You never make any effort to keep peace in this house!
> **SHE:** There is nothing the matter with me!

The idea for her line is in the first part of his speech, but the actress must wait until the cue—"peace in this house!"—before she can speak. Sometimes the idea for one's line does not exist in the previous speech, and the cue must be memorized without the help of logical thought.

> **HE:** How can you do a thing like that? It's ridiculous! You'll make a total fool out of yourself before you are done!
> **SHE:** Are you that jealous of him?

The actress must realize that the idea for her next line is something implied between the lines of the previous speech. Such non sequitur kinds of cues are the most difficult to memorize but often make for the most intriguing scenes in plays.

Also during rehearsals actors must concentrate on other elements of craft, particularly those having to do with the voice and the body. Vocal demands (volume, articulation, breathing, etc.) and physical demands (agility, posture, body language, etc.) are ongoing and cannot be put off until dress rehearsals or performances. Maintaining both of these tools is especially essential while rehearsing a musical. Singing and dancing demands are added to the usual tasks, and neither come quickly or easily. A musical such as *Hamilton* has much more complex characters than, say, a frothy musical comedy of the 1930s, and there is much to explore in the characterizations. Yet the cast of *Hamilton* cannot ignore the tremendous vocal work needed in such a pulsating musical, perhaps the most dangerous kind of play when it comes to maintaining vocal control. The dancing demands of *Hamilton* may not be as great as that of a musical with extended ballet or jazz dance, but it is a very physical show all the same and one that taxes all of the actors' craft. As staged in the original New York production, the cast of *Hamilton* is almost always moving, keeping time with the propelling rhythm of the music. Add to that the rapping and rapid lyrics that some characters have to deliver while moving and there is a demanding amount of craft and stamina needed for performing such a musical.

Late in the rehearsal period the actors begin to wear costumes, wigs, makeup, and other accessories that define their characters. These dress rehearsals add new burdens for the performers, sometimes finding that moves that were polished earlier are now more difficult with a particular costume. Also, adding props such as an umbrella, a cane, purses, and handkerchiefs tends to "throw a person off" at first. Yet if the clothes and such items are consistent with the character being portrayed, they can be very helpful to an actor. Performers often feel that the final clue to understanding their roles comes during these dress rehearsals. This is not just true for period or "costume" plays; even a character in a modern drama can be solidified or strengthened by the right wardrobe or accessory. Essie's ballet tutu and Penny's painter's smock will give those two actors in *You Can't Take It with You* details that help them connect with the character. In the same way, an ornamental period costume and wig might define the character of King George III to the actor in *Hamilton*. In a later chapter, we discuss costume design and the way it speaks to an audience, but one should not forget the way that costumes affect the actors as well.

Sustaining a Performance

The actor's process does not end once the play opens and performances begin. Most amateur actors will only perform a particular play or musical for a handful of times, but professional actors are usually required to repeat a performance dozens, even hundreds, of times. Maintaining a level of freshness and quality during a long run is sometimes as challenging as the process of creating a character the first time. In order for a performance to remain fresh, the actor must keep in shape both physically and mentally. The stamina it takes to perform a play or a musical does not diminish as the run continues, and both vocal and physical exercises are needed. Many casts do "warm-ups" together, while some company members may dedicate a portion of each day to working out. Mentally, the actor must not let the familiarity of the play get in the way of its freshness. Although it may be the fifty-fourth time an actress is playing Lady Macbeth, for the audience it is their first time seeing this particular production of *Macbeth*. The actress must keep mentally alert, making sure that she is still telling the story and portraying her character clearly. Many companies hold line rehearsals every few weeks during a long run. Particularly in modern plays, actors sometimes start to paraphrase or embellish the playwright's words, and these unwanted "improvements" are removed during such brush-up rehearsals. Most actors agree that it is the audience that helps keep their performances fresh. In a comedy, the theatregoers' laughter at lines the actors have heard so many times will remind them that it is all new to the spectators. Even the silent rapport that develops between an audience and the actors during a serious drama is strong enough for the performers to detect, and that encourages them to relive the excitement that prompted them on opening night. For an actor to repeat the same performance over and over again in an empty playhouse would be as tedious as it would be silly, but when the four elements of theatre come together, the actor springs to life and can usually continue to do so as part of the theatre event.

THE BUSINESS OF ACTING

Because one reads about the astounding sums of money that movie and television stars earn, many assume that acting is a lucrative profession. In fact, it is one of the lowest-paying and unstable of all jobs. At any one time, three-fourths of all professional actors are out of work. The actor who works in an office or as a waiter is not a cliché; most actors spend much of their working lives in a job outside of acting. And when actors do get jobs in the theatre, the salaries are much less than those in the other arts. To illustrate how stage actors are paid in proportion to other performers, consider this ratio: If a New York actor is paid $1,000 a week to perform in a Broadway show, an actor making a film in New York City will be paid $1,000 a day, and an actor in network television will get $1,000 a minute. One wonders why an actor would bother with theatre work when the other media pay so much more. Or why would a star, who gets a few million dollars for filming a movie for two months, agree to do a Broadway play for six months for only one-fifth of the money? Actors, both famous and "undiscovered," are drawn to live theatre for the same reasons: the exciting rapport with a live audience, the chance to play great roles, and the sense of accomplishment that comes from performing a character over the course of a evening rather than in bits and pieces that are edited together by others. The one reason you won't find: for the money.

Auditions

The ways that one becomes a professional actor are varied and inconsistent. Someone who graduates from a prestigious college or university with a renowned theatre program will probably have more access to auditions and job interviews than an actor without such a pedigree. Or someone who gets a certificate of completion from a famous acting school in New York will make the right kind of contacts. But no actor, regardless of his or her background, is cast in a play because of a resume or diploma or letters of reference. Actors are cast by what they do at an *audition*. An audition is a prepared or impromptu performance in which an actor demonstrates for a director his or her abilities to act, sing, and/or dance. Auditions are nerve-racking for actors, tiresome for directors, and expensive for producers. They are not even deemed to be very reliable; some fine actors do not come across well at an audition, while some

AUDITIONS The long-running musical *A Chorus Line* (1975) captured the audition process vividly and accurately. The original Broadway cast members are literally "on the line," the white line painted across the stage floor, as they wait to audition for a director. Director-choreographer: Michael Bennett. *Photofest*

flashy, personable performers appear to be more talented than they really are. So why do they keep using auditions in the theatre? Because no one has ever discovered another way to determine if an actor is right for a part. A director can interview a performer, discuss how the character might be played, even review one's credits and survey the type of roles the actor has played in the past. The director or producer might even see the actor give a polished performance in another production. But unless that actor does an audition, actually reading or singing or whatever, one does not know if she or he is going to be effective in a particular role. Major stars do not audition, and some actors might be hired because the director has worked with them in another play, but these are exceptions. Most roles in theatre are filled through auditions.

There are different kinds of auditions, depending on the status of the performer or the type of theatre event being planned. An established actor with substantial credits might get to audition in private with a director and producer. The interview and reading may be very friendly and informal, but the actor still knows that he or she is auditioning. The other extreme is a *cattle call* audition, when dozens or even hundreds of performers are auditioned in groups, only getting a chance to speak a few lines, sing a few bars, or dance a few steps. Singing and dancing chorus members often are cast from a cattle call audition. Sometimes an actor is asked to perform a prepared monologue or a song; other auditions, called *cold readings*, have the performer read aloud a scene that is new to him or her. Actors sometime read with others, sometimes alone. The details may vary, but each audition is a test of sorts. While any person applying for any job goes through an interview, which is a mild form of audition, there is something particularly grueling about an audition in the theatre. You are judged not by your past accomplishments but by what you look like and act like today. A rejection in the theatre is worse than not getting an office job or a sales position because being turned down as an actor is more personal. The director and producer saw you do your best, but it was not good enough. All one can do is keep auditioning for others, waiting for the right role or for a better opportunity.

Professional Union

Most actors working in professional theatres in America are members of *Actors' Equity Association*, the union for actors, singers, and dancers in the theatre. (There are different unions for television and film actors.) One does not join Equity by choice. A performer must first secure a professional job in an Equity theatre or earn enough Equity points working in semi-professional theatres. After paying dues, the Equity actor can get into better auditions and is guaranteed better pay and benefits than that of actors in nonunion companies. What an Equity card does not guarantee is a job. Over half of all Equity members earn less than poverty-level income in a year unless they hold other jobs outside of the theatre. Actors' Equity is a controversial union; many cite it as one of the reasons for rising productions costs, while others argue that it is the only protection that actors have in the very unsettling world of professional theatre. The union was formed in 1912 to combat the way that actors were mistreated by managers: low pay, no benefits, no money for rehearsals or extra performances, being abandoned in outlying towns, being forced to pay for their own costumes, and so on. It took time, but the young union eventually became powerful enough to protect its members. Some feel that Equity has gotten too powerful, but the same may be said for most theatre unions. The fact is, Actors' Equity is an important part of all professional actors' careers, and, like it or not, the union continues to shape the way theatre operates in America.

Once an actor gets into the union and is cast in a role, his or her anxiety does not end. During the rehearsal period (of anywhere from three to six weeks), the director and producer watch cast members closely to see if they are fulfilling the promise that they showed at auditions. Sometimes an actor is deemed incompatible with a role and, regardless of talent, is replaced by someone considered more appropriate. Being replaced in a production is, you can imagine, even more devastating than being rejected at an audition. Yet many accomplished performers have been removed from a production for various reasons usually not having to do with their ability. All the same, actors frequently feel as if they are always auditioning, always hoping and waiting to be accepted. Not until the play opens and that acceptance comes from a live audience can the actor relax somewhat and concentrate on the complex art of acting.

Acting Terms

ad-libbing—dialogue made up on the spot in the case of an emergency, such as a missing prop, a mishap with scenery, a forgotten line, or an actor who fails to enter on cue. The term comes from the Latin *ad libitum*, which means "at pleasure," though theatre folk frown on an actor's ad-libbing unless absolutely necessary.

Alexander technique—a popular series of exercises and breathing techniques favored by actors, many of them attending Alexander classes regularly throughout their careers.

apprentice—a nonunion performer or backstage crew member who works for little or no pay in a professional production in order to get experience and eventually become professional. Apprentices were very common in summer theatres in the past; today they are also found in regional theatres.

articulation—the process of making clear and distinct sounds with the voice so that every word is easily understood. Some performers are blessed with better articulation than others, but all actors have to drill themselves to achieve this ability.

at liberty—a euphemism used by actors to say that they are out of work. Other terms for unemployment are "resting" and "being between engagements."

cheat—to take a body position that allows an audience to see an actor's face even if she or he is looking at another actor onstage. Most actors learn "to cheat out" so that they can be seen and heard clearly, though it looks like their attention is directed to others onstage.

chew the scenery—a slang expression meaning to overact shamelessly.

counter—to move slightly onstage when another actor moves so that both can still be seen by the audience. "To counter cross" is a bolder move, required by one actor because the other has changed his or her position drastically.

downstage—the part of the stage closest to the audience. For an actor to "cross downstage" means to move toward the audience.

George Spelvin—a fictitious name used in a program or in billing to disguise the true identity of an actor. The name is sometimes used by actors who are working illegally in a nonunion production, and producers use the name in the program for characters that do not exist or for actors who play more than one role and want to keep it secret.

go up—an actor's expression meaning to forget one's line. To "go up" is to momentarily blank out and forget what to say, a fear of even the most experienced actors.

green room—a backstage room where actors wait until they go onstage. The origin of the term is unknown, though it might be a distortion of the expression "scene room."

ham—an inferior actor, particular one who overacts. To "ham it up" means to overplay a scene or a speech.

improvisation—an acting exercise in which the performer is the author as well as the interpreter of a scene. Because of improvisations shown on television, audiences tend to think that improv exercises are comic games to show off the quick thinking of actors; but in theatre, improvisations are used in acting classes and sometimes in rehearsals to allow the actors' imaginations to develop and to explore aspects of character beyond what is in the script.

pitch—the position of one's voice on the musical scale. Most women tend to have higher pitches than those of men in their speaking (as well as singing) voices. Experienced actors learn to vary their pitch when speaking, allowing their voice to rise and drop in order to keep it from getting monotonous.

projection—the ability of making the sound of one's words travel a distance. More than just volume, which is the loudness of the voice, projection allows even the softest sounds to reach the audience because of the way the actor has trained his or her voice to be directed to a point far away.

rate—the speed in which one speaks onstage. Actors learn to vary their rate of delivery in order to make their speeches more interesting. One also determines a vocal rate when creating a particular character.

resonance—the quality of the vibration in an actor's voice. Certain vocal exercises can help an actor create an effective resonance that will carry sounds from the throat and out into the audience.

standby—an actor who knows the lines and movements for a major character in a play and is ready to perform the part if the original actor is ill or on vacation. Standbys usually are not in the cast but are "standing by" or available in case they are needed.

swing—an actor, singer, or dancer not in the cast of a musical but one who knows the songs and choreography so that he or she can step in and fill a chorus part or minor role if the original actor is needed to take over a larger role. Swings usually fill in when there is a gap in the chorus due to an understudy's moving into a part.

understudy—a member of the cast, usually in the chorus or in a small role, who knows the lines and blocking of a major character so that he or she can perform the role when the original performer is ill or on vacation.

upstage—the part of the stage farthest from the audience. For an actor to "upstage someone" means to draw attention to oneself and away from another actor onstage.

voice quality—the timbre or vocal characteristics of one's voice. Types of vocal quality include husky, soft, shrill, hoarse, breathy, nasal, and so on. Everyone's voice has a particular quality, but effective actors learn to adopt other kinds of vocal qualities when portraying a character onstage.

Unfortunately, even the most satisfying acting jobs come to an end. Most professional productions are limited engagements, and after performing a month or so, the actor is again out of work and must start the process all over again. Some Broadway musicals, such as *Hamilton*, can run for years, but actors are only contracted for set periods of time. When it is time to renew the contract for a hit Broadway show, actors often feel that again they are being judged. They are.

The life of an actor is continually one of working for acceptance. Much of one's career is auditioning or searching for the next job. It is an existence that is difficult to justify. Of course, all actors hope to become well known and find themselves in the position where several producers are seeking their services. This lucky situation only happens to one in thousands, and all theatre actors know it. The drive to perform on a stage is so great that each year thousands of young men and women enter this most challenging of all professions. Only a small portion will ever make a living out of it, but that does not diminish the power that acting holds on them.

EVALUATING THE ACTOR

The art of acting may be very subjective and open to opinion, but there are still ways to evaluate it. While no two theatregoers need agree on which performer they prefer over another, they can make some accurate observations about acting and come to some form of appreciation of an actor and a performance. There is no checklist or rating system that allows you to evaluate an actor because the qualities of effective acting cannot be categorized or cataloged. Yet when one understands both the craft and the art of acting, it is not difficult to study and evaluate what one sees onstage.

It is not necessary to be an accomplished actor to have an intelligent opinion about acting, just as one does not have to be a writer to appreciate literature. However, it does help to know about acting in order to express a viable opinion.

Since much of the actor's craft is external, audiences do not have to guess what is going on inside the actor's head. By looking at two of the actor's essential tools, the voice and the body, one can objectively observe actors and ask oneself questions about their effectiveness. Was the actor loud enough to be heard? Was his or her articulation clear enough that one could understand the words? Did the actor talk too fast to be understood or too slow to be interesting? Did the actor move effectively onstage? Did the use of the voice and the body help one understand the character? These are valid questions one can ask about any performance. If the play is a musical, one can ask further questions involving the actor's singing voice or dancing ability. Less obvious, did the actor show variety in his or her performance? One hopes for consistency in a performance, but, on the other hand, too much consistency may lead to monotony. Every substantial character in a play, even a silly farce, has different levels—did the actor find and present these levels?

> ### Actor vs. Character
>
> Just as French theorist Denis Diderot first recognized the dilemma an actor faces being oneself while at the same time being someone else, it is sometimes necessary for the audience to make this distinction. We know the actor is pretending, but sometimes we confuse the acting we see with the character being portrayed. If a character is annoying and disagreeable, some spectators are apt to think the acting is off-putting, unpleasant, and, consequently, inferior. It is important to distinguish between what the actor is doing and how the character affects us. The stuffy, conservative Mr. Kirby in *You Can't Take It with You* may be narrow-minded and pompous, so audiences tend not to like him. Yet it is inaccurate to criticize the actor by saying his performance was cold and unfriendly. The opposite is also true. Audiences usually warm up to Penny in the same play because she is cheerful and funny. Yet it is just as inaccurate to praise the actress playing her just because what Penny says and does strikes one as endearing. The skill with which the actor captures Mr. Kirby and the actress brings Penny to life are what really matters in acting. An observant theatregoer can better appreciate fine acting if one is mindful of this distinction between actor and character.

Much more difficult to pin down is the actor's internal process. Members of the audience cannot read the mind of an actor, but they should be able to read the mind of the character if the performance is fully developed. For example, was the character's objective clear? Some plays are more subtle than others, and the character's goals may not be obvious. All the same, an audience should get some sense of what makes a character tick. When a famous role such as Macbeth is performed, the audience may have preconceived ideas of how this power-hungry man should be portrayed onstage; but there is no one way to play Macbeth, and an accomplished actor will explore and find a way that works for him. Sometimes actors surprise us and find effective ways to portray a character that we had not considered before. Perhaps Grandpa Vanderhof in *You Can't Take It with You* is jovial and performs his part as a stand-up comic; or he is easygoing, low-key, and even rustic. Or maybe one actress sees Lena Younger as a more forceful, demanding woman than usually presented in *A Raisin in the Sun* and finds levels of strength in a character sometimes played as weak. These are the surprising joys of watching live actors reveal new levels of characterization for us.

Perhaps the most encompassing question one can ask oneself about an actor's performance is: Was it truthful? There is a truth in all characters in all plays, and it is the actor's task to make that truth come alive. In a realistic drama we might compliment actors on their believability, but many plays are not realistic and believability is a relative thing. The poetic thoughts of Macbeth or the vibrant musical stream of consciousness of Aaron Burr in *Hamilton* may not be realistic or even believable; one performance is in poetry and the other in song with lyrics. Yet both portrayals must have a truthfulness. The audience will accept an actor playing a lion or a ghost, not because a performance is believable, but because it is true—not true to real life but true to the conventions of theatre, which state that anything can be re-created onstage by humans. Theatre is based on such conventions, and it is the actor's power to bring such truth to life.

The Superstitious Actor

Actors have always been very superstitious people. Perhaps the art of acting is such a delicate and intangible thing that they fear anything that might affect it. Whistling in a dressing room, for instance, is thought to bring bad luck to a production. Even saying "Good luck" on opening night is not tolerated; instead, the expression "Break a leg!" is used, even though it sounds unlucky to nontheatre people. Actors are particularly superstitious about the play *Macbeth*. One never says its title while rehearsing any play; in fact, one is not supposed to mention it in any theatre. Actors and other theatre practitioners refer to it as "the Scottish play" even if they are actually presenting *Macbeth* onstage. How this phobia may have started is unclear. There have been disastrous occurrences while performing *Macbeth* but not any more than other plays with plenty of fighting and violent murder onstage. Some believe that the play is haunted by the ghost of the real Macbeth, who remains angry over how Shakespeare turned him into a villain when historically there is no evidence that he killed the king. All the same, generally actors do not discuss the situation. Just talking about *Macbeth* raises their superstitions.

Before closing this chapter on the actor, let us return to the fictional actress Kristen Jones and her long day one more time. It is now about ten thirty at night, and the cast of *Macbeth* is taking its curtain call. This is a very important part of the evening's performance and not because the actors crave applause and the audience likes to applaud. The curtain call is an essential aspect of the theatre event. The actors come out onstage, not as the characters they portrayed, but as artists. They stand as themselves before the spectators and acknowledge the audience's appreciation. Characters have died in the story, but the actors portraying them return and take a bow. The audience accepts and salutes the convention of acting; no one is shocked or even surprised that Macbeth, who was beheaded in the last scene of the drama, now stands before the audience and bows. The cruel then pathetic Lady Macbeth bows, and the spectators applaud Kristen, relaying to her that they know she is not really like the Scottish queen. Kristen is now back to role-playing. She is no longer Lady Macbeth but is now playing the role of an actress, and as such she takes her bow. In a few minutes she is in her dressing room removing her costume, wig, and makeup. This is a simple but powerful ritual for any performer: one takes off the mask, figuratively speaking, and becomes oneself again. Kristen spent weeks creating and developing her character, but now she removes it from her own self each evening after the curtain call. Using her craft and the art of acting, she may return to it again and again to become Lady Macbeth. She is an actress.

TOPICS FOR GROUP DISCUSSION

1. Determine a possible *spine* or *objective* for Lena Younger in *A Raisin in the Sun*, Lady Macbeth in *Macbeth*, Essie in *You Can't Take It with You*, and Alexander Hamilton in *Hamilton*.
2. What external features (voice, movement, dialect, gestures, etc.) might an actor consider if playing Grandpa Vanderhof in *You Can't Take It with You*, Eliza in *Hamilton*, Beneatha in *A Raisin in the Sun*, and the title character in *Macbeth*?
3. After watching a scene on video involving two actors, determine the range of reactions in your group to the two performances.

POSSIBLE RESEARCH PROJECTS

1. Using the union websites at the end of the book, determine what the current wage scale is for actors in the theatre, in films, and on television.
2. View the 1951 film *A Streetcar Named Desire* and contrast Marlon Brando's Method acting with the non-Method performance of Vivien Leigh.
3. Watch a contemporary film and evaluate one actor's performance in terms of craft, objective, and truthfulness.

FURTHER READING

Adler, Stella. *The Technique of Acting.* New York: Bantam, 1990/2000.
Benedetti, Robert, and Cicely Berry. *The Actor at Work.* Englewood Cliffs, NJ: Prentice-Hall, 2008.
Boleslavsky, Richard. *Acting: The First Six Lessons.* New York: Theatre Arts Books, 1933/2013.
Cohen, Robert, and James Calleri. *Acting Professionally: Raw Facts about Careers in Acting.* New York: Harper and Row, 2017.
Cole, Toby, and Helen Krich Chinoy, eds. *Actors on Acting: The Theories, Techniques, and Practices of Great Actors of All Times as Told in Their Own Words.* New York: Crown, 1995.
Cole, Toby, and Lee Strasberg, eds. *Acting: A Handbook of the Stanislavski Method.* New York: Crown/Three Rivers Press, 1995.
Deer, Joe, and Rocco Dal Vera. *Acting in Musical Theatre.* Abingdon-on-Thames, UK: Routledge, 2015.
Diderot, Denis. "The Paradox of Acting." In *Masks or Faces?* by William Archer. New York: Hill and Wang, 1957.
Goudsouzian, Aram. *Sidney Poitier: Man, Actor, Icon.* Chapel Hill: University of North Carolina Press, 2011.

Hagen, Uta, and Haskell Frankel. *Respect for Acting*. Hoboken, NJ: Wiley-Blackwell, 2008.
Hirsch, Foster. *A Method to Their Madness: The History of the Actors Studio.* New York: Norton, 1984.
Hischak, Thomas. *Enter the Players: New York Stage Actors in the Twentieth Century.* Lanham, MD: Scarecrow, 2003.
Lewis, Robert. *Advice to the Players.* New York: Harper and Row, 1980.
Linklater, Kristin. *Freeing the Natural Voice.* New York: Drama Book Specialists, 2014.
McGaw, Charles. *Acting Is Believing.* New York: Holt, Rinehart and Winston, 2013.
Poitier, Sidney. *This Life*. New York: Alfred A. Knopf, 1980.
Rafael, Mark. *Telling Stories: A Grand Unifying Theory of Acting Techniques*. Hanover, NH: Smith and Kraus, 2008.
Spolin, Viola. *Improvisation for the Theatre.* Evanston, IL: Northwestern University Press, 2013.
Stanislavsky, Constantin. *An Actor Prepares.* Translated by Elizabeth Reynolds Hapgood. New York: Theatre Arts Books, 1989/2015.
———. *Creating a Role.* Translated by Elizabeth Reynolds Hapgood. New York: Theatre Arts Books, 1977.
———. *My Life in Art.* Translated by Elizabeth Reynolds Hapgood. New York: Theatre Arts Books, 1952.

5

THE PLAY MAKERS I: THE DIRECTOR AND THE CHOREOGRAPHER

BEHIND THE SCENES

If the actor is the most visible person to an audience during a theatre event, then the director is the least visible. Not only do theatregoers not see this person, but also most of the audience is not even sure what directors do. Mention the term *director* and many think of the movie director sitting in his canvas chair and shouting, "Action!" But what do they actually do? An actor acts and can been seen and heard doing so onstage. The playwright's words are also heard, and the designer's work is seen. Yet when watching a play, what can one see or hear of the work done by the director? If you go to an orchestra concert, you can see the conductor conducting the symphony. At a sporting event, you can see the coach during the game, giving directions, shouting orders, and whispering strategies to the players. We see the conductor or the coach doing their job (or at least part of it), but a theatre director does not direct during a performance. If fact, the director might not even be present during the theatre event.

    Directors have unusual tools available to them. Actors, we have seen, use their voice and body, and playwrights put a written blueprint down on paper. In later chapters, we will see how designers create visual and aural designs using paper, wood, fabric, light, and other materials. A director has only one kind of tool: other people. A director does not have to act, write, or design, but he or she must work with and inspire actors, writers, and designers. The directing tools are artistic people, and the talent for directing lies in getting a final, polished product on the stage using these artists.

    We have seen earlier that theatre is a collaborative process and that it is nearly impossible for one person to create and perform a theatre event. Yet for a collaborative art form to look as if it has one unified vision rather than a collection of various art forms onstage, the collaboration must be supervised and channeled into one cohesive whole. This is the job of the director. In the next chapter, we will explore the job of the producer, the person behind the financial and business part of a theatre production. Each job has specific areas to attend to, but, in the most general definition of their jobs, directors and producers bring all the elements of the theatre event together. The director concentrates on what happens on the stage, while the producer must also see that there is an audience and a theatre to perform in. There are areas of overlap, and sometimes both jobs are done by the same person, but the talents of a director are distinct enough from those of a producer that we will look at them separately. Yet one cannot ignore the fact that, in the theatre today, both directors and producers are the true play makers.

WHAT DOES A DIRECTOR DO? Acclaimed director-choreographer Susan Stroman uses mirrors to help instruct the actors in rehearsal for the Broadway musical *Big Fish* (2013). Working with actors is only one aspect of stage directing. *Sara Krulwich/New York Times/Redux*

THE ART OF DIRECTING

The director's job is to supervise all the creative elements of a theatre event. The art of directing, on the other hand, is less concrete. A director usually chooses the play, casts the actors, approves the designs, and rehearses the play. These are straightforward tasks that involve knowledge of the various aspects of theatre production and the ability to work with different people. Yet directing is so much more than just a supervisory job. The modern director must take the playwright's blueprint and, using actors and designers, turn it into a conceptualized piece of art. It might be a highly personal vision of truth, or it may be a finely crafted product that reflects a particular style or period; often it is a combination of both. Some directors put a distinctive stamp on all their work, making the theatre event as unique to themselves as a painting is to a particular artist. Other directors hide their personal character in the production, letting each theatre event have its own individuality. In either case, a director must have some kind of vision for a production. Some call this vision the production *concept*, the idea that drives the whole theatre event. Some concepts are bold, easy to recognize, or even controversial; other concepts are subtle, subliminal, or completely hidden. The important thing is that the director has a particular vision for the play and that all the performances and designs conform to that vision.

Consider the variety of concepts available to a director staging *Macbeth* today. Some directors might approach the piece historically. The costumes, props, and even the scenery might re-create what primitive, early Scotland was like. The fight scenes might be realistic, graphic, and bloody, and the poetic dialogue could be turned into a brutal form of expression that allows the actors to play the characters with blunt simplicity. Another director might use aspects of the original production of *Macbeth* in Shakespeare's day. There would be no concern about the historical accuracy of the costumes, and the locale would only be suggested by a few platforms and scenic pieces. The actors might deliver the verse in a highly lyrical style, just as the fighting might be more stylized than realistic. Yet another director might set *Macbeth* in a totally different period, perhaps even in a modern setting, and let the themes of the play dictate the production, rather than the details of the plot, characters, and setting. In one production, the thane Macbeth can be a cruel, manipulating villain; in another, he might be a very haunted individual, the words of the witches forcing him in directions he may not want to go. In some productions Banquo's ghost is never seen, and Macbeth's peculiar behavior at the banquet is viewed as the other guests see him. Sometimes the witches are portrayed literally as ragged hags who crawl out of the mists. Other times they are more symbolic, played by masked actors or even puppets. The different conceptional ideas for *Macbeth* are endless. One of the many reasons that Shakespeare's works remain so popular on the contemporary stage is that directors are always finding fresh and exciting ways to interpret the plays.

A modern realistic play, such as *A Raisin in the Sun*, offers less possibilities for boldly different interpretations, but the director must still offer a vision of Lorraine Hansberry's drama. The decisions might be subtler, such as directing an actor to play Walter in a particular manner or with a distinct character objective. The setting is a small Chicago apartment in the 1950s, but the director can interpret that realistically or not. For example, working with a designer, a director might make the decision to only suggest the apartment and surround the acting area with images or projections of the ghetto neighborhood that is suffocating the Younger family. The original New York production, directed by Lloyd Richards (one of the first African Americans to direct a play on Broadway), emphasized the reality of the situation. For white theatregoers in 1959, this was a world that they had never experienced before, so Richards wanted the play to seem as real and natural as possible. A director today may wish to point out the period of the story, emphasizing 1950s clothes, props, and hairstyles and playing 1950s music so that a contemporary audience is constantly reminded of what the world was like for African Americans at that time.

A director's concept for *You Can't Take It with You* can vary greatly, depending if the play is seen as a comedy or a farce. A realistic approach with a detailed 1936 living room and accurate period clothes will re-create the era in which the play was first presented. The characters might be quite real even in their unconventionality. Grandpa Vanderhof might be played as a gentle, easygoing figure that will be familiar to audience members. Another director might see *You Can't Take It with You* as a riotous farce with exaggerated characters wearing colorful costumes. The Vanderhofs could be frantic cartoons who often explode with enthusiasm for their odd lifestyle. The Kirbys might not be everyday people but hardened, inflexible figures of wealth and power. There are many possibilities in how the Kaufman and Hart characters can be played, and a director is needed to narrow these possibilities into a unified vision.

Hamilton is about true events and historical people during the end of the eighteenth century and the beginning of the nineteenth century. Thomas Kail, who directed the original New York production, made no attempt to present this time frame realistically. Working with the designers, he placed the action in an open space surrounded by a wooden gallery. The events in the musical were set in this space, which suggested the streets of colonial New York, battlefields, meeting rooms, a ballroom, and the homes of some of the characters. The time period was defined by the costumes and furniture pieces. The performers did not move or speak like colonial characters, but more like modern-day rappers or pop singers. This concept, mixing contemporary elements into a period story, was a bold one and contributed much to the success of the musical. Future productions of *Hamilton* will most likely approach the musical in different ways, each director finding a distinct manner in which to tell the story and present the characters.

THEATRE STYLES

Once a director decides on his or her concept for a play, it is time to select the *style* in which to convey that concept. *Style* is a very tricky word, meaning everything from fashion in clothes to a way of behaving to an attitude. Architecture, furniture, painting, music, and other artistic forms are said to be done in a particular style. Style might be broadly defined as the way in which something is done. In theatre, style is the form of presentation that a director uses to express his or her vision. There are many styles, and no one kind is the only correct style for a particular play. It is the director's job to consider the different ways in which a play can be presented and choose the one that fulfills the directorial concept.

Realism

The style we are all most familiar with is realism. Any time an artist attempts to re-create the real world in a true-to-life manner, some variation of realism is used. Although this style is relatively new (about 150 years), it is the predominant style seen in most plays, movies, and television today. Characters speak in realistic dialogue, as opposed to poetry or witticisms; they dress appropriate to the period and

REALISM Playwright Tennessee Williams created characters with a poetic temperament and way of speaking, but they were often firmly placed in a realistic world. In the 2003 Broadway revival of *Cat on a Hot Tin Roof*, it is the real world that Brick (Jason Patric) tries to escape from, but his wife Maggie (Ashley Judd) is determined not to let it happen. Director: Anthony Page. *Joan Marcus/Photofest; photographer: Joan Marcus*

location of the action; and the setting looks like an actual locale. Some plays are written in a more realistic mode than others, but again it is the director who really determines realism onstage. Yet true realism in the theatre is difficult to achieve because we know by the very nature of theatre that what takes place onstage is pretend. As realistically as a fight or a murder is staged in the theatre, it cannot hope to be as realistic as in a film or television drama. Theatre audiences know this and understand the limitations of the stage, accepting the convention of realism just as they accept the other theatrical elements.

Romanticism

One of the most prominent styles before realism came in was romanticism. This style takes an idealized view of the real world and presents truth in a larger-than-life way. Romanticism is not so much about romance as about romanticizing characters, plots, language, and even ideas. The passions and the goals of the characters are not everyday ones: the stories are filled with action and complex plotting; the language is poetic (if not in poetry itself); and the themes are often penetrating and exciting. Romanticism was a specific movement in art, music, and theatre in the nineteenth century that advocated a freedom of expression that embraced nature and even mysticism. Today the term refers to a style of presentation that views life in a grand, poetic, and unrealistic manner. In theatre, romanticism is the directing style most used in presenting classics of the past and musicals. Since the arrival of realism, theatregoers consider romanticism somewhat artificial, yet it is often that unrealistic quality that is wanted in certain theatre productions.

Expressionism

In the early decades of the twentieth century, a style was developed that fought against realism yet did not wish to hark back to romanticism. This style had various schools of thought, each with a different name, but the term we will use to encompass the ideas of the movement is *expressionism*. As the name suggests, this style wishes to express an inner truth, as all art wishes to, but in expressionism, it is done by ignoring the surface and delving into the psychological. In an expressionistic play we see people and places not as they are in real life, nor as they are idealized in romanticism, but through the eyes of one person's psyche. This person might be a character in the play who sees the world as it appears in his or her mind, or it can be the playwright's depiction of a world that is disturbed, distorted, or menacing. Dreams, hallucinations, and fantasies are typical devices used in expressionism because they are essentially truthful without being realistic. Scenery, costumes, props, and makeup might be exaggerated in an expressionistic production, sometimes going so far as to be grotesque. The acting might be unrealistic, with the voices and bodies of the actors being used symbolically or mechanically to make a point about the depersonalization of modern society. Lighting and sound effects may be startling and exaggerated. The ways that one can use expressionism onstage are endless, and directors often find the possibilities for this style very invigorating. As with other styles, there are plays that are specifically written to be staged in an expressionistic manner. Yet it is also a style that a director can use to stage a play written by a playwright who was not aware of expressionism, such as Shakespeare. As long as the director is seeking to discover the truth in a play, even such an exaggerated style as expressionism can sometimes reveal that truth in a new way.

EXPRESSIONISM Frank Wedekind's 1891 play *Spring Awakening*, about rebellious and sexually frustrated youth, is considered a classic example of German expressionism. The 2006 musical version by Duncan Sheik and Steven Sater retains the expressionistic elements of the original, with the addition of stylized song and dance. Directed by Michael Mayer, with choreography by Bill T. Jones. *Geraint Lewis/Alamy Stock Photo*

Other *Isms*

There are many other directorial styles, and new ones are being developed all the time, but they are usually offshoots of one of the three predominant ones of realism, romanticism, and expressionism. *Naturalism*, for example, is an extreme form of realism in which the sensory details of life are put onstage. A production done in the naturalistic style might have dirt on the floor, scientifically accurate lighting effects coming from the moon, the realistic sounds of nature filling the air, and even the smell of cooking or the presence of real livestock onstage. It is a style that is difficult, not to say expensive, to create on a stage, and naturalism was never a widely popular movement. Yet there have been some outstanding productions over the years that have experimented with the style.

Absurdism and *theatre of alienation* are two more recent styles that are offshoots of expressionism. The German playwright and director Bertolt Brecht developed the idea of alienation in the 1930s as a way to fight both realism and romanticism and to turn the theatre into an instrument to make audiences think about sociopolitical issues. The idea behind "alienation" was to remove or "alienate" the audience from the traditional conventions of theatre by appealing to their intellects rather than their emotions. Brecht's productions used slides, projections, songs, loudspeakers, harsh lighting, and a declamatory kind of acting to get the message across. This highly theatrical style is not only used in staging Brecht's plays today but is also a style that has proved effective with other works as well, particularly musicals. Absurdism arose in the 1950s as a way to define new plays from France that presented the world as nonsensical, filled with characters that had no objective and plots that had no stories. Samuel Beckett's two most produced works are *Waiting for Godot*, which takes place in an undefined space where two tramps wait for a mysterious figure but are not sure why, and *Endgame*, in which the characters seem trapped inside a room, two of them living in trash cans. As a directing style, absurdism can be used to present plays that emphasize the desolate predicament of man and woman, and absurdist settings and lighting can be found in many productions of plays that are not strictly classified as absurdism.

Now that you are somewhat familiar with a handful of the different styles available to a director, let us consider our four sample plays. Because of its poetry, bold characterizations, and complex plot, *Macbeth* seems an ideal candidate for romanticism, and many directors have chosen to present the play in that style. But, as we saw in discussing the directorial concept, a director may choose to approach *Macbeth* in the style of realism with authentic costumes, sets, fights, and acting. Another director may select expressionism as the style, looking at the play through the eyes of the haunted Macbeth. The sets, costumes, fights, and performances will be far from realistic, and the themes of the play will be expressed in a bold and theatrical manner. *A Raisin in the Sun* calls for realism, but, again, one director may select romanticism, idealizing the characters and turning the drama into a lyrical piece, while another director might employ some expressionism in the setting, sound, and lights. Realism might seem to be the obvious style for *You Can't Take It with You* but a nostalgic approach to the script could use romanticism, re-creating the 1930s and presenting the Vanderhofs in a warm glow of a bygone time. Finally, *Hamilton* suggests romanticism because of its songs and larger-than-life emotions, but it can also use expressionism to show the world as seen through the eyes of Alexander Hamilton or Aaron Burr. Which of these styles is the correct one for each play? Obviously, some will work better than others, but it comes down to the director and the way he or she uses a particular style to create a vision that illuminates the play.

ABSURDISM Samuel Beckett's tragicomedy *Waiting for Godot* has intrigued audiences and theatre artists since it premiered in Europe in 1953. Sean Matthias directed this acclaimed 2009 London production, in which Patrick Stewart (left) and Ian McKellen played the two tramps lost in an illogical world. The production was later a success on Broadway in 2013. *Geraint Lewis/Alamy Stock Photo*

A BRIEF HISTORY OF DIRECTING

The director is the most central and pivotal job in the modern theatre. Yet for thousands of years plays did not have directors. If you recall the four essential elements of a theatre event (actors, script, audience, and place), you will notice that a director is not called for. For centuries the supervision of a theatrical production was done by playwrights, producers, stage managers, or even the actors themselves. Rehearsals, as we know them today, were few and far between. Actors learned their lines independently, then the stage manager brought everyone together a few times to decide on entrances and exits, stage the fight scenes, and clean up movement problems. The star stood center stage, the less prominent actors to the sides. There was no concept and rarely any cohesiveness. Designers worked independently from the actors (in many cases the actors had to come up with their own costumes), and it all came together at the dress rehearsal. This was a satisfactory arrangement for hundreds of years. In the eighteenth and nineteenth centuries, famous actor-managers ran their own theatre companies, and often they served as a director of sorts. Yet most of their energy was concentrated on producing the plays and performing the leading roles rather than staging them.

The First Director?

The first director, in the modern sense of the word, was a German aristocrat who started to present plays that were thoroughly rehearsed with a particular vision in mind. Georg II, the Duke of Saxe-Meiningen (1826–1914), did not like the star system of his day and thought that the placement and movement of actors onstage was artificial and unrealistic. The duke started his own theatre troupe that toured throughout Europe in the mid-1800s, and his productions were immediately recognized as unique and innovative. His company employed no stars but featured an ensemble that had been directed meticulously, each member of the cast given specific positions, moves, and even gestures. By using the stage as a painter uses a canvas, the duke was able to control the visuals of his productions and place focus where he wanted. Most of his productions had large casts, but, through precise direction and lengthy rehearsal periods, he made the action clear, and the attitudes and feelings of even the crowd members were defined. Georg II also worked with his designers, coordinating all the visual elements of the production into a unified whole. Many of his directorial sketches survive, and they are stunning to behold, much like a detailed storyboard for a modern movie. The look of the Duke of Saxe-Meiningen's productions did not go unnoticed, and both audiences and theatre people realized for the first time the importance of a director.

Just as Konstantin Stanislavsky revolutionized stage acting, he also had a great influence on modern directing. While much of his lengthy rehearsals were concerned with character development and getting sincerity from his actors, Stanislavsky was also concerned with stage movement; how scenes could be best presented; the use of realistic props and furniture; and coordinating the sets, costumes, and lights. When his productions by the Moscow Art Theatre toured Europe and America in the early twentieth century, the reaction was overwhelming. Many theatre companies patterned themselves after the Russian troupe, and directing started to become the all-important job that it is in theatre today. Throughout the century, renowned directors helped shape the direction of theatre production. Both new and old plays were approached with a conceptual eye, and often the mark of the director became as important as the script or the actors. In fact, powerful directors sometimes influenced the writing of plays. The respected director Elia Kazan staged the original productions of many of Tennessee Williams's and Arthur Miller's plays and insisted on specific changes in the scripts during rehearsals. As famous as these two playwrights were, Kazan was more powerful, and they complied to his wishes, usually strengthening the plays in the process.

By the middle of the century, the musical theatre saw the rise of the director-choreographer. By having one person stage both the book scenes and the dances, the musicals took on a unified persona never seen before. The most innovative of these director-choreographers was Jerome Robbins whose dynamic staging of such musicals as *West Side Story* and *Fiddler on the Roof* were landmarks in theatre directing. In the last decades of the century, some distinctive director-choreographers became the stars of their own shows. The casts and writers were secondary in several musicals staged by Gower Champion, Bob Fosse, Michael Bennett, and others. One went to see the new "Fosse musical," for example, because it was his staging that was the real attraction.

THE MODERN DIRECTOR The Broadway musical theatre changed with the rise of the director-choreographer in the 1950s and 1960s, with the work of Jerome Robbins, Gower Champion, and others. In 1981, Michael Bennett put his personal mark on the staging of *Dreamgirls*, in which even the scenery moved in time with the musical Motown tempo. Pictured are members of the original cast, led by Jennifer Holliday (in the foreground). *Photofest*

In today's theatre, whether it is a high school production or a Broadway blockbuster, the director is firmly in charge. A job deemed unnecessary for centuries has now become indispensable.

THE DIRECTING PROCESS

Different directors work in different ways, and there is no one correct way to direct a play or musical. Just as actors differ in their approach to a character, directors differ in their approach to carrying out their vision for a script. Some will spend a great deal of time on the psychological aspects of the play and its characters, while others may emphasize the movement and the look of the production. Many directors leave room for the actors to discover the characters and the concept of the production, while others dictate precise ways to portray a character and follow through on the directorial style and concept. Regardless of which particular method is employed, all directors must go through a series of steps to bring a production from idea to opening night. The order of these steps may vary, but the process of directing usually covers the same tasks.

Play Selection

In professional theatre a director is usually hired for a production already decided on, with, possibly, the designers and cast already chosen. But in educational, community, and sometimes regional theatre, the director selects the play. Choosing a script to direct for a particular theatre group or school is a major decision because all of the director's and actors' work will be hampered by doing a play that is not appropriate. It is certainly helpful if the director has great affection and respect for the script, but that does not mean that the play is a wise choice for the situation at hand. Directors must make other considerations as well and ask if the script is a good choice for the actors, the likely audience, the theatre space, and the financial demands. The success of the production will largely rest on the actors, so one must question if the play can be adequately cast. Is the cast size for the script too large or too small for the number of actors at one's disposal? Are they experienced enough to handle the difficulties of the production? Are there enough actors of the appropriate age, sex, or type? If a musical is attempted, are the actors capable of the singing and dancing required of the score?

Even if one can answer yes to all these questions, the director must then consider the audience and who it will most likely be. It is always admirable to challenge an audience and broaden its theatre experience, but sometimes a particular play may not have any appeal to a certain audience, or, if it should attract them, it may confuse or disappoint them once they are in the theatre. As for the theatre space, some plays are not appropriate for all spaces. An auditorium holding over a thousand spectators might not be an ideal venue for an intimate, small-cast play, just as a small, intimate theatre may prove problematic for a large-scale play or musical. Finally, the expenses of a production are always a concern to both professional and amateur theatre groups. Some plays require elaborate costumes and detailed sets while others have more modest demands. We will see later that finances are the major concern of the producer, but directors must know the type of expenses involved in a play in order to make a wise selection.

Analysis

Once the play has been chosen, the director can then start to develop a concept for the production and create a vision for the script. This might involve researching the production history of the play and reading literary criticism about the piece. After analyzing the script and outside sources, the director must come to a decision about the concept and the directorial style. Only after these are set can he or she meet with the designers and discuss ways to bring this concept to life. Often scenic, costume, lighting, and other designers can be very helpful in solidifying the director's ideas and offering ways to visualize the concept. All this is done before auditions and rehearsals begin because the decisions made regarding vision and style will affect the way the play is cast. Also part of the analysis is the director's *prompt book*—a copy of the script in which a director makes detailed notes regarding character, movements, and technical effects. This highly annotated script becomes the director's reference guide during rehearsals and helps keep the production in line with the directorial concept. Stanislavsky kept very complete prompt books, and theatre historians studying them today can almost re-create the original production from his notes and sketches. While not all directors believe in preparing a detailed prompt book before auditions—many prefer to discover the play during the rehearsal process—most productions end up with a prompt book that documents on paper what was attempted onstage.

Casting

We have already seen how auditions work from an actor's point of view. For a director, the audition process is almost as nerve-racking. Actors are anxious to be liked and accepted; directors are anxious to find the best possible actor for each role. One can envision exactly what one wants for a character, but it is unlikely, even in professional theatre, for one actor to fulfill all those expectations. Instead, an experienced director looks at each auditioning actor as a possibility for how the character might be played. There are always compromises to be made, and one must consider the cast as a whole, not just a series of individuals, in order to come up with the best possible company of actors. Many a production is blessed or cursed from the moment a play is cast. It is such an important step yet one that cannot be objectively or coolly carried out. The director often must go with his or her instinct, hoping that the cast chosen is the one that will work best.

Nontraditional Casting

Most theatre companies today believe in nontraditional casting, though not all use it as frequently as some might wish. Nontraditional casting means that characters are played by actors who may not fit the literal description of the role in the script. The play might call for an elderly male doctor, but the director may envision the character as a younger female doctor. Another character might be a prosperous white male in the nineteenth century, but the director may cast an Asian or African American in the part. The character of a lawyer in a courtroom might be cast with an actor in a wheelchair. In each case, the director departs from the traditional presentation of the character yet does not sacrifice the integrity of the play.

The belief behind nontraditional casting is that one should cast the best actor for the role, regardless of gender, race, or other factors. The tax inspector in *You Can't Take It with You*, for example, could effectively be played by a woman, just as in *Macbeth* King Duncan can be enacted by an African American with his son Malcolm being played by a white actor. (The use of such racial types is sometimes called *color-blind casting* in the theatre.) Sometimes a script does not leave room for such departures from the usual. The Younger family in *A Raisin in the Sun* must be played by African Americans because the whole point of the drama is about the plight of black Americans in the 1950s. Schools have long been more readily accepting of nontraditional casting, while such use of actors did not become usual in professional theatre until the late 1960s. Today audiences are quite used to nontraditional casting, and it may someday become so common that it will not be considered nontraditional at all.

NONTRADITIONAL CASTING In the 2014 revival of *You Can't Take It with You*, African American actor James Earl Jones (seated) played Grandpa Vanderhof, while the rest of his family was portrayed by white actors, a notable example of color-blind casting on Broadway. Director: Scott Ellis. *Sara Krulwich/New York Times/Redux*

Rehearsals

The order of, and the emphasis during, rehearsals is an area in which directors most often differ. Most rehearsal periods begin with a *read-through*, in which the entire cast sits in a circle and reads the play aloud, with each actor reading his or her own part. A read-through rehearsal is the first time the director hears the complete play with the voices he or she has selected, and this reading, no matter how smooth or bumpy it may go, tells the director a great deal about the strengths and weakness of the cast, allowing one to come up with a plan for rehearsals. A read-through is also an excellent way to begin the rehearsal process because it unifies the cast and they start to think as an ensemble instead of a group of individual actors. Many directors will then begin *blocking* rehearsals. *Blocking* is the theatrical term for movement onstage; where entrances and exits are made; and how actors maneuver among furniture, steps, and other obstacles. Some directors give the actors very specific blocking, telling them on which part of which line they are to move. Others are more general in their blocking direction, letting the actors work out the details as long as the general flow of movement is correct. There are even some directors who do not believe in formal blocking and leave all such movements to the actors' discretion—something not to be attempted with inexperienced performers. Blocking may take anywhere from five to ten rehearsals, depending on how complicated the movement is in the production. It is always useful for a director to have *retrace* rehearsals before moving on. These rehearsals allow the actors to retrace their movements and correct their blocking. Most actors memorize their lines after a scene has been blocked and retraced because they can then put both the words and the movements to memory at the same time.

Once the cast members know their lines and are "off book," the director can spend rehearsal time working with the actors on their characterizations. This period of the rehearsal process is called *character* or *interpretation* rehearsals. It is usually the rehearsal time that both actors and directors most enjoy because, having gotten the mechanics of movement completed, there is time for discussion and coaching. *Interp* rehearsals concern how the lines are spoken, what level of emotion is attempted, the pace or urgency of a scene, and, most important, the relationship between characters. At various points during the rehearsal process (and particularly after a series of interp rehearsals), the director will hold a *run-through* rehearsal. As the name suggests, the entire play is rehearsed without stopping (except for intermissions) so that the actors get used to performing the script in the manner that it will be done for an audience. Run-throughs are very demanding and often frustrating because the actors are put into performance conditions before they are ready to perform the play as a whole. But such rehearsals are necessary to prepare the cast for opening night.

Before all the technical aspects are added to the production, the director will often put aside a few rehearsals for polishing the performances. At these so-called *polish* rehearsals, the actors work with props, furniture, and even costume pieces such as hats and shoes so that they can get accustomed to them and smooth out any awkwardness. A director will also use polish rehearsals to work on the tempo of scenes and to clean up any moments in the play that are still rough. It is also the director's last chance to work solely with the actors; from this point on his or her attention will be divided between the cast and the design elements of the production. *Technical* rehearsals are used to add these elements: lights, sound, scene changes, costumes, and makeup. In many professional theatres, this is the first time that the cast leaves the rehearsal space and begins to rehearse on the actual stage. Technical run-throughs are time-consuming, draining on the cast and crew, and vitally necessary. The last technical rehearsals, in which the costumes and makeup are added, are called *dress* rehearsals and represent the end of the rehearsal process. This whole process may take from two to seven weeks, depending on the length and number of rehearsals, so the pace of development varies greatly. If all of the steps are taken and all of the kinds of rehearsals are sufficiently covered, the production should be ready for an audience.

> **Sample Rehearsal Schedule**
>
> For a college production of *You Can't Take It with You**
>
> | Day | Month | Date | Activity |
> |---|---|---|---|
> | Mon. | Sept. | 21 | Auditions |
> | Tues. | | 22 | Auditions |
> | Thurs. | | 24 | Read-through |
> | Fri. | | 25 | Discussion; costume measurements |
> | Sun. | | 27 | Blocking act 1, scene 1 |
> | Mon. | | 28 | Retrace act 1 scene 1; blocking act 1, scene 2 |
> | Tues. | | 29 | Retrace act 1, scene 2 |
> | Wed. | | 30 | Blocking act 2 |
> | Thurs. | Oct. | 1 | Blocking act 2 |
> | Fri. | | 2 | Retrace act 2 |
> | Sun. | | 4 | Blocking act 3 |
> | Mon. | | 5 | Retrace act 3 |
> | Tues. | | 6 | Run-through |
> | Wed. | | 7 | Interp; select characters and scenes |
> | Thurs. | | 8 | Interp; select characters and scenes |
> | Fri. | | 9 | Interp act 1, scene 1 |
> | Sun. | | 11 | Interp act 1, scene 2 |
> | Mon. | | 12 | Interp act 2 |
> | Tues. | | 13 | Interp act 3 |
> | Wed. | | 14 | Interp; select characters and scenes |
> | Thurs. | | 15 | Run-through |
> | Fri. | | 16 | Polish act 1, scene 1 |
> | Sun. | | 18 | Polish act 1, scene 2 |
> | Mon. | | 19 | Polish act 2 |
> | Tues. | | 20 | Polish act 2 |
> | Wed. | | 21 | Polish act 3 |
> | Thurs. | | 22 | Polish act 3 |
> | Fri. | | 23 | Run-through |
> | Sat. | | 24 | Tech; add sound, props |
> | Sun. | | 25 | Tech; add lights |
> | Mon. | | 26 | Tech |
> | Tues. | | 27 | Dress rehearsal; add costumes |
> | Wed. | | 28 | Dress rehearsal: add makeup/hair |
> | Thurs. | | 29 | Performance |
> | Fri. | | 30 | Performance |
> | Sat. | | 31 | Performance |
> | Sun. | Nov. | 1 | Performance |
>
> *based on evening rehearsals three hours long

Performance

Many theatre groups, both amateur and professional, find it useful to do one or more *previews*. These are like dress rehearsals, but an audience, either invited or paying, is present. Both actors and directors find previews very helpful. It gives the cast the chance to get used to an audience and to start to develop that special rapport between actor and spectator that makes the theatre event come alive. Previews for comedies are particularly important because it allows the actors to get used to laughter, though any experienced actor will tell you that laughs differ from audience to audience. Also, directors can use previews to survey the production and continue to give notes to the cast, crew, and designers about details that need to be corrected or polished. If the play or musical is new and has never been produced before, major changes are sometimes made during previews. Scenes may need to be rewritten or songs added or dropped, all based on the reactions the production is getting from a live audience. On the play's official opening night, the director's job comes to an end, though many directors will return to long-running plays to check on the quality of the production and even give some further notes. Once the play begins performances, the production belongs to the actors, not to the director. He or she has led the cast through a creative process, and now it is the actors who must keep the theatre event alive.

Musicals

The rehearsal process for a musical is complicated by the fact that the director is working not only with actors and designers but also with a *musical director* and a *choreographer*. It is the musical director's job to teach the cast the score, rehearse both actors and musicians, and (usually) conduct the orchestra. Obviously, the musical director needs plenty of time with the cast, so several music rehearsals are scheduled for individuals and for the chorus. Many of these sessions come near the beginning of the rehearsal period because actors must know the music before the songs or dances can be staged. These musical numbers are the job of the choreographer, the person who often becomes the director when music plays. Not only do choreographers develop, stage, and rehearse the dances, but many of them also block musical numbers that do not involve dance. Dance rehearsals are perhaps the

REHEARSING A MUSICAL Because of the triple task of staging and rehearsing the book, songs, and dances, directing a musical is the most complicated of theatre challenges. Trey Parker and Casey Nicholaw directed and choreographed the popular musical *The Book of Mormon* (2011), and they made the efforts of dozens of artists look unified and whole. *Sara Krulwich/New York Times/Redux*

most time-consuming of all because performers learn choreography much slower than they do lines or songs, and dance takes much more time to polish. Whenever possible, musicals use multiple rehearsals utilizing three different spaces: the music director is working with one actor on his or her songs while at the same time the director is staging a book scene with a handful of other actors and the choreographer is rehearsing the chorus in a dance number. In older musicals, the book scenes and the musical numbers (especially dances) are quite separate, and it is clear where the director's job ends and the choreographer's starts. In more recent musicals, such as *Hamilton*, there is little if any separation between song/story and dance, and the roles of the director and choreographer overlap. This situation helped give rise to the director-choreographer, a single person who stages the musical as one entity.

THE BUSINESS OF DIRECTING

A career as a theatre director is as difficult and unstable as that of an actor, perhaps more so. Each theatre production will involve three or thirteen or thirty actors but needs only one director, so the opportunities for work are scarce. Also, directors cannot audition as actors do or submit a script or designs as playwrights and designers do. Since the director's tools are other artists, there is no way to demonstrate one's abilities as a director without staging an actual production. Young or inexperienced directors are not hired because they have not directed, and they cannot direct because no one will hire them. It is a vicious circle that is unique to theatre directing. But like most theatre jobs, directing is a very rewarding experience (artistically, if not financially), and there is never a shortage of artists willing to attempt the difficult road to becoming a professional director.

The training to be an effective theatre director is broader and more challenging than perhaps any other theatre job. Because a director works with a variety of other artists, he or she must be very familiar with all aspects of theatre production. The director may not be able to write a play, perform a part, or design a costume, but the director must certainly "understand" playwriting, acting, and designing. It is important for fledgling directors to study all these arts, even attempting them so that they will become familiar with the process that each artist goes through. The inexperienced director will say what he or she would like, describing it in vague or theoretical terms; the experienced director offers ways for an actor or designer to achieve the directorial concept. This does not mean that the director dictates specifically what others should do. The very best directors suggest ideas in a way that inspire other artists to explore bold and exciting possibilities.

The best training for a future director is to study at a theatre or school that allows for a variety of experiences. Most directors have acting experience, perhaps the best preparation for working with actors in rehearsals. But fledgling directors should also learn how plays are written, scenery is built, costumes are made, lighting is achieved, and so on. In most colleges with a theatre program, students can take courses in directing and actually stage a student production. Although the production might be small scale and very amateur, the experience is invaluable. Once such a training is completed, one can start to pursue a directing career. Many do this by becoming an assistant to an established director or getting hired as a *stage manager*. Such jobs involve recording the director's blocking and technical cues, assisting in rehearsals, attending production meetings, and running the play after it opens. Although these positions usually do not include any directing, they allow the would-be director to get involved with professional productions and create contacts for future employment as a director. Another means to a directing career is to stage small semiprofessional productions called *workshops*. In New York City these might be found in humble and out-of-the-way venues, but again valuable contacts can be made. Since most directors are hired because the producer has seen his or her work somewhere, staging such minor productions for little or no money becomes a form of auditioning. One can invite interested producers or theatre managers, with the hopes that they will come and like what they see. Yet just as most actors are usually out of work, so too is directing a very unstable profession. At least actors have a job for months if a play is a success; the director is only needed for the rehearsal process, no matter how long a play runs. In order to gain steady employment as a director, one must be willing to move from theatre to theatre, which usually means traveling from city to city. Very few directors are in such demand that they can settle in one place, such as New York, and work continuously.

The plight of choreographers is not very different from that of directors. Most theatre choreographers begin as professional dancers in musical theatre. While choreographers need not have as broad a training as directors, they must be very experienced in theatre dance and be able to communicate ideas to performers in terms of both dance and character. Theatre choreography today is so much more than just dance steps, often telling a story and developing a character, so in essence a choreographer becomes something of a director as well. No wonder so many choreographers have made the transition to director-choreographer. Yet like directors, choreographers cannot audition in order to be hired and can only hope that producers see their work in other productions. Also like directors, they are only needed during the rehearsal process, so they too are always job hunting.

CHOREOGRAPHY Although the role of dance in the theatre has evolved throughout the years, there is still great entertainment value in the traditional forms of stage choreography. Randy Skinner reconstructed some of Gower Champion's original choreography for the 2001 Broadway revival of *42nd Street* and provided some original dance routines as well. Director: Mark Bramble. *Joan Marcus/Photofest; photographer: Joan Marcus*

The financial rewards of directing and choreographing are similar to those of a playwright: few make a reasonable living, but another few can make a killing. Directors and choreographers are usually paid a flat fee for staging a production, but if the play is done on Broadway, a percentage of the box office income might be offered to a well-established director. Some high-profile directors and choreographers may get up to 10 percent of the box office, which, for a Broadway hit, might translate into $10,000 a week for a play and twice that for a musical. Although directors and choreographers do not have a trade union as such, most professionals belong to the Society of Stage Directors and Choreographers (SSDC), which helps in setting minimum fees and arranging for royalty percentages.

As the roles of the director and choreographer have grown, so too has the importance of the two jobs, and producers know that an outstanding director/choreographer can mean the difference between a hit and a flop. But there are only a handful of directors or choreographers that rank this highly, and most others have to try to live off the usual flat fee. Just as many actors are lured away from theatre for the more lucrative salaries in film and television, many talented directors find that the work is more steady and pays much better in these media, and frequently they leave live theatre and cannot afford to return. Yet the satisfaction of directing in the theatre is strong, and there are always new and willing artists anxious to pursue it.

EVALUATING THE DIRECTOR AND CHOREOGRAPHER

Since directing is the least visible and least understood job in theatre, it is difficult for many to evaluate it. Even professional theatre critics are often uninformed about what the director does, blaming directors because the script is too confusing or praising them because the jokes are funny and the scenery is attractive. Yet it is possible to make intelligent judgments about theatre directing if one considers the very essence of the job: supervising all the creative elements and bringing them together in one concept. As an audience member, you may not be able to put your finger on that concept or label the directorial vision, but it is possible to observe how successfully that vision works. Does the acting serve the script, or does it seem wrong for that kind of play? Are all the actors performing in the same kind of style, or do they seem to be in different plays? Was the movement in the production too static or too busy for the story? Do the scenery, costumes, lights, and other technical elements seem consistent with each other, or do the exaggerated clothes seem out of place in the realistic set? Does the play move along at a pace that seems appropriate for the script, or does the comedy drag and the dramatics seem rushed and contrived? What style did the production use, and was it consistently used? These are the kinds of questions that one can ask about theatre directing. Like judging any piece of art, evaluating the direction of a play or musical is a subjective task, but with enough knowledge of what a director is responsible for, one can make valuable observations and express a valid opinion.

Some believe that, since the director is responsible for overseeing all creative aspects of the production, he or she should take the credit (or the blame) for everything that happens onstage. If the acting is overdone or too dull, it is the director's fault for not coaching the cast better. If the scenery is ugly or the lighting too dim, the director can be blamed for not having it changed. If the script is faulty or overlong, the director should have had the playwright change or cut it. Such criticisms are a bit extreme; not even the most effective directors can get exactly what they want in any one production no matter how much available talent or money. On the other hand, there is some truth in this kind of thinking. The director is the controlling force, and an evaluator must consider the director when looking at any and all aspects of the production.

It is somewhat easier to evaluate the work of a choreographer because dance is so visual. One does not need to know anything about ballet or tap or jazz dance to form an opinion about what is effective and what is not. Yet dance is a deceptively difficult art: some dance moves and routines easily impress an audience, while others are extremely difficult to perform, yet that difficulty is rarely evident to the novice. One can certainly say whether the dancing in a musical was entertaining, funny, dramatic, evocative, exciting, romantic, and clever. These are subjective emotions and difficult to argue with. A better question might be, how did the dance enhance the production? Was it there as an escapist piece of entertainment only? For many older musicals, this was the primary reason for dance onstage. Or did the dance reveal something about the story or the characters? This can be asked of most musicals written in the past sixty years. Sometimes the talent of the dancers is more interesting than the choreography they perform. Conversely, some choreographers can create combinations and movement that make even mediocre dancers look good. Can you detect this in the production?

During the past six decades, some directors or choreographers have been labeled *auteur* artists. *Auteur* is French for "author," and the term implies that the director or choreographer has such a distinct style that one can easily identify the creator of the direction or the choreography just by looking at it. Director-choreographer Bob Fosse, who staged such stylized dance shows as *Sweet Charity* and *Chicago*, is perhaps the most notable example of this kind of artist. Other auteur directors or choreographers are less easy to identify because their versatility is so great that they are always creating fresh ideas that do not obviously resemble their other work. Yet they are definitely "authors" because their ideas are as important as those of the playwright. The aforementioned Elia Kazan and Jerome Robbins are outstanding examples of this kind of auteur. Some feel that it is less difficult to evaluate the work of these auteurs because their contributions to the production are so much greater. But any artist who fulfills the difficult and all-encompassing job of a director is equally important. This one person, who hopes to make the work of many look like the work of one creative mind, is still the backbone behind every modern theatre production.

TOPICS FOR GROUP DISCUSSION

1. Select two directorial styles and discuss the ways in which two different productions of *Macbeth* might be if directed in these styles.
2. Discuss how the rehearsal process for *A Raisin in the Sun* would differ from that for *Hamilton*.
3. Discuss which of the four sample plays would require the most blocking rehearsals and which the most interp rehearsals.

POSSIBLE RESEARCH PROJECTS

1. View two different film or video productions of *Macbeth* and determine which directorial styles were used in each one.
2. View the episode about Julie Taymor directing a production of Shakespeare's *The Tempest* in the 1992 documentary *Behind the Scenes* and note the different kinds of rehearsals that are shown.

FURTHER READING

Bartow, Arthur. *The Director's Voice: 21 Interviews.* New York: Theatre Communications Group, 1993.
Berry, Ralph. *On Directing Shakespeare: Interviews with Contemporary Directors.* London: Hamish Hamilton, 1990.
Bradby, David, and David Williams. *Directors Theatre.* New York: St. Martin's, 1988.
Catron, Louis E., and Scott Shattuck. *The Director's Vision.* Mountain View, CA: Mayfield, 2015.
Clurman, Harold. *On Directing.* New York: Macmillan, 1972/1997.
Cole, Susan Letzler. *Directors in Rehearsal: A Hidden World.* New York: Routledge, 1992.
Cole, Toby, and Helen Krich Chinoy, eds. *Directors on Directing.* Brook Park, OH: Allegro, 2013.
Crook, Paul B. *The Art and Practice of Directing for Theatre.* Abingdon-on-Thames, UK: Routledge, 2016.
Daniels, Rebecca. *Women Stage Directors Speak.* Jefferson, NC: McFarland, 2000.
Deer, Joe. *Directing in Musical Theatre: An Essential Guide.* Abingdon-on-Thames, UK: Routledge, 2013.
Fliotsos, Anne, and Wendy Vierow. *American Women Stage Directors of the Twentieth Century.* Champaign: University of Illinois Press, 2008.
Guthrie, Tyrone. *A Life in the Theatre.* London: Harrap, 1987.
Hischak, Thomas S. *Enter the Playmakers: Directors and Choreographers on the New York Stage.* Lanham, MD: Scarecrow, 2006.
Hodge, Francis, and Michael McLain. *Play Directing: Analysis, Communication, and Style.* Boston: Allyn and Bacon, 2009.
Innes, Christopher, and Maria Shevtsova. *The Cambridge Introduction to Theatre Directing.* Cambridge, UK: Cambridge University Press, 2013.
Johnson, Albert, and Bertha Johnson. *Directing Methods.* South Brunswick, NJ: A. S. Barnes, 1970.
Jones, David Richard. *Great Directors at Work: Stanislavsky, Brecht, Kazan, Brook.* Berkeley: University of California Press, 1986.
Kazan, Elia. *A Life.* New York: Knopf, 1988.
Koller, Ann Marie. *The Theatre Duke: Georg II of Saxe-Meiningen and the German Stage.* Stanford, CA: Stanford University Press, 1984.
Leiter, Samuel L. *The Great Stage Directors.* New York: Facts on File, 1994.
Mitter, Shomit, and Maria Shevtsova, eds. *Fifty Key Directors.* New York: Routledge, 2005.
———. *Systems of Rehearsal: Stanislavsky, Brecht, Grotowski and Peter Brook.* New York: Routledge, 1992.
Schneider, Alan. *Entrances: An American Director's Journey.* New York: Viking, 1986.
Sievers, W. David, Harry E. Stiver Jr., and Stanley Kahan. *Directing for the Theatre.* Dubuque, IA: William C. Brown, 1974.
Wills, Robert J., ed. *The Director in a Changing Theatre.* Palo Alto, CA: Mayfield, 1976.

6

THE PLAY MAKERS II: THE PRODUCER

WHAT IS A PRODUCER?

The simplest definition of a producer is a person or group who raises the money for a play. A more thorough definition would add that the producer provides all the elements needed for a theatre production: actors, script, audience, and the space. Since all four of these cost money, the more accurate definition of a producer's job is, in essence, the first one. Producers hire the director, designers, actors, and other creative personnel, but they also provide the business personnel as well, from box office clerks to carpenters to publicists to ushers. If the director is responsible for everything that goes onto the stage, the producer is responsible for everything that supports the production. And while directors are a recent phenomenon, producers have been necessary since the ancient Greek theatre.

Someone has always been needed to sponsor or fund a theatre production. For the popular theatre festivals in Athens, a *choregus* was the person who paid for the costumes and funded the actors. In the Middle Ages, trade guilds such as bakers and tailors provided the scenery and costumes for the annual religious pageants.

PRODUCING IN THE PAST The Shubert Brothers built dozens of theatres on Broadway and throughout the nation during the first three decades of the twentieth century and produced more than five hundred Broadway productions between 1901 and 1954. Their flagship playhouse, the Sam S. Shubert Theatre, is still one of Broadway's favorite houses, seen here for the 2017 revival of *Hello, Dolly!* featuring Bette Midler. *Photofest*

During Shakespeare's day, shrewd businessmen invested in theatre companies and in theatre buildings in the hopes of sharing in the profits. Actors such as Richard Burbage, who originated many of Shakespeare's most famous roles, ran their own companies, just as the renowned actor-managers of the eighteenth and nineteenth centuries were the stars onstage and the producers offstage. Whenever a theatrical event took place, there was some person or a group of people who provided the funds and made the production possible. Today that is still true, in both professional or amateur theatre. In educational theatre, the producer might be the school itself, a drama club, a theatre department, or an arts committee. In professional resident theatre it is probably an artistic or producing director, who represents a board of trustees. In commercial theatre, the producer is a businessperson (on Broadway, more likely several of them), who raises money to pay for all the expenses of the production. It is this last kind of producer that we will look at more closely.

There is much more to operating a business than finding money and hiring people; a manager must know how to run the business if it is to succeed. So too with the theatre producer. In addition to securing a staff, the producer must find and pay for a script, arrange for a theatre space, budget the production, see that it is advertised, and manage the incoming money in order to pay bills and see that the enterprise turns a profit. The job calls for a person who understands both business and the theatre. Producers need not be creative people, but they must understand creativity and must hire and work with artists rather than mere employees. Because presenting an arts event is something like selling a product or providing a service, producers also have to understand the audience as well as the staff. The professional for-profit theatre producer must be something of a wizard to pull it all off.

Women in Directing and Theatre Management

In the nineteenth century and for much of the twentieth century, it was very rare to find women in powerful positions in business in America. Banking and industry were strictly male bastions, and even when women inherited a business, they let men manage it for them. Yet in theatre there have been women managers and directors since the 1850s, some of them quite famous and successful. Actresses on the stage, of course, were a common thing, and society would not question women in that position. But some enterprising women moved beyond acting and started to manage their own companies, also serving as the director of the plays. Perhaps the most famous of these early actress-managers was Laura Keene (1826?–1873) who found renown as a performer and who, in 1855, opened her own theatre in New York, where she employed some of the most popular stars of the day. Her company toured to several cities, where they were warmly welcomed until fortune turned against her in 1865. Keene and her players were performing the comedy *Our American Cousin* in Ford's Theatre in Washington when Abraham Lincoln was assassinated. She and her company never recovered from the incident. One of the most respected managers of the later half of the nineteenth century was Mrs. John Drew (1820–1897), who ran the celebrated Arch Street Theatre in Philadelphia for over thirty years. Her productions rivaled those in New York, and all of the most talented actors of her day wished to perform in her company. In the twentieth century, it was not uncommon to find women producers and directors. Some, such as Eva Le Gallienne (1899–1991), were actresses who broadened their talents to direct and manage, while others, such as Cheryl Crawford (1902–1986), were known first and foremost as producers and managers. Later, the professional regional theatre movement was pioneered by women in the 1950s. Today there are still, proportionally speaking, fewer women directors than men, but as producers women continue to be a strong presence.

PRODUCING TODAY Perhaps North America's largest theatre-producing organization today outside of New York City is the Stratford Theatre Festival in Ontario, Canada. The Festival Theatre, the largest of the four playhouses in the organization, began in 1953, as a tent. The 1957 permanent theatre, seen here, still retains the structural suggestion of a tent. *Performance Image/Alamy Stock Photo*

THE BUSINESS OF PRODUCING

Let us go through the process of producing a play on Broadway today. Such a venture is only a small portion of all the theatre activity going on across America, but theatrical producing in New York remains one of the most fascinating of theatre jobs. Some productions start with a star or an idea for a play, but most begin with a script, that blueprint that the playwright sends to possible producers. You may recall that, in the business, that script is referred to as a *property*, as if the play is a piece of land that one hopes to develop. The fictional producer Margaret Barnes receives a script from a playwright's agent, and she is interested in presenting it on Broadway. It is a drama with a small cast, and the playwright is unknown. Margaret knows that these are not ideal conditions, as audiences prefer comedies or musicals, and it is always easier to raise money for an established writer's work. But she feels the script is exceptional, and she embarks on producing it, estimating that it will cost $2 million to produce and knowing that the chances for failure are high. The first thing she must do is secure the rights to the property by taking an option on the play, as we saw earlier in the chapter on the playwright. Margaret gives the playwright $20,000, and both sign an agreement that no other producer can present the play while she tries to raise the money for the production. The agreement is for one year; at the end of a year, if Margaret cannot raise the $2 million, the rights to produce the play revert back to the playwright, who keeps the $20,000 and can approach another producer.

During that year, Margaret will try to raise the $2 million by going to investors, or *backers*, who will contribute to the production with the understanding that they will share in the profits, if there are any. One backer may invest $200,000 in the venture; having provided 10 percent of the capital, he or she will enjoy 10 percent of the dividends that will come if the play is a hit. This transaction, called a *limited partnership agreement*, is not unlike buying stock in a company, with the hopes of getting dividends from the company's profits. As both Margaret and the backers know, the risk level for theatre investing on Broadway is very high. Approximately 85 percent of all plays and musicals presented there fail to make any kind of profit, and the chance of losing one's entire investment is very likely. Theatre backers are usually in the investment game for reasons other than money, and, despite the risks involved, it is still possible to raise money for a production.

After ten months Margaret has gotten a dozen people to invest in the play, and she has the $2 million. She then signs a contract with the playwright to produce his play, agreeing how much royalty he will be paid. A royalty, you might recall from an earlier chapter, is the money paid to authors and composers every time their work is produced. Margaret will contract with the playwright and the Dramatists Guild, the organization for professional playwrights, for a royalty amount that will be a percentage of the box office income. Her rights to present the play are exclusive, meaning that no other producer can open a different production of the play on Broadway at the same time as hers. This agreement will last as long as the play runs, then the rights for other productions (a national tour or a movie version) will have to be renegotiated.

With the rights in hand, Margaret can now hire a director, who will in turn be part of hiring the designers and auditioning the cast. Although most creative decisions fall upon the director, many producers have some say in the casting and in the approval of the designs. Margaret will also attend many of the rehearsals and make

PRODUCING ON BROADWAY When the elaborate and innovative musical *Follies* opened on Broadway in 1971, it cost producer-director Harold Prince $800,000 to produce. Today large Broadway musicals cost at least twenty times that amount, and it often takes several producers and organizations to find the money to finance such an expensive operation. On Broadway today, $800,000 would not even cover the cost of Florence Klotz's magnificent *Follies* costumes. *Photofest*

Play-Producing Terms

aislesitter—a slang term for a theatre critic. In the past, most newspaper critics were given seats on the aisle so that they could leave the theatre quickly after the curtain call and make their copy deadline.
angel—an investor in a play or musical. It is an affectionate name for a backer.
break-even point—the week in the run of a commercial production when the box office income has paid off the initial investment and the show starts to make a profit.
comp ticket—a free ticket to a production, short for "complimentary." In the past, a comp was punched with a hole and was sometimes called an "Annie Oakley" because it looked like the famous sharpshooter shot a hole through it.
dress the house—to sell reserved seat tickets in such a way so that the audience is spread out and the theatre looks fuller than it really is.
front of house—the nonstage operations in a theatre, such as the box office, ushers, concessions, and so on.
ice—a bribe or a kickback paid to a box office person to buy hard-to-get tickets for a show. Like scalping, it is illegal but still happens. Modern accounting and computerized tickets have cut back on ice considerably.
nut—the amount of money it costs to pay the weekly expenses of a production. A show that "makes the nut" each week earns more than it spends. The term comes from the days of traveling players when the sheriff took the axle nut from the actors' wagon and would not return it until they paid their bills.
paper the house—to give away free tickets so that the theatre will be full for opening night or some other special occasion.
play doctor—a writer or director that the producer brings in to fix a show that is in trouble in rehearsals or in previews.
scalper—a person who buys tickets to a hit show then illegally resells them to willing theatregoers at an inflated price.
sleeper—a surprise hit on Broadway, one no one was expecting to succeed.
SRO—"standing room only." It means that the theatre has sold all its seats and that there is only room for standees.
success d'estime—a play or musical that is praised by the critics but does not do very good business at the box office.
TKTS booth—a ticket service located on Times Square that sells discounted tickets to shows for that day only. The booth was started in 1973 by the nonprofit Theatre Development Fund and today sells millions of Broadway and Off-Broadway tickets each year.
turkey—a play or musical that closes quickly and deserves to. The expression came from the early years of the 1900s, when producers would try to foist a terrible show on the public around Thanksgiving time to take advantage of the brisk holiday business.
Variety—the weekly magazine that gives facts and figures on all areas of show business, including theatre news and box office statistics for Broadway and touring companies.

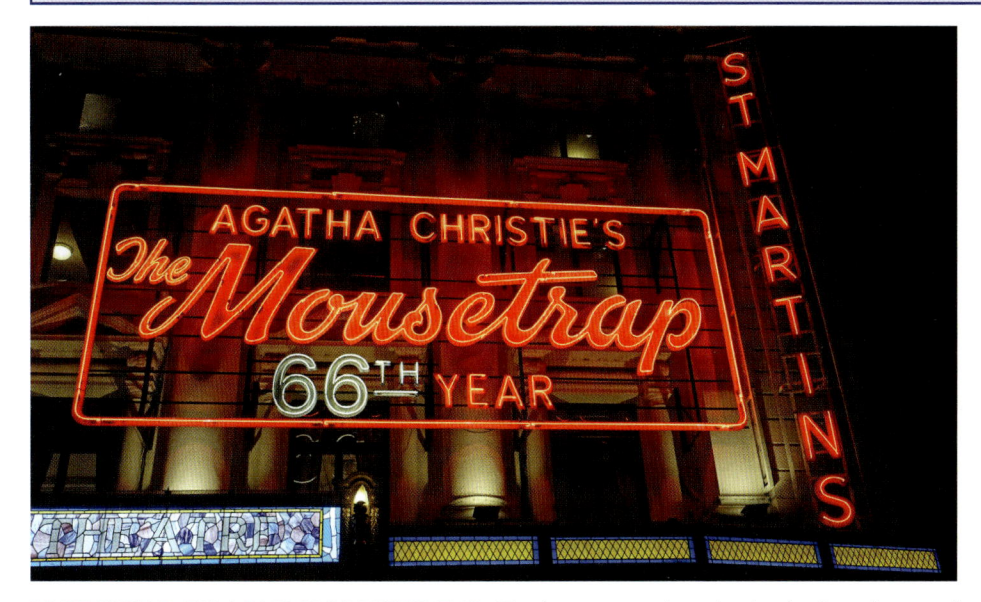

PRODUCING ON LONDON'S WEST END The longest-running play in the Broadway and London record books is Agatha Christie's mystery *The Mousetrap*, which opened in 1952, and is still running in the West End, London's version of Broadway. Shown here is the sign on St. Martin's Theatre in 2018, when the production celebrated its sixty-sixth anniversary. *Ian Macpherson London/Alamy Stock Photo*

suggestions and authorize changes. Some producers insist on having a say about every detail of the production, from the hairstyle of an actor to the cutting of a whole scene; many others put their trust in the director and only involve themselves in case of emergencies. As the rehearsals proceed, Margaret is busy paying the bills as they come in, organizing the publicity campaign to sell the show, and working out the details for leasing the theatre and its staff. By opening night, both the creative and the business aspects of the production converge, and soon the success of the venture will be determined. If the play is popular and business is healthy, the producer and the backers eventually share in the profits. If the show is struggling at the box office, Margaret must make the decision whether to put more money into advertising and hope that the play catches on or to close it. It is her decision alone, not that of the director or the investors, and it is the most difficult one that a producer faces. Many Broadway shows failed because they were not given enough time to find an audience; yet, just as many productions proceeded to go deeper into debt when they should have cut their losses and closed.

Although Margaret did not invest her own money into the $2 million, she did invest a year of her life and the expenses of an office and staff into the venture, and she takes a severe loss if the play closes in the red. On the other hand, she could make a great deal of money if the play is a hit, even more than the playwright, director, and others. Producers normally share in one-half of the profits, and for a Broadway hit that can easily add up to hundreds of thousands a week. So we see a Broadway producer is something of a speculator, using other people's money to experiment and gamble. The losses can (and usually are) substantial, but every once in a while, like any speculator, it is possible to strike gold.

TOPICS FOR GROUP DISCUSSION

1. Select one of the four featured plays and make a list of all the jobs onstage, backstage, and throughout the theatre building that a producer would need to fill for a professional production of that play.
2. Create a budget for one of the four featured plays by listing all the items (but not the dollar amounts) that a producer must pay for, from theatre rental to wigs.

POSSIBLE RESEARCH PROJECTS

1. Mel Brooks's 1967 and 2005 films *The Producers* spoof how plays are presented on Broadway. View one of the films and discuss how the two producers follow the process as outlined in this chapter.
2. One of the most revealing documentary films ever made about producing on Broadway is the 1997 documentary *Moon over Broadway*. After viewing the film, comment on the ways in which the producer and director might have saved the production from failure.

FURTHER READING

Adler, Steven. *On Broadway: Art and Commerce on the Great White Way.* Carbondale: Southern Illinois University Press, 2004.

Crawford, Cheryl. *One Naked Individual: My Fifty Years in the Theatre.* Indianapolis, IN: Bobbs-Merrill, 1977.

Epstein, Helen. *Joe Papp: An American Life.* Lexington, MA: Plunkett Lake Press, 2011.

Farber, Douglas C. *From Option to Opening: A Guide to Producing Plays Off Broadway.* New York: Limelight, 1989.

Hirsch, Foster. *The Boys from Syracuse: The Shuberts' Theatrical Empire.* Lanham, MD: Cooper Square Press, 2000/2013.

Goldman, William. *The Season: A Candid Look at Broadway.* New York: Limelight, 1984.

Greenberg, Jan Weingarten. *Theatre Business: From Auditions through Opening Night.* New York: Holt, Rinehart and Winston, 1981.

Hunter, Martin. *Romancing the Bard: Stratford at Fifty.* Toronto: Dundurn Press, 2013.

Jacobs, Susan. *On Stage: The Making of a Broadway Play.* New York: Knopf, 1972.

Langley, Stephen, ed. *Producers on Producing.* New York: Drama Book Specialists, 1976.

Langley, Stephen, and David M. Conte. *Theatre Management and Production in America.* New York: Drama Book Publishers, 2007.

Long, Robert Emmett. *Producing and the Theatre Business.* London: Continuum Publishing, 2007.

MacDonald, Laura, and William A. Everett. *The Palgrave Handbook of Musical Theatre Producers.* New York: Palgrave Macmillan, 2017.

Marshall, Norman. *The Producer and the Play.* London: Davis-Poynter, 1975.

Mordden, Ethan. *Ziegfeld: The Man Who Invented Show Business.* New York: St. Martin's Press, 2008.

Ostrow, Stuart. *A Producer's Broadway Journey.* New York: Praeger Press, 1999.

Stamas, Stephen. *Lincoln Center: A Promise Realized, 1979–2006.* New York: Wiley Press, 2006.

Turan, Kenneth. *Free for All: Joe Papp, the Public, and the Greatest Theatre Story Ever Told.* New York: Anchor Press, 2009.

Weiss, Mitch, and Perri Gaffney. *The Business of Broadway.* New York: Allworth Press, 2015.

7

THE PLAY BUILDERS I: THEATRE ARCHITECTURE AND SCENIC DESIGNERS

THEATRE ARCHITECTURE

While it is possible to do a play without scenery, costumes, or lights, one must have a place for a theatre event to occur. As noted earlier, the nature of that place has changed over the centuries. Today, there are a variety of kinds of performance spaces, each of which has its roots in some past model or theory. By looking at the four basic kinds of theatres that are used today, one gets a sense of the history of theatre spaces. As performance places developed and changed over time, new aspects of production were invented and incorporated into the theatre event. For example, when plays moved from outdoor to indoor spaces, theatrical lighting came into existence. As the configuration of the actor-audience positions changed, different types of scenery were created. Theatre architecture shaped the history of theatregoing as much as the playwrights and actors who worked in those spaces.

Proscenium Stage

The most traditional and frequently seen kind of performance space used today is the proscenium stage. Most theatres, from a majority of Broadway houses to just about every high school auditorium, use the proscenium model. A proscenium is an arch that frames the acting area, putting the actors inside a sort of picture frame. The audience looks into the frame from one direction and views the performance as if looking at a framed painting or at a movie screen. A proscenium theatre divides the playhouse into two distinct sections: the stage and the audience. We call the spectators' section the *house*; from it comes such terms as *full house* or a *house manager*. So that the audience can comfortably look into the picture frame, the floor of the house is raked or slanted so that *sight lines* are not obstructed. A sight line is the path that the eye travels from each seat in the house to the stage. Some theatres have better sight lines than others, but every proscenium playhouse should be designed so that all the spectators can clearly see into the frame.

There are both advantages and disadvantages to the proscenium model. Because the actors are being viewed by the audience from only one direction, it is fairly easy to stage a play so that each performer's face is seen by all the spectators. Proscenium theatres allow for plenty of scenery because of this picture-frame construction. Also, lighting designers can control light better in a proscenium theatre and create effects not possible in other theatre configurations, such as silhouettes. While not as many proscenium theatres today use a front curtain as in the past, one can see the advantage of lowering a drape across the frame to allow for scene changes or to surprise the audience with a scenic effect. There are also some disadvantages to the proscenium stage. A proscenium arch divides the actors and the audience; there is an invisible barrier between them. Obviously, some spectators are going to be closer to the actors than others, and, in very large playhouses, the rapport between actors and spectators can be diluted by distance. Also, proscenium stages require scenery and the expenses it entails. The audience looks into the frame, and there must be something there besides the actors. This is not true of other models of theatre space. Yet the proscenium stage remains popular, and it shows no signs of going out of favor.

This popular design is among the newer forms of theatre architecture. It was invented by the Italians in the Renaissance as a way to show off elaborate scenery and to use the newly discovered phenomenon of *perspective*. When something on a flat surface tricks the eye and looks like it has depth, it is said to be drawn in perspective. We are so used to perspective in art today that it is difficult to realize that for thousands of years artists had no way to create depth on a canvas or a wall painting. Even the inventive Greeks could not figure out that a figure drawn smaller in relation to another figure will look like it is in the distance. But the Renaissance Italians did discover it, and perspective was born. Of course, perspective only works if one views the piece of art from one direction. Therefore, the proscenium stage was developed. The stage became a painting, and the actors were placed in front of scenery like the figures in a landscape. In many modern theatre productions, particularly those with plenty of spectacle, this is still true. The proscenium is the frame through which most of us today see the theatre event.

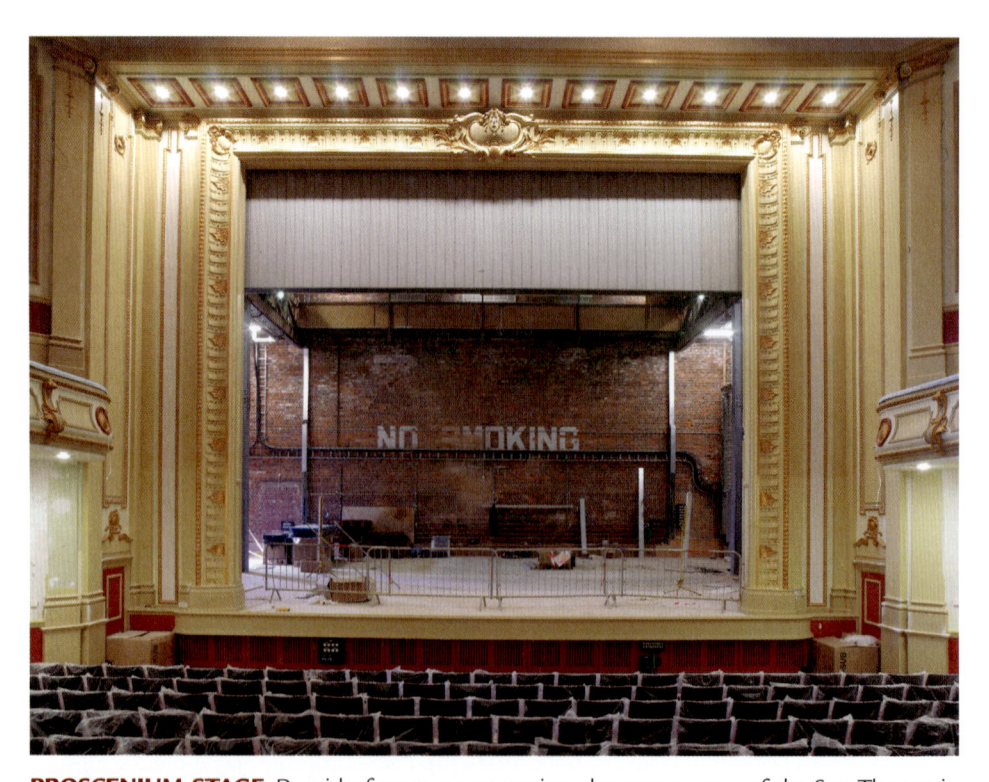

PROSCENIUM STAGE Devoid of scenery or curtains, the empty stage of the Spa Theatre in Bridlington in Yorkshire, England, reveals how the proscenium arch divides the theatre into two sections: the acting area and the audience. Viewing a play through this arch remains the most common architectural structure for theatres in Western culture. *Arcaid Images/Alamy Stock Photo*

Thrust Stage

The second most common form of theatre architecture today is the thrust stage, often called a *three-quarter stage*. As the names suggest, the stage "thrusts" out into the audience, and the spectators sit on three sides of the acting space. Several regional theatres, most Shakespeare festivals, and many Off-Broadway playhouses use this arrangement. The audience now views the action from one of three sides. It is a bit more difficult to direct actors on a thrust stage because sight lines are complicated by some actors blocking other actors from being seen by one-third of the audience. The action on a thrust stage needs to move in such a way that no one part of the audience is ignored and sees only the backs of a lot of performers. The main advantage to the three-quarter arrangement is the actor-audience relationship. With the spectators wrapped around the playing space, the rapport is stronger, and every seat in the house is closer to the action. While some scenery can be used, it is limited to the side of the stage where there is no audience. Perspective does not work in a thrust-stage arrangement; rather than being figures in a distant landscape, the actors are instead closer and directly linked with the audience.

Forms of the thrust stage go back to the ancient Greeks, whose semicircular acting area was lined with spectators. In the Middle Ages, actors performed on platforms or wagon stages, and the theatregoers surrounded them on three sides. Perhaps the most effective use of the thrust stage was the Elizabethan playhouses in London, where hundreds of spectators watched the action from the ground and from three levels of galleries, all of them wrapped around the thrust stage and none very far from the action. Shakespeare's plays were all first presented on such a stage, and, although his works are performed today in all kinds of theatres, it is clear that the famous playwright wrote specifically with the thrust stage in mind.

Arena Stage

Perhaps the simplest form of theatre architecture is the arena stage, better known as *theatre-in-the-round*. In this arrangement the audience completely surrounds the acting space, little or no scenery is used, and more members of the audience are closer to the actors than in any other model. (Despite its name, these stages are usually square or rectangular rather than round.) Sight lines "in the round" are very tricky because no matter which direction an actor faces, half of the audience cannot see his or her face. It is also difficult to put very many actors on an arena stage; one must keep them moving to maintain clear focus. Yet no other kind of stage is better for developing the actor-audience relationship. Sometimes the performers must go through the audience to enter or exit, totally breaking down any barriers between performers and spectators.

Arena stages can be found today in a number of regional, college, and summer theatres. When it was introduced in America in the 1940s, the arena stage was considered highly experimental. Ironically, it is probably the oldest of all theatre spaces. The very first theatre events probably took place around a campfire with the spectators encircling the chorus or storytellers. In some ancient civilizations, it is believed that early forms of theatre took place in temples, with the "actors" surrounded by other participants. Old or new, arena staging presents plenty of challenges for all the theatre artists, from the director and actors to the scenic and lighting designer. Yet there is something immediate and vibrant about theatre-in-the-round, and many feel it creates the most engaging of all theatre events.

THRUST STAGE Inspired by the ancient Greek amphitheatre, the thrust stage of the Guthrie Theatre in Minneapolis allows for variety in staging, a practical space for actors, and an intimacy between audience and performance. The theatre, which opened in 1963, was designed by Tanya Moiseiwitsch and founder Tyrone Guthrie. *AP Photo/Andy King*

Flexible Space

The fourth kind of theatre architecture is a combination of the previous three models. Sometimes called a *black box* theatre, this kind of flexible space is a room with four walls and no permanent seating, stage platforms, or scenery. The space is turned into a proscenium, thrust, or arena stage by the arrangement of the portable seating platforms. The acting area may be raised or on the floor and can be situated anywhere in the room. The seating capacity changes with each new arrangement and each new production. Sometimes these arrangements are variations on the types mentioned earlier: the audience can sit on two sides of the acting area, or the stage may be oddly shaped and the spectators are in five or more sections. One can even present *environmental staging* in which the whole room becomes the setting of the play and the audience is clustered in different parts of the space. The possibilities for creativity in a black box are endless, and many colleges and regional theatres have such a space as an alternate performance place. In fact, most theatre centers—those building complexes in which there are two or more theatres—will usually have a flexible space theatre somewhere in the building. It is perhaps the most useful of all forms of theatre space because the theatre architecture conforms to the production rather than the other way around.

    Let us consider our four sample plays and see how they might fit into these different kinds of performance space. As mentioned earlier, *Macbeth* was first presented to the public at the Globe Theatre, which was a thrust stage. Yet when it was produced privately for King James I and his party, it was done inside the palace and was probably staged on a platform closer to a proscenium theatre. In the eighteenth

Shakespeare's Globe Theatre

Perhaps the most famous and most efficient playhouse in the history of Western theatre is the Globe Theatre, which stood right outside the city limits of London from 1599 to 1642. It was octangular in shape, open to the sky in the middle, and consisted of three galleries that surrounded a thrust stage, allowing for over two thousand theatregoers to either stand on the ground below or sit on benches above. The stage itself had three levels: the main stage, which stood about five feet off the ground; a balcony stage behind and above it; and a musicians gallery above that, which was used for music and sound effects. Behind the thrust stage was an inner stage, called the discovery space, that had a curtain across it so that actors could be "discovered" in position by pulling back the drapery. Actors were able to enter the acting area through doors on either side of the thrust stage or above on the balcony. The Globe Theatre required little scenery; the efficient acting space could be a palace, a battlefield, a public street, or a private bedroom, all by adding one or two pieces of furniture. The two columns that held up the roof over part of the thrust stage could be trees, hiding places, or whatever the script described. Since there were no elaborate scene changes, the action on the Globe stage was uninterrupted and very practical.

As famous as the Globe Theatre was, no one quite knows the details of its architecture. Since it was made of wooden beams, plaster, and straw, no evidence survives of the original playhouse. Scholars have argued for over one hundred years about the exact number of spectators, the dimensions of the structure, and what exactly was on the stage. Even the precise location of the theatre has been argued, theatre historians having placed it in various spots on the south bank of the River Thames. We know much more about some other Elizabethan playhouses nearby, such as the Rose Theatre, whose foundations were discovered late in the twentieth century. As for Shakespeare's famous Globe, it will always remain somewhat of a mystery.

In 1997, a new theatre patterned and named after the Globe was erected in London in the general area of the original, and it is used today for outdoor performances much in the style of the Elizabethan era, even utilizing some of the same building materials as the first Globe. Spectators can stand on the ground or sit on benches; no modern lighting instruments are used except for general illumination for night performances; and the actors perform classical plays by Shakespeare and others in an open style that approximates the theatre events of the Elizabethan era.

GLOBE THEATRE One of many conjectural reconstructions of Shakespeare's famous playhouse, this sketch includes most of the features believed to have existed in the original: the thrust stage, a discovery space behind curtains, two doors used for entrances and exits, a balcony stage, and a roof that covered some of the acting area. The sketch also shows the three rows of galleries for seated patrons and the standing room surrounding the stage for the "groundlings." *Photofest*

BLACK BOX and **ARENA STAGING** A flexible theatre space, or black box theatre, offers the greatest variety in performer–audience relationships. Moisés Kaufman's documentary drama *The Laramie Project* was produced arena style in the black box at Morehead State University in Kentucky. The intimate production was directed by Greg Carlisle, with scenic design by Andy Baker, lighting design by Paul Denayer, and costumes by Ashlee Colins. *Paul Denayer*

and nineteenth centuries, *Macbeth* was a favorite of European theatre companies, all of whom used elaborate proscenium stages. Today the tragedy can be done in the round (such as at the Arena Stage theatre in Washington, D.C.) or in a black box (as it is at many colleges). *You Can't Take It with You* was originally presented on Broadway in a proscenium theatre. The setting, interior rooms in the Vanderhof house, is called a *box set*. This kind of interior was invented in the nineteenth century and given that name because the set resembled a box with one side removed. The missing side was called the "fourth wall," and it was through this invisible wall that the audience watched the action of the play. A box set is similar to a doll house in which all the rooms are viewed by looking through the missing wall. Yet the Kaufman and Hart comedy has been successfully produced on thrust and arena stages as well as proscenium theatres. *A Raisin in the Sun* was also first seen on Broadway in a box set in a proscenium theatre, but a production in the round or on a thrust stage might even intensify the power of the play. Finally, *Hamilton* has a loose, free-flowing structure and makes few specific demands about its staging. Although it played in a proscenium theatre Off Broadway and then on Broadway, its future life will be in every kind of performance space. Is there such a thing as the correct kind of theatre for a particular play? Just as these four plays will come to life in any kind of theatre architecture, it can be assumed that any theatre event can take place in any kind of venue. It all goes back to the theatre's ability to change and evolve.

The four kinds of theatre architecture represent formal theatre spaces. But what about informal theatre events? In our definition of theatre, we said that there must be a *place*, not a theatre building. Any place that actors and audience gather to present a story can become the theatre space, whether it be a storefront, garage, church, street, public park, warehouse, or other nontraditional locale. Some refer to such places as "found space" because they were not intended for performance, but the actors and audience found them and used them for a theatre event. Many Off-Off-Broadway theatres in New York are located in found spaces, as are alternative performance companies in cities across the nation. (We will see later that street theatre and guerrilla theatre usually avoid formal theatre spaces and take place "on location.") While one will usually find experimental or nontraditional works produced in such spaces, sometimes the offerings are very traditional. For example, Shakespeare's popular comedy *A Midsummer Night's Dream* takes place mostly in a forest, and many productions of the play have been successfully presented in parks. *Macbeth* has been produced in castles in Europe. Similarly, there will probably be outdoor revivals of *Hamilton* in historic districts that provide an accurate background for the musical's period. Theatre has never been limited to a formal performance space, and it is not likely that it ever will be.

SCENIC DESIGN

After the actors, scenery is perhaps the most visual element of theatre. Some productions are more visual than others; there is a major difference between spectacular sets in a musical comedy and the drab living-room setting in a domestic drama. In either case, scenery connects with an audience and provides a visual reinforcement of the director's concept for the play. We refer to stage scenery as *sets* and talk about the *setting* of a play, but scenery is more than that. The actors and the story they re-create are seen in a setting prepared by the director and scenic designer. In a way, scenery is the environment in which we see the story unfold. Even a play with a simple or minimalist set still has scenery; the bare stage becomes the visual *setting* for the piece. Just as we accept the convention of actors pretending to be characters, we accept that canvas walls, pieces of furniture, or painted backdrops are the locale of the story. Scenery is the visual image that prompts our imagination.

There are as many kinds of scenery as there are theatre spaces and directorial styles. Over the centuries, certain kinds of scenery were popular; others were dismissed as old-fashioned; and some were deemed too experimental. For example, when the play *Our Town* opened on Broadway in 1938, it was presented on a bare stage, something which struck theatregoers as very odd since they were used to detailed scenery. Theatregoers today can expect to experience all forms of scenery, from a realistic, elaborate interior of a home to a stark, nondescript void. There is no one common or accepted form of stage scenery today as there has been in times past. The ancient Greeks expected to see a simple stone structure that remained the same for comedies and tragedies. Medieval audiences knew only colorful wagon stages or decorated platforms. Spectators in the eighteenth century saw large-scale painted scenery. In the twentieth century, some past styles of scenery were rediscovered and were adapted to contemporary tastes. Most of the theatres may have been proscenium stages, but what took place on those stages was as variable as it was unexpected. This picking and choosing from different styles is called *eclecticism*, and it best describes modern scenic stage design today.

Consider the options available for our four sample plays. Just as there are different directorial approaches to producing *Macbeth*, *You Can't Take It with You*, *A Raisin in the Sun*, and *Hamilton*, there are various ways to design the scenery for them. You will recall that the director chooses the style for the production. The designers work with that style to bring the directorial concept to life. A nonrealistic, psychological approach to *Macbeth* using the style of expressionism will lead the scenic designer to create an environment onstage that will let the audience know that they are looking beyond the surface of the story and characters. A director who decides to use realism and to present *A Raisin in the Sun* in as lifelike a manner as possible will enable the stage designer to re-create a Chicago tenement apartment with as much detail and authenticity as possible. The director's concept is the jumping-off point for a scenic designer, and it is his or her job to turn that concept into tangible and practical scenery.

Functions of Scenery

Regardless of style, stage scenery should fulfill three very basic functions to be truly effective. The set should, first of all, immediately tell an audience the *location* of the action. When the curtain rises or the lights come up on a set, the audience must learn something about where the play takes place. Some sets will give specific information while others will only suggest a locale in the mind of the spectators. For example, a ritzy penthouse apartment with a view of the Chrysler Building will tell the audience that the play takes place in a wealthy high-rise apartment in New York City. The furniture and interior decor might even tell them that the setting is the 1930s. But often scenery cannot be so specific. When the lights rise on the small, dingy apartment of the Younger family, theatregoers can guess that the residents are not rich, but they will not know that it is Chicago and that it is an African American neighborhood in the 1950s. As the play progresses the details about the location will become clearer through dialogue, but the initial impact has been made. Scenery sets the locale in the audience's mind and creates a visual formation, either specifically or suggestively.

Just as important as the location is the *mood* of the play. Even if the specifics of where the action is are not clear, the tone of the production should be. Is this going to be a comedy or a melodrama or a farce? Is it going to be realistic or exaggerated or romanticized? Some spectators might be familiar with the script before the play begins and are already thinking along the lines of a particular type or style of play, but the function of scenery is to relay this information visually and let the audience know what the mood of the play will be. Neil Simon's play *Brighton Beach Memoirs* takes place in the crowded, dingy home of a family during the Depression, a locale not very different from the one for *A Raisin in the Sun*. Could the two plays use the same scenery? The set for Simon's nostalgic comedy-drama must set a mood that is very different from that for Lorraine Hansberry's drama; the locations might be similar, but the tones are not. It is the scenic designer's job to create this specific mood in the use of color, shape, texture, space, and other artistic tools. While it might be easy to convey location, it is more difficult to convey tone.

THEATRE TECHNOLOGY The technical theatre elements of scenery, costumes, and lighting come together beautifully in the wedding dance scene in the original Broadway production of *Fiddler on the Roof* (1964), directed and choreographed by Jerome Robbins. Boris Aronson designed the scenery, Patricia Zipprodt the costumes, and Jean Rosenthal the lighting. *Photofest*

The third basic function of scenery is to provide a *practical playing space* for the actors. Modern scenery is not merely to be looked at; it is to be used. Actors must be able to move through the space and use the doors, steps, windows, platforms, furniture, and whatever else is placed onstage. The script may state what is needed scenically to tell the story, and the director might suggest some scenic elements that will illustrate the concept, but it is up to the designer to create an environment that is practical for the action of the play. An experienced designer develops what will be put onstage and how it should be built. If the play calls for multiple settings, it is the designer's task to figure out how scenery will be moved on- and offstage, and where it will be stored when not in use. It is also the designer's concern that the scenery creates no sight-line problems for the audience; each spectator should be able to see every actor and all the pieces of scenery without one blocking the other. A set designer must function as an architect as well as an artist because even in the most well-equipped Broadway theatres space is limited. This is particularly important in plays or musicals that have multiple sets. The practicality of scenery should not be underestimated. Impressive scenic designs on paper are useless unless they can be realized on a real stage.

Kinds of Scenery

Modern scenery comes in so many forms and styles that it is not possible to list all the options available to designers, but some basic concepts can be explained. For example, most scenery can be divided into *interior* or *exterior* sets. Interior settings usually involve a room with furniture and one or more entrances. An interior might be suggested by a wall or a frame or even just a few pieces of furniture in a space. If the room is presented more realistically, with three walls and perhaps a ceiling, it is called a box set, as we have already seen with the original Broadway productions of *You Can't Take It with You* and *A Raisin in the Sun*. Exterior sets refer to any location outdoors, be it a detailed forest with trees or simply a bench to denote a park setting. Realistic scenery is always more detailed (and expensive) than suggestive scenery, and realistic exteriors are particularly difficult. Many exteriors rely on painted drops, or *backdrops*, in which a landscape is re-created. Drops are usually made of a thin form of canvas and are stretched taut by a pipe at the top and the bottom. Because drops can be raised up into the space above the stage, called the *fly loft*, they are easier to store than three-dimensional scenery. The Italians first developed painted drops in the fifteenth century when they invented perspective, and for many years drops were the most popular form of stage scenery.

Some stage sets are neither interiors nor exteriors but an open, unspecified space that can be used to create different locales through lighting and a few set pieces. This flexible kind of scenery is often called a *unit set* and is ideal for plays such as *Macbeth* and *Hamilton,* which require many locations to tell the story. The most effective unit sets have different levels with a variety of acting spaces on the stage. The witches may appear on a raised platform to suggest the heath where they meet Macbeth and Banquo. Another part of the unit set may have an archway and an area that serves as a room in the castle where Lady Macbeth urges her husband to go down the hall and murder the king in his sleep. Unit sets are highly practical and much less expensive than a series of detailed interiors and exteriors. They also allow multiscene plays to move more smoothly because there is no cumbersome changing of scenery at the end of every scene. The action in *Hamilton* moves to many locations in the colonies and even takes place briefly in England when King George II appears. So a unit set that offers a variety of playing spaces is essential.

Scenery can also be divided by its construction. A set can be made of flats or three-dimensional pieces. A *flat* is a rectangular piece of scenery that is joined with other pieces to make interior walls, exterior facades, and other structures. Flats sometimes have window, arch, or door openings in them as well. Although a flat may be sixteen feet high, they have very little depth (therefore the name *flat*), and when they are stacked together, many flats can be stored in a reasonably narrow space. They are also thin and light enough that they can be flown up into the fly loft when not needed. A flat is constructed much like an artist's canvas: material called *muslin* is stretched over a frame and fastened in the back. This is known as a soft flat. While theatre flats used to be made of cloth over a wooden frame, today a variety of materials are used, from steel frames to a thin form of plywood for the surface. These are known as hard flats. A series of painted flats can be formed to create a box set with depth, but the result is still considered flat scenery. An exterior setting can have cutout trees and shrubbery which are also considered flats, though they are often painted to give the illusion of depth. It is possible to design and build scenery that doesn't use flats. A set may consist of only platforms, furniture, three-dimensional trees, or other objects. It is possible to combine flat and three-dimensional scenery, as with an exterior that has some artificial trees placed in front of a backdrop that continues the illusion of depth by showing painted trees in the distance. Also, designers today are not limited to traditional flats and drops. Scenery can be made of rough-hewn wood (as in *Hamilton*), steel, plastic, Plexiglas, and other materials that the Renaissance Italians did not have when they first developed stage sets for the proscenium.

Finally, most set designs can be divided into *symmetrical* and *asymmetrical* scenery. Like a painting, a stage set should be balanced so that it is aesthetically pleasing to the eye. The easiest way to balance a setting is to make both sides of the stage exactly the same. This is symmetrical balance, a formal and classical method of unifying a set

SCENIC DESIGN RENDERING Among the many drawings and plans the scenic designer makes in preparing the scenery is a rendering of what the set will look like. Boris Aronson's rendering for the original Broadway production of Tennessee Williams's drama *The Rose Tattoo* (1951) captures not only the Gulf coast locale, but also the mood of the drama. *Photofest*

that goes back to ancient Greece and to Shakespeare's Globe Theatre but one that still works well. A series of columns with a door center, a room with identical windows and furniture on each half of the stage, and an exterior with a row of trees left and right balancing each other are examples of symmetrical scenery. When a setting is balanced without the two sides of the stage mirroring each other, it is said to be asymmetrical. A room with a large fireplace on the left might be balanced by an oversized archway on the right, or a staircase on one side of the stage might be balanced with tall windows on the opposite side. Asymmetrical balance is achieved by considering the "weight" of individual scenic features and distributing that weight evenly across the stage. Since much of what we see in the real world is not symmetrical, it makes sense that most theatre scenery is asymmetrical. There is also something dynamic about positioning dissimilar pieces on a stage and still achieving balance.

THE SCENIC DESIGNER'S PROCESS

Identifying scenery as interior or exterior, flat or three-dimensional, and symmetrical or asymmetrical is just the beginning to understanding the various ways that scenic designers work. There is more to a painting than composition and balance, just as there is more to music than identifying notes and scales. So too, the art of theatre scenery is more complex and mysterious than categorizing kinds of stage sets. Looking at the steps a scenic designer goes through in the creation of a set will give you a better understanding of this unique art form.

Research

Once a scenic designer meets with a director and the concept and style for the production has been discussed, he or she rereads the script several times, looking for images that will evoke the period and place. The designer also makes notes about the practical needs of the scenery. Something as simple as the placement of a door or the direction in which that door opens can help or hinder a production. The designer will also research the location and period of the play. Looking at sketches, paintings, and photographs of architecture and furniture is necessary, even if the production is not going to be in the realistic style. For example, a scene might take place in an English tavern in the 1800s, and the plan is to suggest the location with a table and some stools and with a few wooden beams overheard. Since these few pieces need to tell the audience the time and place, they must evoke the environment and do the job of a complete stage setting. The furniture might be thick and bulky, and the beams may be oversized and carved in a certain way to create an old-world feeling. This is the approach that David Korins used in designing the scenery for *Hamilton*. The designer's research should cover everything from architectural building styles to details such as window curtains and the type of mantle clock that should appear over the fireplace.

Graphic Designs

When designers feel that they have a grasp on the material, the next step in the design process is the production of a series of concept drawings. These help the director visualize what the scenery will look like. Also, the technical director, who will be building the scenery, can look at the concept drawings and estimate the cost of the materials and labor and see if the proposed designs can be built with the money budgeted. After adjustments have been made, the designer creates a series of drawings that act as

UNIT SET The acting space for the musical *Hamilton*, designed by David Korins, is a unit set that suggests its colonial period setting with wooden beams, stairs, and galleries. Period furniture, props, and costumes are then added to depict each locale in the story. *David L. Moore—US NE/Alamy Stock Photo*

the scenic plan's "blueprint." Some of these drawings might view the stage from the audience's point of view; others may illustrate particular walls or sections of the set. The most important of these early drawings is the *ground plan* (often called the *floor plan*), a bird's-eye view of the playing space. Much like the layout in a house design, the ground plan indicates walls, windows, doors, stairs, and other permanent features. The placement of furniture is also indicated in a ground plan since it will tell the director what objects will affect the actors' movement. For exterior sets, a designer may include trees, bushes, steps, and other features. Directors usually work with designers to solidify the final ground plan, making sure that the space will be practical. After the director reviews and makes comments on all the sketches, the designer will then create a *rendering* of the set. This is a color sketch that shows what the scenery will look like from the audience's point of view. Not only should an effective rendering show walls, furniture, and color, but it should also somehow evoke the mood of the set. If the designer cannot suggest the mood on paper, it is unlikely that it can be done onstage with a real set. Many designers will go one step further and build a model of the scenery. This is a small-scale but three-dimensional model that might be painted as in the rendering, with miniature furniture made and placed in the space. Models help the director and the actors visualize the performance space, but they are also useful for figuring out how the set might be built and how scene changes will be accomplished. The technical director, the person in charge of constructing the scenery, cannot depend on renderings or even models to get the information needed to build the set accurately. For this step the designer must draw construction plans, sometimes called *elevation drawings*, that give exact dimensions and instructions on how the scenery is to be made. Some of these drawings will indicate the way a staircase is to turn while others will give painting instructions that show what colors are to be used where. A designer might have to create dozens of such drawings before construction can begin.

THE PLAY BUILDERS I: THEATRE ARCHITECTURE AND SCENIC DESIGNERS • 133

SCENIC DESIGN The original Broadway production of the musical fable *Guys and Dolls* (1950) had scenic and lighting design by the celebrated Jo Mielziner. The crap game scene in the sewers is depicted in Mielziner's color rendering and then the actual production is seen as it appeared on the stage of the 46th Street Theatre. Director: George S. Kaufman. *Photofest*

Implementation

Even after all of these graphic designs are completed, the designer is still needed during construction, load-in, and rehearsals. The technical director is in charge of implementing the scenic designs but experienced designers frequently visit the scene construction shop to answer questions and make decisions on details too small to show up on a drawing. The load-in is when the scenery is moved from the scene shop and positioned on the stage. In schools and community theatres, scenery might be built right on the stage, but in professional theatre the scene construction shop may be miles away from the theatre building. The designer is often needed during load-in because problems usually arise and must be solved. For example, not until the set is onstage can the designer be sure that there are no obstructed sight lines.

Designers must also attend the technical and dress rehearsals, in which the actors first begin to work within the design, and the previews, when the play is first performed in front of an audience. While it may be too late to make major changes to the scenic structure, there are usually many minor adjustments to be made, from the way a window curtain hinders a piece of business to the too-soft cushion on a sofa that impedes an actor's movement. By opening night the designer's job is done. During a long run, the set may need repair or retouching on occasion, but mostly the designer's work remains unchanged and as potent as it was during the first performance.

TOPICS FOR GROUP DISCUSSION

1. List the challenges and advantages of producing *Macbeth* in a theatre-in-the-round.
2. Discuss the different kinds of materials (steel, wood, cloth, plastic, etc.) that might be used in creating a scenic design for *Hamilton*.
3. What kinds of furniture and other objects on the set of *You Can't Take It with You* could be used to tell the audience that the comedy is set in 1936?

POSSIBLE RESEARCH PROJECTS

1. View the opening ten minutes of Laurence Olivier's film *Henry V* (1945), supposedly set in the Globe Theatre, and the final twenty minutes of the movie *Shakespeare in Love* (1998), placed in the Rose Theatre, and discuss the similarities and differences between these two Elizabethan reconstructions.
2. Going through the script for *Macbeth*, list the various interior and exterior locations in the story and decide which pieces of scenery are necessary to denote each locale.
3. Much of *A Raisin in the Sun* takes place in a 1959 kitchen. Determine what items might be found in such a kitchen and how it differs from a modern kitchen.

FURTHER READING

Adler, Phoebe. *Behind the Scenes: Contemporary Set Design.* New York: Black Dog, 2013.

Aronson, Arnold. *American Set Design.* New York: Theatre Communications Group, 1985.

Bablet, Denis. *Revolutions of Stage Design in the Twentieth Century.* New York: L. Arnie, 1985.
Bay, Howard. *Stage Design.* New York: Drama Book Specialists, 1974.
Carter, Randolph, and Robert Reed Cole. *Joseph Urban.* New York: Abbeville, 1992.
———. *Theatrical Design and Production.* New York: McGraw-Hill, 1999.
Condee, William F. *Theatrical Space: A Guide for Directors and Designers.* Lanham, MD: Rowman & Littlefield, 1995.
Davis, Tony. *Stage Design.* Hove, East Sussex, UK: Rotovision, 2001.
Di Benedetto, Stephen. *An Introduction to Theatre Design.* Abingdon-on-Thames, UK: Routledge, 2012.
Gillette, J. Michael. *Theatrical Design and Production.* New York: McGraw-Hill, 2012.
Gorelik, Mordecai. *New Theatres for Old.* New York: Octagon Books, 1962.
Henderson, Mary C. *The City and the Theatre: The History of New York Playhouses.* New York: Back Stage Books, 2004.
———. *Mielziner: Master of Modern Stage Design.* New York: Back Stage Books, 2001.
Hildy, Franklin J., ed. *New Issues in the Reconstruction of Shakespeare's Theatre.* New York: Peter Lang, 1990.
Hodges, C. Walter. *The Globe Restored.* New York: Oxford University Press, 1968.
———. *Shakespeare's Second Globe.* New York: Oxford University Press, 1973.
Izenour, George C. *Theatre Design.* New Haven, CT: Yale University Press, 1997.
Kiernan, Pauline. *Staging Shakespeare at the New Globe.* New York: St. Martin's, 1999.
Leacroft, Richard, and Helen Leacroft. *Theatre and Playhouse: An Illustrated Development of Theatre Buildings from Ancient Greece to the Present Day.* New York: Methuen, 1985.
Lewandowski, Elizabeth J. *The Complete Costume Dictionary.* Lanham, MD: Rowman & Littlefield, 2011.
Mielziner, Jo. *Designing for the Theatre.* New York: Atheneum, 1965.
Morrison, William. *Broadway Theatres: History and Architecture.* New York: Dover, 1999.
Oenslager, Donald. *Scenery Then and Now.* New York: Norton, 1936.
———. *Stage Design: Four Centuries of Scenic Invention.* New York: Viking, 1975.
Parker, W. Oren, and R. Craig Wolf. *Scene Design and Stage Lighting.* New York: Holt, Rinehart and Winston, 2008.
Payne, Darwin Reid. *Computer Scenographic.* Carbondale: Southern Illinois University Press, 1994.
———. *Scenographic Imagination.* Carbondale: Southern Illinois University Press, 1993.
Reid, Francis. *Designing for the Theatre.* New York: Routledge, 2013.
Rich, Frank, and Lisa Aronson. *The Theatre Art of Boris Aronson.* New York: Knopf, 1987.
Rufford, Juliet. *Theatre and Architecture.* New York: Palgrave Macmillan, 2015.
Smith, Ronn. *American Scene Design 2.* New York: Theatre Communications Group, 1991.
Strong, Judith, ed. *Theatre Buildings: A Design Guide.* New York: Routledge, 2010.
Svoboda, Joseph. *The Secret of Theatrical Space.* New York: Applause Theatre Books, 1993.
Turner, Cathy. *Dramaturgy and Architecture.* New York: Palgrave Macmillan, 2015.
Van Hoogstraten, Nicholas. *Lost Broadway Theatres.* New York: Princeton Architectural Press, 1997.

8

THE PLAY BUILDERS II: THE OTHER DESIGNERS

COSTUME DESIGN

Certain plays are identified as *costume* pieces because they are set in the past and the clothes are radically different from contemporary dress. Yet every play, no matter what its time or location, requires costumes. One will certainly notice the Scottish wardrobe of the thanes in *Macbeth* or the colonial-period clothing of the characters in *Hamilton*, but just as important is the 1930s wardrobe of the New Yorkers in *You Can't Take It with You* and the everyday 1950s clothes of the Younger family in *A Raisin in the Sun*. Stage costumes are not like Halloween costumes, which are used in dressing up to be something or someone you are not. Stage costumes are the clothes that a certain character would wear at a particular place during a specific period of time. Obviously, costumes from past times are more noticeable to modern audiences than are contemporary clothes onstage, but anything that an actor wears is important to the success of the production.

Functions of Costume Design

Scenery is all about the location; costume design is all about the *characters*. Just as the audience should be able to figure out where the action is taking place by looking at the sets, they should learn something of the character the moment they see a costume onstage. The primary function of stage costumes is to reveal something about the characters, either with a broad and satirical flourish or with subtle suggestion. What the strong-willed Lady Macbeth wears might suggest an unfeeling and unfeminine woman of power; on the other hand, the practical housedress with a touch of color that Penny wears in *You Can't Take It with You* might suggest the flamboyant side of her that writes plays and paints portraits. Just as a playwright must find a distinctive language and manner for each character in a play, the costume designer must create clothes that point out the unique qualities of each character. All of the costumes in a play must be true to the period and the style that the director has chosen, but it is the individuality of each character's clothes that is the real challenge to a designer. The slight difference between the costumes for Mrs. Younger and Ruth in *A Raisin in the Sun* should point out how the two women are different, even though both are in the same economic class and both might shop at the same discount or secondhand store. Macbeth and Macduff are both Scottish thanes and men of some wealth, but the costume designer should indicate how different these two characters are by choices of color, fabric, and design. If the costume does not help describe the character in some way, the design fails.

COSTUME DESIGN Costume designer William Ivey Long and director-choreographer Tommy Tune made the unusual decision to have all the characters in the musical *Nine* (1982) dressed in black, allowing for a bold contrast when the actors appeared in Lawrence Miller's mostly white Italian spa setting. *Photofest*

The second function of costume design is the *indication of time*. Because we associate different periods with what people wore, it is through the costumes that the audience is made aware of the play's time frame. Scenery is not always able to designate time: The wooden galleries and early American furniture would look pretty much the same in the mid-1700s and the mid-1800s, but the costumes in *Hamilton* should specifically re-create the 1776 to 1804 time frame in the audience's mind. Occasionally, time recognition is obvious, such as the 1950s poodle skirts in *Grease* or the World War II uniforms in works such as *Mister Roberts* or *South Pacific*. Yet more often than not, period clothes do not suggest a specific decade, and the designer must help solidify the period in the audience's mind. No character in *A Raisin in the Sun* wears a poodle skirt, so the designer must indicate the 1950s setting in less obvious ways. The example of the swank penthouse apartment in New York that was used earlier can be used to tell a story in the 1930s, 1940s, or even today; it is when the characters enter and the audience sees their clothes that the period is established.

Finally, costumes should serve the directorial concept and help illustrate the *style* of the production. Everyday but accurate costumes for *A Raisin in the Sun* might suggest realism, while stark, exaggerated costumes for *Macbeth* would indicate expressionism. A costume designer can work on three different productions of the same play and come up with very different costumes for each, depending on the directorial style in each case. Costumes can also support the type of play being produced. Bright colors, for example, work better for comedy while somber tones are best for melodramas. It is possible to present a play on a bare stage and still re-create a period and style through the costumes. In fact, many of the Shakespeare festivals around the world present the plays on simple unit sets and let the costumes tell the audience all they need to know about time, place, and character.

THE COSTUME DESIGNER'S PROCESS

The steps that a costume designer goes through for a theatre production parallel those of the scenic designer. Meetings with the director will determine the concept for the production and the directorial style to be used. With that information the costume designer can begin to research the period of the play, even if a historically accurate approach is not taken. Whereas the scenic designer studies architecture, decoration, and furniture of the period, the costume designer concentrates on the era's clothes, using paintings, sketches, and photographs of the time. One must understand what the fashion of the time was even if that fashion is going to be satirized or presented expressionistically onstage. Costume designers must pay particular attention to the details of fashion: hats, handbags, gloves, parasols, walking sticks, handkerchiefs, and other accessories. Not only will these bring life to the designs, but they are also useful in developing the character through such details. Also, like all designers in theatre, one must consider the budget and determine what is possible with the money available for costumes.

With sufficient research, the costume designer then draws a series of sketches showing each character in costume and, if needed, the different costumes that one character might wear throughout the play. The designer makes a chart called a *costume plot*, which shows which characters are in which scenes and when costume changes are required. Such a chart is needed for practical reasons but also for aesthetic ones. If Alice is wearing a brown and yellow costume for the first scene in *You Can't Take It with You*, then Essie might be costumed in a contrasting blue. The designer usually goes over the costume plot and the preliminary sketches with the director before making the *costume renderings*. Like scenic renderings, these are in color and include such details as hairstyle and accessories. Often the designer will attach one or more sample pieces of fabric to the corner of the rendering to indicate the texture or pattern of the material to be used in making the costume. Not only the director but sometimes the actors are shown these renderings to help them visualize the costumes and aid in developing their characters.

The implementation phase of costume design differs from that of the scenery. Costume designers do not do construction drawings or indicate how a costume is to be made. Instead, experienced craftspersons, called *drapers*, make the costumes. They figure out how to translate a two-dimensional sketch into a three-dimensional costume. Drapers create patterns on paper or directly on a *dress form*, a life-size torso that serves as a kind of giant pincushion. Drapers are highly valued in the theatre because they understand how fabric folds, falls, and drapes and they know the best way to sew material so that it looks like the rendering. The patterns are then turned over to a cutter or assistant, called *first hand*, who cuts a mock-up of the costume on inexpensive fabric to get the fit and proportion correct before using the final fabrics. Costumes are often built right on the dress form until it is complete enough for a fitting. The designer is usually present when the actor tries on the incomplete costume at a fitting, making notes on what changes or adjustments must be made. Sleeves, collars, hems, or other parts of the costume may not be finished at the first fitting, but it is an essential step in making a theatre costume. Since each costume is tailor-made for a particular actor, more than one fitting may be required. By the time the actor wears the costume at the first dress rehearsal, he or she is usually very familiar with it and can start to get comfortable wearing the costume.

At the first dress rehearsal, some directors hold a *dress parade*. This is a chance for each actor to wear each costume onstage under the lights while the director and costume designer make notes about possible changes or adjustments. It is not

COSTUME RENDERING Christopher Hampton's 1985 stage adaptation of Choderlos de Lacois's French novel *Les Liaisons Dangereuses* requires the costume designer to re-create the apparel of the aristocratic class of the late eighteenth century. Designer Elaina Wahl-Temple's costume renderings for the two major characters contain pieces of fabric that indicate not only color and pattern, but also the texture of the material to be used. The same two costumes are seen worn by Justin Register and Dani Fattizzi in the production by Flagler College. Director: Andrea McCook. *Nikki Falaco*

a parade as such, but the entrance of a line of actors in costume might suggest a parade of sorts. The designer will also watch the dress rehearsals and note costume problems that arise when the actors move about in the clothes or when they have a quick change offstage. Like scenic designers, costume designers are finished with their work by opening night. Costumes require much more maintenance and repair during the run of the play than does scenery, but this is taken care of by a wardrobe master or mistress, who keeps the costumes clean, pressed, and in good repair. Sometimes duplicate versions of the same costume (but in a different size) are made for understudies or standbys, and costumes that receive a lot of wear and tear during a performance might have to be totally remade. When a production closes, the costumes usually go into storage to be used again or altered for a future production in the same period. Costumes from Broadway shows are usually sold or donated to costume companies who rent them out to schools and other theatre groups. The life of a costume may be limited, but it is sometimes surprising how many productions it may be used in before it is reduced to rags and remnants.

Quick Changes

Audiences are often amazed at how quickly actors can change costumes, particularly in a musical that requires the main characters to be in different clothes for each scene. Quick changes in the theatre is an old art form and one that has not changed very much over the years. An actor who has a quick change will usually be assigned two or three dressers who assist in the rapid transition from one costume into another. Dressers assist in undressing and redressing the actor, having different parts of the costume ready in a methodical manner so that the change uses the few moments available efficiently. Sometimes the actor wears one costume over another, and the dressers help in removing the outer layer of clothes. Quick changes must be meticulously rehearsed before the dress rehearsal in order to work. Once the best sequence is determined and both actor and dressers know what they must do, the rapid change is possible.

Quick changes are also accomplished by constructing the costumes with quick changes in mind. Clothes that open from the back; shirts, vests, and jackets that are sewn together; period costumes that have rows of buttons hiding a modern zipper; and other costuming tricks are developed to make the change easier. For many years the most useful invention to help quick changes was Velcro, the sticky material that can be used to fasten everything from fabric and collars to shoes. But Velcro is noisy and sometimes not very precise. More recently designers have started using magnets as a reliable fastener. Small magnets or magnetic tape is sewn into the costume and are very effective in fastening and unfastening. Using such tricks and employing dressers can make a complicated costume change take half a minute while it would take an individual several minutes to do it unassisted.

LIGHTING DESIGN

Few people in theatre work harder and get less recognition than do lighting designers. The better they do their job, the less the audience notices it. Unlike costumes and scenery, lighting is not visual in the same way. One does not see light, only what is lit. Since everyone has lighting in their home or school or office, they take lights for granted. Yet stage lighting is deceptively difficult to achieve, and what it can do to enhance a theatre production is not generally understood. While the scenic and costume designers can provide drawings and other concrete evidence of what their work will look like, the lighting designer cannot show to others (or even see for himself or herself) what the finished product will be like until the technical rehearsals. The lighting designer plans, plots, and charts how the lighting will be achieved for a particular production, but it is only numbers and circles on a page. Yet the best lighting designers can see the final results in their heads, from the way different colors will combine to achieve a desired effect to the manner in which shadows and angles will create different moods. Lighting designers are painters whose paint is colored light in space.

A BRIEF HISTORY OF THEATRE LIGHTING

Since stage lighting was not necessary until theatre moved indoors, it is one of the newer elements of theatre production. Plays presented outdoors made no effort to denote time of day visually; instead, the dialogue in the play told the spectators that it was a dark, moonless night or that the hot sun was beating down. Recall the scene in *Macbeth* when the three murderers wait in the darkness for Banquo and his son Fleance. When the play was presented at the Globe Theatre, everyone, actors and audience, was highly visible in the midafternoon sun; theatregoers just accepted the convention and pretended that it was dark. When theatre was first presented indoors, the convention continued. Both the stage and the house were lit with candles or oil lamps during the entire performance, and one still pretended that there was darkness or moonlight or other lighting effects. Later some pioneering theatre companies experimented with silhouettes and lighting only the stage, leaving the spectators in partial darkness. It was not until the introduction of gas lighting in the nineteenth century that stage lighting as we know it today began. Since one could control the intensity of a gas lamp by regulating the flow of gas, designers were able to create certain effects for the first time. A sunset or the evening sky could be suggested by dimming the lights somewhat, making sure that the audience could still see the actors and the necessary action. It was even learned that a gas lamp on low gave off a yellowish tint while one at a high intensity was closer to blue. Yet gas lighting had its limitations, and it was extremely dangerous; many theatres in the eighteenth and nineteenth centuries burned down due to the fickle nature of the early gas lights.

The invention of electricity in the late 1800s solved the problems of safety and flexibility. Ironically, the public feared electricity because they did not understand how it worked. Theatre owners were hesitant to install electric lights at first, afraid that it would hurt business. But after a while the public's prejudice against electric light faded, and playhouses were wired for electricity; it is still the method used in theatres today. Electricity could be controlled even more than gas, and the levels of intensity were much broader. It was then possible to have dozens of lights at various levels working together to create a variety of effects. About the same time electricity was developed, designers came up with ways to control the direction of light and how to add color to light. These early lighting instruments, which allowed one to focus the light on a small area and not let it spill all over the house, were a major breakthrough for stage lighting. In fact, the current high-tech lighting instruments used today are not that far removed from these primitive but effective devices.

THE FUNCTION AND ELEMENTS OF THEATRE LIGHTING

While stage lighting can indicate time of day, create mood, and offer special effects such as moonlight and lightning, its main function is to provide focus by lighting who or what should be seen by the audience at a particular point in the performance. If theatregoers cannot clearly see the actor or the object that they must see, all of the others qualities of lighting are useless. Throwing light on something may seem like a simple task, but theatre lighting does not simply illuminate a space as in a home or public place. It may take anywhere from a dozen to one hundred lighting instruments to light one portion of the stage, and the light from all those instruments must blend together so that an actor walking across the set will not move in and out of shadow. A bare lightbulb throws light in all directions equally; a theatre light goes in one direction. Lighting a large space onstage is like using hundreds of pieces of tile to cover a floor, except not all of the floor should be tiled at all times and each tile must be able to change colors at different times. Stage lighting is an intricate puzzle, and when it is done well, it looks easy.

The best way to light an actor onstage is from a lighting instrument that is 45 degrees to the side and 45 degrees higher than the person. One instrument will cast a shadow on the side of the actor not lit, so a second light is added from 45 degrees from the other direction. Now the actor is sufficiently lit . . . until he or she moves. Walking five feet to the left, the actor must now be covered by at least two more instruments, each at 45 degrees. When you consider all of the places on the set that the actor can go, you begin to see why so many instruments are needed. Then you must double that number if one scene is during the day and requires bright, sunny light and another scene is at night and calls for moonlight. It sounds like an endless task just to illuminate one actor, but you must remember that all those instruments give a designer the opportunity to light only the section of the stage that is needed and to paint with light, bringing in different colors at different intensities to create the mood that the play requires in each scene.

LIGHTING DESIGN Because *The Lion King* (1997) is set in Africa, the color palette for the costumes and, particularly, the lighting is richer and more vibrant than in most musicals. Donald Holder's lighting also makes use of shadows, silhouettes, and contrasting lights and darks, as demonstrated in the opening sequence. Director and costume designer: Julie Taymor. *Joan Marcus/Photofest © Walt Disney Productions*

Intensity

Let us consider the three basic elements of stage lighting: intensity, distribution, and color. The amount of electricity that is sent to a theatre lamp will determine the intensity of the light it produces. Electricity is controlled by a dimmer board, a more complicated version of the simple light dimmer that one might have at home to dim a dining room chandelier. Each circuit leaving the dimmer board will go to two or more instruments. If that circuit is brought up to level 10, the lights connected to it are shining at their brightest. At level 5 they shine only half as bright, and at level 2 they will only cast a glow on the stage. Before dimmer boards were computerized in the 1970s, all of these circuits were operated manually. Today the computer can control hundreds of lighting instruments and keep in its memory the levels needed for hundreds of lighting cues. As helpful as this is, the computer cannot determine the effect that is achieved by combining different levels of intensity. The experienced lighting designer knows, for example, that ten instruments on level 10 do not cast the same kind of light as twenty instruments on level 5. Stage lighting is scientific in that one must understand wattage and how electric power is distributed, but it is not scientific in that the results cannot always be calculated. Only by experiment and experience do lighting designers learn how to use light creatively.

Distribution

Where one hangs a lighting instrument and at what angle its beam of light hits the stage determines the distribution of light. Distribution is as delicate a matter as intensity. Light coming from directly over an actor, called *downlighting*, will cast long shadows on the face and make the character look sinister. Lighting that hits an actor's face head-on will give the character a flat, featureless appearance. Light that comes from behind a person, called *backlighting*, gives the actor strong definition and, consequently, strength. How a designer chooses to distribute the available light will greatly affect the nature of the lighting. Consider the complex lighting needed for *Hamilton*, where certain areas of the stage must be visible while others are not; with no walls with doors or windows, the lighting in the musical becomes the scenery.

Even in the most technically equipped theatres, there are limits to the number of places to hang lights. Most lighting positions are in the house with the instruments fastened to pipes in the ceiling, on the side walls, or in front of the balcony ledge. Then there are a limited number of positions backstage, either overhead or from the sides. It may not be possible to hit every inch of the stage with the ideal 45-degree angle, especially when one adds scenery that may obstruct the path of light. How lighting instruments are distributed throughout the theatre is a practical problem for the designer, but the effect of all these different lighting positions also means that the combinations are numerous, and sometimes being forced to hang a light at an awkward angle can provide interesting results.

Color

The most noticeable element of stage lighting is color. In everyday life we expect lamps, chandeliers, and overhead lights to be a soft white. In theatre, white light is rarely used, because it is too harsh and it washes out an actor's facial features. Theatre instruments use *gels* to create color. A gel is a sheet of plastic or glass that is tinted with a particular color. It is placed in a slot in the front of a lighting instrument so that the light passing from the lamp is a particular color. Gels come in dozens of different colors, just as a painter's palate can mix together all kinds of paint colors.

Yet the colored light from a theatre instrument is affected by other lights with other colors and by the colors of the sets and costumes being lit. Lighting designers do not choose the gel colors for their design until they have seen the set and costume designs because some colors change their quality depending on the object of their focus. White costumes are particularly a problem since they tend to reflect the color that shines on them so that a white dress can become pink or yellow. A box set that includes a busy wallpaper pattern on the walls will become too distracting under certain colors of light. Like a painter, lighting designers divide the color palette into warm and cool colors. Generally, warm colors work best for comedies while cool colors add texture to melodramas. Color is also used to denote time of day, with a more yellowish tint for mornings, a deeper orange for sunset, and a blue-green for evening. Color is very psychological, and how it is used in the lighting design for a production is essential in creating mood.

THE LIGHTING DESIGNER'S PROCESS

Although the lighting designer meets with the director early in the production process, there is little he or she can do until there are scenic designs to look at and study. Lighting does not require the same kinds of research as scenery and costumes do, but there is still plenty of preparation, including reading the script carefully for details such as time of day and season of the year, weather conditions, and mood. The designer will examine the ground plan and decide the best way to divide the stage into lighting areas. Then he or she will watch rehearsals to see how the stage is being used by the actors. When the designer can begin to mentally picture the production, it is time to create a *light plot*. This is a complicated diagram of the theatre showing each instrument and what type, color, and wattage are to be used; where each light will be hung; and to what area onstage it will be focused on. As the time for technical rehearsals approaches and there is enough scenery on the stage to light, the designer, the master electrician, and the lighting crew will hang, wire (called *cabling*), and focus all the lighting instruments.

After the color gels are inserted, the designer can write the *light cues*, indicating which lights at what intensity will be used at each specific moment of the production. It is only while writing and watching the cues performed that the designer finally sees exactly what the lighting design will look like. During the final rehearsals, the addition of costumes may require altering some cues, and there will be fine-tuning throughout the preview performances as well. Because the entire lighting design is in the memory bank of the computer, the designer can be reasonably confident that the lighting for the play will be consistent at each performance, provided that the stage manager and the dimmer board operator cue the computer correctly. Yet, despite all this work, most audience members and even many actors will not notice the lighting unless there are some special lighting effects or if something goes wrong and someone or something is left in the dark. The very best stage lighting is so unobtrusive that everyone takes it for granted.

Even more than scenic and costume design, the technology for stage lighting has changed rapidly over the past forty years. The introduction of computer lighting boards and new kinds of lighting instruments have made the job of lighting designer more complicated than ever before. The ephemeral and even mysterious art of theatre lighting has been made more intricate and the job of the lighting designer more high tech. Some of these technological changes will be discussed later in the chapter.

LIGHTING EFFECTS J. B. Priestley's 1947 drawing room melodrama *An Inspector Calls* was turned into a surreal nightmare by British director Stephen Daldry at London's Royal National Theatre and for the 1994 Broadway revival. His concept was visualized by Ian MacNeil's expressionistic scenery and Rick Fisher's dreamlike lighting design. *Joan Marcus/Photofest; photographer: Joan Marcus*

SOUND DESIGN

It may seem that actors speaking loudly enough onstage to be heard is all the sound that a theatre event requires, but most productions today involve sound design in some manner or form. Sound designers are needed for a variety of tasks, from amplifying the actors' singing voices over an orchestra to creating the clamor of a thunderstorm. Musical instruments, gunshots offstage, the patter of rain, the noise of an approaching crowd are examples of basic sound effects, all of which were done manually before the invention of recorded sound. Today's sound design can be quite sophisticated, even altering the voices of the actors with, for example, an echo effect. Every playhouse is filled with a variety of sounds during a performance, and we can categorize them into three types.

Acoustics

The way that sound travels over space and within a confined space has fascinated scientists for centuries. The study of sound movement within a theatre or concert hall is called *acoustics*. Although there are many principles and theories about acoustics, it is not a very exact science, and no one knows for sure if the acoustics in a playhouse filled with spectators will be acceptable until the first public performance. Sound is affected by everything from the shape of the ceiling to the type of building materials used on the walls to the fabrics on the seats. Since ancient times theatres have been built in certain ways to help the flow of sound from the stage to the audience. The ancient Greeks and Romans placed their outdoor theatres on the side of a hill or at a specific angle so that the actors' voices would carry; most of these surviving theatres still have remarkable acoustics. Theatre builders later learned that adding draperies and ornamental accessories to the interior of the playhouse would help avoid an echoing effect. Today architects make all kinds of provisions to ensure the acoustical quality of the space. Still, there are many examples of multimillion-dollar theatres that were built, only to be discovered later that they had dreadful acoustics; additional money had to be spent to add acoustical tiles or rebuild sections of the interior.

Amplification

Although it was unheard of until the 1960s, sound amplification in live theatre has become very common today. Any time that the sound of an actor or orchestra is reinforced through a microphone, it is said to be *amplified*. Loudspeaker systems for public gatherings have existed for nearly one hundred years, but the consensus was that actors performing in an acoustically efficient playhouse did not need such amplification. Even musicals with actors singing over large orchestras in the pit caused few problems, and audiences heard everything clearly. But some actors (often movie stars who had never needed to project their voices) in the 1960s were "mic'd" unobtrusively, and the sounds carried better. By the end of that same decade, rock music was introduced to the Broadway musical, and it became necessary to mic performers if they hoped to be heard over electronic musical instruments. Soon designers developed *body mics*, small microphones hidden in the actor's costume or hair, which broadcast sound waves to a receiver at the back of the house. One was now able to control the level of the actor's voice just as one was controlling the intensity of lights. Orchestras, now mostly hidden under the stage, also needed to be amplified. It seems that the meaning of "live" theatre has changed. While many lament the arrival of amplification in the theatre, there are definitely some advantages to it. Every seat in the house now hears the dialogue and music equally well, and the distance that one is from the stage is more a visual factor than an aural one. Yet it has been argued that what everyone is hearing is not the human voice but an electronically re-created human voice, as one would get from listening to a CD, film, or television program. Today, for all Broadway musical productions, including *Hamilton*, the cast wears headpiece microphones. The debate about theatre amplification will continue, but it seems that amplification, at least for musicals, is here to stay. Most theatre artists and theatregoers will agree, however, that one need not and should not amplify actors in a nonmusical production, although it has been done on occasion.

Sound Effects

Whether it is created manually or electronically, the use of sounds not coming from the actors is considered a sound effect. It can be as simple as a telephone ringing, a clap of thunder, background music, or a montage of voices and noise used in an expressionistic nightmare scene. Before the development of recorded sound, theatre special-effects workers had to be very clever in re-creating particular noises backstage. A barrel of nails turning sounded like rain; paper being crumpled up suggested a crackling fire; and thunder was achieved by shaking a long thin sheet of galvanized iron. Today thousands of special effects are available, and through a computer the sounds can be run directly into the theatre's speaker system. Yet many sound effects are still done "live," and not recorded, because they can be more accurately placed and seem more spontaneous. Slamming doors, gunshots, doorbell chimes, and other effects are often done manually, even in theatres with the most sophisticated sound systems. Consider the sound effects in *You Can't Take It with You*, such as the fireworks going off in the basement and the gunshots of the FBI agents. And imagine how the sounds of battle or the eerie chanting behind the witches' scenes can heighten the drama in *Macbeth*. The sound design for a production can sometimes be very complex, with hundreds of special-effects cues or sounds that overlap, such as the roar of waves heard throughout a scene with seagull cries added at specific points. Sometimes an entire music score is composed and recorded for a theatre production, much like a music soundtrack for a film. The use of sound in the theatre is so effective that few productions will forgo the opportunity of creating mood and colorful details that come with expert sound design.

THEATRE PROPERTIES

A theatre property (usually abbreviated to the word *prop*) is any object on the stage that is not scenery, be it as small as a handgun or pencil or as substantial as a bicycle or sofa. Props are an extension of the set, and often scenic designers will also design the props for the production. During the run of a play, all of these props are cataloged and organized by the props master or mistress. Tables are set up backstage on both sides of the stage where the props are waiting for the actor to pick up before entering a scene or to deposit after exiting one. Like lighting, props are rarely noticed by audiences unless they are very unusual or they are missing and the mistake is obvious. Some productions may have hundreds of props, while another might do with a sword and a chair. In either case, stage properties are not to be casually dismissed. They provide the necessary details that add so much to a production.

Theatre properties can be roughly divided into two categories: *set props* and *hand props*. Any prop that is attached or considered dressing for the scenery is called a set prop. Most furniture would come under this type, as well as framed pictures hanging on the walls, a telephone sitting on a table, or a trash can in the park. Sometimes there is a fine line between the set and a set prop. A log lying on the ground in a forest might be considered part of the scenery, yet if it is moved and two actors sit on it, it might be classified a set prop. The kitchen table in *A Raisin in the Sun* and Grandpa's favorite easy chair in *You Can't Take It with You* are set props, as would be Macbeth's throne. The other kind of property is a hand prop, and, as suggested by its name, it is small and mobile enough that it can be handled by an actor. The insurance check in *A Raisin in the Sun*, Essie's candies, the bloody daggers that Lady Macbeth takes from her husband, and other handheld objects are good examples. Sometimes part of a costume can become a hand prop. A character might drop a glove on the floor; another takes it and hides it in her pocket to show it later to her husband. The glove is now more than a costume accessory; it is a hand prop that is important to the action of the play. Generally, hand props are kept on the properties tables backstage, while the set props remain onstage, though there are many exceptions (particularly in multiset productions). The distinction between a set prop and a hand prop is used for organizational purposes; the importance of theatre properties lies in the way that they support the plot and the characters in a play.

MAKEUP IN THE THEATRE

If properties are an extension of scenery, then stage makeup is related to costumes. Sometimes costume designers suggest the hair and makeup style to be used for each character, but it is usually the makeup artist who does the actual work. People have been highlighting and accentuating the human face with makeup since the ancient Egyptians, long before it was used in the theatre. Once masks were abandoned, actors started to apply makeup to exaggerate their facial features and indicate character types by the choice of color and accent markings. In Asian theatre, makeup is an elaborate art form in which the face becomes a canvas for intricate designs that both beautify and stylize the actor. When theatre moved indoors and artificial light was used, makeup was needed to highlight features that were not as visible as they were in sunlight, such as eyes and mouths. The invention of stronger but harsher electric light caused a problem when the actors' faces appeared to be pale and washed out, so color was added to the makeup to restore normal skin tones. The materials used in stage makeup have also changed over the years. Performers have used everything from primitive stains to powders to oil-base pigments to today's more efficient pancake makeup.

Makeup in the theatre is used for many purposes, but we divide makeup designs into two categories: *straight makeup* and *character makeup*. When actors play characters that are close in age and type to themselves, they apply straight makeup. This kind of makeup does not attempt to change the face in any way but rather helps define its features by highlighting eyes, adding color to cheeks, and providing other everyday cosmetic techniques. The makeup that many people use in everyday life is a mild form of straight makeup, though in theatre it is called *street makeup* to distinguish it from that used onstage. When the makeup artist attempts to change the face in any way, it is called character makeup. Making a young actor seem older, a healthy actor look sickly, or a well-groomed person appear unshaven and slovenly

STAGE MAKEUP Both straight makeup and character makeup are evident in this scene from the popular musical *Wicked* (2003), still running on Broadway. Glinda (Kristin Chenoweth, left) wears straight makeup, which makes no attempt to change her features, while the outcast Elphaba (Idina Menzel) is born with green skin and, consequently, requires character makeup to change the actress's natural skin color. Joseph Dulude II designed the makeup for *Wicked*, which has costume designs by Susan Hilferty and is directed by Joe Mantello. *Photofest*

are examples of character makeup. Such a treatment might be used, for example, on the drunken actress in *You Can't Take It with You* or the wounded Captain in *Macbeth*. In the popular Broadway musical *Wicked*, the actress playing the witch does not need to look any older than she is, but she does need to have green skin. Character makeup is much more difficult to apply effectively, but there are tricks of the trade that make such changes more feasible in a large theatre than in a film or on television. Many people can recall seeing special-effects makeup, such as the disfigured face of the phantom in various versions of *The Phantom of the Opera* or the horrid features on characters in science fiction movies. While these images are memorable and certainly take great artistry to achieve, most stage makeup is more subtle and character based.

Related to makeup but usually done by other artists is hair design. Period plays require period hairstyles, some of which are very difficult to re-create. Even contemporary plays might call for a particular color or style of hair that is very different from the performer's own. Hairstylists in theatre might use the actress's existing hair and copy styles that have been researched beforehand. Other times it is more efficient to purchase wigs or hairpieces and style them on head forms. Wigs are not limited to women, though, and during certain historical periods upper-class males also wore them. Whether a hair design is fashioned from the person's own hair or from wigs or hairpieces, the same criteria as costuming apply: it must reflect the character being portrayed. The way that Lady Macbeth wears her hair might be very different from the style that Lady Macduff uses, just as Ruth Younger might straighten her hair while the younger Beneatha would sport an early form of "Afro" hairstyle. Also like makeup, hair design can sometimes be very memorable in an obvious way, such as the exaggerated 1960s hairdos of some of the characters in the musical *Hairspray*. Both makeup and hair design should help the audience understand the character; otherwise, each is just surface dressing.

Tech Theatre Terms

apron—the part of the stage in front of the proscenium that projects out into the audience. Also called the *forestage*, it is the best place for an actor to be seen and heard.

body mic—a small microphone that an actor wears in the hair or on the costume.

border—a flat piece of material or scenery that hangs horizontally above the stage to hide lighting instruments. In the past, a series of borders in a proscenium theatre were sometimes painted to look like tree branches or clouds; combined with wings, it gave the illusion of a forest or sky.

counterweight—a heavy iron bar that hangs from a pulley and is used to help raise and lower scenery. The weight is balanced with the drop or scenic piece being lifted so that it moves up and down easily. Counterweights used to be sandbags until iron was found to be more efficient.

cyclorama—a large piece of fabric stretched by pipes at the top and the bottom that is used behind scenery. Familiarly called a cyc, it serves as a screen of sorts for projections, sunsets, lightning, and other special lighting effects.

fly loft—the area above the stage into which drops and other scenery are "flown up" when not needed.

gobo—a piece of tin or other material that has designs cut into it and that is placed in front of a lighting instrument to create a pattern of light onstage. There are hundreds of gobo effects, but perhaps the most common is a leafy pattern that makes the stage look as if the sun is shining through the leaves of a tree.

greasepaint—an oily cream form of stage makeup that comes in a variety of colors and is still used on occasion. Its name is also a synonym for the theatre profession, as in "the world of greasepaint."

limelight—an early form of stage lighting in which the combustion of oxygen and hydrogen over a surface of lime created a bright light. The expression "to be in the limelight" survives, meaning to be the center of attention.

periaktoi—a three-sided piece of scenery with a different scene or design painted on each side. By turning a series of periaktois, the designer can quickly change the look onstage. The device goes back to the ancient Greek theatre, hence the archaic foreign name.

scrim—a thin, gauzelike fabric that becomes somewhat transparent when lit from behind. A scene played behind a scrim will seem to disappear into thin air if the lighting behind it fades out.

shotgun mic—a microphone, usually hung from above, that aims itself at the stage to capture sound and project it through the speakers. This kind of mic works best for the singing chorus and the pit orchestra. Individual actors usually have *body mics*.

swatch—a small piece of fabric, usually no longer than an inch or two, that the costume designer attaches to a rendering to show the texture, color, and pattern of the material to be used in the construction of the costume.

trap—a theatrical term for a trap door in the stage floor for the raising and lowering of actors or scenery. In Shakespeare's day, for example, ghosts would enter through a trap in the floor of the Globe Theatre.

turntable—another term for a revolving platform. It may cover part or all of a stage and can be used for scene changes or dramatic effects, such as seen in the popular musicals *Les Miserables* and *The Lion King*.

wiggle lights—a slang term for the flexible automatic light instrument because the instrument seems to wiggle itself into position when it changes direction.

wings—flats or curtains that hang down on either side of the stage to conceal the offstage space from the audience. Generally, actors enter the stage "through the wings." The term has come to mean the entire backstage space; hence, actors are "waiting in the wings."

NEW TECHNOLOGY

Throughout its long history, theatre has used the new technology available, particularly in design. In some cases, theatre artists developed technology that was later used outside of theatre, such as treadmills and electric dimmers. Ironically, when the computer was first developed and started to be used in business and education, theatre was hesitant to embrace it. It was generally thought that a machine that could remember numbers and store information was of little use in theatre production. Long after most companies were using the computer for billing and accounting did Broadway start to utilize it for printing tickets and keeping records. The first computerized dimmer board was not seen on Broadway until 1975, many years after film and television had started to take advantage of computer imaging. It took a while before theatre caught up with other arts and businesses, but today the new technology that is available is readily and eagerly utilized.

No computer can write or direct a play, design a set or a costume, or replace a live actor onstage. Yet computers can certainly assist a playwright, director, designer, and even actors. Word processing alone has aided all kinds of writers, including playwrights, and actors today can download scenes or entire plays and print out speeches especially tailored to their use. A box office or ticket service can sell, print, and account for a theatre ticket in several locations outside the theatre's box office, and websites can allow theatregoers to select seats totally on their own. Yet the area that has most benefited from the new technology of computers is design. Without diminishing the creativity of the designer, computers have removed much of the drudgery of drafting; allowed designers to visually experiment with color, shape, and form without costly construction; and given designers endless visual information and ideas for solutions to tactical problems.

The most frequently used technologies in theatre design are computer-aided design (CAD) and computer-aided manufacture (CAM) programs, both of which came into wide usage in the 1990s. A scenic designer can use such programs to see what the scenery might look like from different angles, creating a virtual reality tour of one's own work. The painstaking labor of checking sight lines and creating dozens of construction drawings is also simplified, and designs can easily be altered without going back to square one. Costume designers can view clothes from different periods and download sleeves or collars and apply them to original designs to consider different options. Lighting designers have perhaps benefited the most from such technology, not only in facilitating the tedious task of making charts, amperage distribution, and lighting plots, but also in experimenting with color and determining the shadows created by using different angles. Theatre lighting used to consist of a half dozen basic instruments that came in a few sizes. Today the hardware and software is much more encompassing and the lighting designer has to keep up with the latest developments. The lighting for rock concerts was behind many of these changes and today's theatre lighting has been altered significantly. The use of LED (light-emitting diodes), video and pixel mapping (creating images onstage using small lighting instruments programed like a video screen), and complex laser lights

THE TOTAL LOOK Exaggerated early 1960s hair and makeup styles are an essential part of the musical *Hairspray* (2002). Paul Huntley did the hair and wig design for the original Broadway production, and Randy Houston Mercer did the makeup design, all of which supported William Ivey Long's outrageously funny costumes. Director: Jack O'Brien. *Photofest*

has given some Broadway shows a whole new look. Even the use of projections, which used to look like a static slide show on stage, are being used in new and inventive ways. The projected images now move and can be projected onto all kinds of surfaces on stage. While a production of *You Can't Take It with You* or *A Raisin in the Sun* might not find any use for such lighting effects, productions of *Macbeth* and *Hamilton* certainly can.

One might wonder if such technology has reduced the designer to a doodler who plays on a computer screen until a finished design appears. In fact, the role of the theatre designer has changed little because of computers. The training and creativity needed to design for the stage have not been altered, and only the proficiency of using the computer programs has been added to the required talents. The artist is still an artist; only some of the tools have changed.

THE BUSINESS OF THEATRE DESIGN

The ways that one becomes a professional scenic, lighting, or costume designer differ greatly from the pattern followed by actors, directors, or choreographers. While all of these jobs require training and talent, the designer must follow a specific path of study to hope to compete in the professional field. Scenic designers usually attend an art school or a college with an art program. They then sharpen their skills by studying at a university graduate school that specializes in scenic design. By graduation, he or she has not only designed many sets but has seen some of those designs realized in an actual production. All of these works are put into a portfolio, a collection of designs used when being interviewed for a job. Many would-be designers next work as an assistant to a practicing designer, getting more experience and making contacts in the business. Fledgling designers also work for small or low-budget theatres, sometimes without pay, just to build up their portfolios and to allow others to see their work. Most scenic designers work for a flat fee, but if the production is on Broadway and the designer has earned some name recognition, he or she might also get a small percentage of the box office income. All the same, few set designers are wealthy, and most have to be working on three or four projects at once in order to earn a steady income.

Costume designers often come from art schools or fashion design schools, and many attend university programs in stage costuming in order to get further training and to build an impressive portfolio. Not all theatres can afford to design and build new costumes for each production, so they hire costumers, people who "pull" and alter existing costumes or rent costumes from other theatres or professional rental companies. While this kind of work allows for little original design, fledgling costume designers can learn a great deal about the business from these jobs and, again, make valuable contacts. Often a production that is pulled or rented may require an original costume or two, and the costumer will not only design it but "build" it as well. Most costume designers must be adept at sewing and tailoring because many of the jobs that lead one to a design position require such skills. Even the top Broadway costume designers know all about costume construction, even though they may have drapers and others who actually make the costumes.

Lighting designers rarely come from art schools; instead, they receive their training at colleges and universities where there are specific degree programs in stage lighting. Although they might develop a portfolio filled with charts and photos of productions designed, a lighting designer can only demonstrate his or her true talent in an actual production. Like scenic designers, would-be lighting designers often work as assistants or take jobs in out-of-the-way venues, hoping that their work will be seen and contacts will be made. Of the three kinds of design, lighting is perhaps the most difficult business to break into. Also, only one of each kind of designer is needed for each production, so design positions are more scarce than, for example, acting jobs.

Scenic, lighting, and costume designers belong to the same trade union, United Scenic Artists (USA). Unlike Actors' Equity, in which a professional job immediately allows you to enter the union, designers must take a lengthy and rigorous test in order to be admitted. (Only in a few cases are designers requested by a producer and admitted without taking this examination.) Once one becomes a member, jobs are not guaranteed; but the union is not as unwieldy as Equity, and members, in a way, have proven their knowledge and craft just by passing the test, so the union card is respected by most theatres. Like directors and actors, professional designers must be willing to travel to where the work is. A New York–based designer hired to design a production in Denver will have to travel to that city for preliminary meetings with the director, return a month later to show designs, return again a few months later to check on the progress of the construction or light hanging and to observe some rehearsals, and then travel one last time for the technical rehearsals and preview performances. The theatre company will pick up some of these travel expenses, but the time and money spent on the job is significant. As stated earlier, there are few wealthy designers.

EVALUATING THEATRE DESIGN

Because they are visual, any theatregoer can form an opinion about the scenery, properties, lighting, costumes, makeup, and hair in a production. Anyone can say that the setting was impressive or the costumes were pretty or the makeup was scary. But evaluating theatre design should go beyond an instinctual reaction to what is pleasing to the eye or the emotion. The scenery for *Macbeth* might be dark, mysterious, and far from attractive, while the lighting for *You Can't Take It with You* may be so quietly subtle than no one notices it. Some judge costumes by their attractiveness, so none of the clothes worn by the cast of *A Raisin in the Sun* would be appealing. On the other hand, a theatregoer might like the costumes in *You Can't Take It with You* because of a nostalgic interest in 1930s fashion. Since everyone has a personal reaction to things like places, clothes, and hair, there is always the danger that one cannot separate preference in fashion from the creative product by a designer.

It helps to know something about these areas of design in order to make an intelligent judgment about them. Having learned a little about scenery, costumes, and lighting, you are already in a position to offer a more valid opinion than that of the average spectator. More important, a theatregoer can use certain criteria when looking at theatre design and make an even better judgment. When looking at scenery, for example, consider the functions of scenic design and ask questions about how well the sets fulfilled those functions. Did the scenery tell you what you needed to know about the location and the environment of the play? Was the design approached realistically or not, and how well did it succeed? Did the set create a mood or give one an idea of the tone of the production? Was it a practical playing space for actors, or did it seem too crowded, too awkward, or too inefficient? Did the furniture and other props accentuate the scenery, or did they seem out of place or inconsistent with the scenic design?

When considering the lighting design of a production, first ask if the light was sufficient. Were you able to see what you were supposed to see? Did you find an unevenness in the lighting, such as actors moving in and out of bright light, that was distracting? Was the lighting purposely unobtrusive, or did it demand attention? Did the special lighting effects add to the atmosphere, or were they glaring and awkwardly noticeable? Did the colors create the appropriate tone for a comedy, melodrama, or whatever type of play was being performed? There are two primary questions regarding costume design: Did the costume reveal the character's personality? Did the costumes help denote the period of the play? The same questions can be asked about the makeup and hair as well. Finally, one can evaluate the sound in a production by questioning the clarity of the acoustics in the theatre, the reinforcement of the actors using mics, and the use of created sounds, such as music and sound effects. Unlike staring at a painting in a museum and deciding whether one likes it or not, theatre design must serve several purposes, and it is possible to judge it in terms of those purposes.

TOPICS FOR GROUP DISCUSSION

1. Discuss which of the four sample plays might require the most complicated technical and dress rehearsals and why.
2. Describe the kind of costumes the three female characters in *A Raisin in the Sun* might wear.
3. Discuss which actors in a production of *Macbeth* would require character makeup as opposed to straight makeup.

POSSIBLE RESEARCH PROJECTS

1. Go through the script of *A Raisin in the Sun* and create a complete list of hand props needed for a production of the drama.
2. Research the hairstyles of women in the 1930s and select styles that would be appropriate for four of the female characters in *You Can't Take It with You.*
3. Make a list of the various kinds of sound effects necessary for a production of *Macbeth.*
4. Look up on the internet one of the major theatrical lighting companies, such as Stage Lighting Store or Kinetic Lighting, and report on the various kinds of lighting instruments that you find.

FURTHER READING

Abulafia, Yaron. *The Art of Light on Stage: Lighting in Contemporary Theatre.* Abingdon-on-Thames, UK: Routledge, 2015.
Anderson, Barbara, and Cletus Anderson. *Costume Design.* New York: Holt, Rinehart and Winston, 1998.
Bergman, Gosta M. *Lighting in the Theatre.* Totowa, NJ: Rowman & Littlefield, 1977.
Collison, David. *The Sound of Theatre.* New York: Drama Book Specialists, 2008.
Corson, Richard, and James Glavan. *Stage Makeup.* Englewood Cliffs, NJ: Prentice Hall, 2009.
Davis, Gretchen, and Mindy Hall. *The Makeup Artist Handbook.* New York: Focal Press, 2012.

Delamar, Penny. *The Complete Makeup Artist.* Evanston, IL: Northwestern University Press, 2002.
Emery, Joseph S. *Stage Costume Technique.* Englewood Cliffs, NJ: Prentice Hall, 1981.
Fraser, Neil, and Richard Attenborough. *Stage Lighting Design.* Marlborough, UK: Crowood Press, 2018.
Gillette, J. Michael. *Designing with Light.* New York: McGraw-Hill, 2002.
———. *Theatrical Design and Production.* New York: McGraw-Hill, 2012.
Hart, Eric. *The Prop Building Handbook.* New York: Focal Press, 2013.
Ingham, Rosemary, and Liz Covey. *Costume Designer's Handbook.* Portsmouth, NH: Heinemann, 1992.
James, Thurston. *The Theatre Props Handbook.* Studio City, CA: Players, 2000.
Kaye, Deena, and James LeBrecht. *Sound and Music for the Theatre.* New York: Focal Press, 2015.
Leonard, John A. *Theatre Sound.* New York: Routledge, 2001.
Motley. *Designing and Making Stage Costumes.* London: Studio Vista, 1964.
Palmer, Richard H. *The Lighting Art: The Aesthetics of Stage Lighting Design.* Englewood Cliffs, NJ: Prentice Hall, 1993.
Parker, W. Oren, and R. Craig Wolf. *Scene Design and Stage Lighting.* New York: Holt, Rinehart and Winston, 2008.
Pecktal, Lynn. *Costume Design.* New York: Back Stage Books, 1999.
Pilbrow, Richard. *Stage Lighting Design.* New York: Van Nostrand and Reinhold, 2000.
Reid, Francis. *Discovering Stage Lighting.* New York: Focal Press, 1998.
———. *The Stage Lighting Handbook.* New York: Routledge, 2013.
Rosenthal, Jean, and Lael Wertenbaker. *The Magic of Light.* New York: Theatre Art Books, 1972.
Russell, Douglas A. *Stage Costume Design: Theory, Technique and Style.* Englewood Cliffs, NJ: Prentice Hall, 1985.
Shelley, Steven Louis. *A Practical Guide to Stage Lighting.* New York: Focal Press, 2013.
Strawn, Sandra. *The Properties Director's Handbook.* Abingdon-on-Thames, UK: Routledge, 2012.
Swift, Charles I. *Introduction to Stage Lighting.* Englewood, CO: Pioneer/Meriwether, 2004.
Swinfield, Rosemarie. *Stage Makeup Step-by-Step.* Cincinnati: Betterway Books, 1995.
Thudium, Laura. *Stage Makeup.* New York: Back Stage Books, 1999.
Wilson, Andy. *Making Stage Props: A Practical Guide.* Marlborough, Wiltshire, UK: Crowood Press, 2003.

9

THE PLAYGOERS I: THE AUDIENCE

THEATRE TODAY

In this chapter we will examine who the theatre audience is in America and what kinds of theatre events they are attending. Sometimes people make generalizations about who attends what kind of event. Highbrow urban types go to the opera; lowbrow rural folk like country music concerts; blue-collar workers go to boxing matches; artsy, educated people visit art galleries; and so on. These clichés are often far from the truth, and anyone can find many exceptions to such blatant categorizing of American audiences. So when we try to speculate on who goes to the theatre in this nation, we are faced with the diverse character of America and how impossible it is to generalize about the modern theatregoer. Those who go to see a musical on Broadway are not necessarily the same people who attend a Latinx performance in a community center in Miami. Many spectators at a high school play in a midwestern town, or the audience at a free Shakespeare performance in Central Park, might never see any other kind of theatre production elsewhere. All theatre is not for all people, but for each American there is at least one kind of theatre event that is probably a perfect fit.

THEATRE TODAY Times Square has been the center of Broadway theatregoing since the early years of the twentieth century. Since the early 1970s, the focal point of the "crossroads of the world" for theatre lovers is the TKTS booth, which sells discounted tickets to Broadway shows.
Ann E Parry/Alamy Stock Photo

The only way that we can begin to determine who goes to the theatre in this country is to look at the wide variety of places where theatre is produced. Each location and form of theatre will attract certain kinds of audiences. A successful theatre organization is one that realizes this and does its best to provide theatre events that are appropriate and satisfying to its audience. A film that opens in hundreds of movie houses across the country cannot possibly appeal to everyone, but it makes no distinction. The movie playing in a Wisconsin city is the same one shown in a New Mexico town. Although some films seem to cater to urban audiences and others to rural ones, Hollywood assumes that a movie is national, not regional. Most American plays can be produced anywhere in the fifty states, but the venue might be very different from place to place. *Oklahoma!* produced by a Vermont high school cannot be the same theatre experience as a professional theatre production of the musical in Detroit or as a star-studded revival on Broadway. Each is a different event for a different audience, and it should be that way. All three groups are theatregoers, but it would be difficult to generalize and say what they have in common.

Before looking at the places where theatre happens, let us clarify three distinctions about theatre events today. Every production is either a new work or a *revival*. The first time that an original script is premiered, it is considered new. It used to be that most new American plays and musicals were first presented on Broadway. That is no longer true, and new scripts often come from professional regional theatres. If a new play from a regional theatre goes to New York and is produced, it is still considered new. The same New York production might tour to other cities; it also is considered new. When the play is given a different production at a later date, it is said to be a revival. To "revive" a play may sound like bringing back to life something that was sickly or dead; in reality, most revivals are of plays that are very much alive and probably have been so for quite some time. Productions today of *Macbeth*, *You Can't Take It with You*, and *A Raisin the Sun*, no matter where they are produced, can be labeled revivals. The original production of *Hamilton*, which is still playing on Broadway and touring in cities in the United States and Europe, is considered a new work. But some future day when *Hamilton* is done by colleges and community theatres, it will be considered a revival. Most theatre events today are revivals. This is not necessarily a bad thing. It just means that hundreds of scripts are durable enough to be revived over and over again.

A second distinction: a theatre organization and its productions are either for-profit or nonprofit. Only Broadway and some other New York theatres, most touring companies, and a number of summer and dinner theatres hope to make a profit. On Broadway they rarely break even, but they are still on a for-profit basis. Most theatre in America is nonprofit. The school, community, summer festival, and professional resident theatres are all on a nonprofit basis. They continue to operate only because they are funded by some organization, or they engage in fund-raising to pay all the bills. This explains the vast difference between the price of a Broadway ticket, which must pay all the expenses of the production or it closes, and the cost of admission to these nonprofit theatres. Sometimes a school or community theatre might put on a play as a fund-raiser, and it may indeed turn a profit. But the organization is a funded one, and the theatre productions it sponsors have a nonprofit status.

Finally, all theatres and their productions can be divided into professional and amateur standing. *Professional* means that all the personnel, from the actors to the box office staff, are paid, regardless if the participants belong to one of the theatre unions or not. The word *amateur* may seem to be a derogatory term to some (as in something being "amateurish"), but the word comes from the Latin for *love* and "amateur" actually means someone who does something out of love for it. When the participants in a theatre event are not paid—whether they are students or adults, experienced or newcomers—the production is classified as amateur. It has nothing to do with quality. In fact, there are many cases when an amateur production can rival or even surpass a professional one. Yet the distinction is important in understanding the next section, which looks at places where professional and amateur, for-profit and nonprofit, and new works and revivals are presented.

WHERE THEATRE HAPPENS

At different times in theatre history, the range of theatregoing was very narrow, and there were few choices for the public. Not so today. Never in its long history has there been such a wide selection of theatre events available to theatregoers. Let us look at the variety of venues for producing theatre in America today, from the most expensive and famous to the most everyday and accessible.

Broadway

The expression "Broadway" is a street, a district, a form of theatre, a union classification, and a state of mind. The street runs the length of Manhattan, north and south, and New York playhouses have been clustered close to the thoroughfare since the 1730s. Today the Theatre District is centered near Times Square, with some thirty playhouses on the street itself or on the side streets east and west of Broadway. As a form of theatre, Broadway is a highly polished, highly publicized, professional, for-profit theatre that once meant the finest to be found in America. The various theatre unions classify these playhouses as "Broadway houses," and everyone working in them, from the actors to the ushers, have a "Broadway contract." Finally, the term *Broadway* means glamour and fame to many theatregoers. It is a form of theatre that suggests opulent musicals; glittering stars; and renowned playwrights, directors, and designers. Some of that glamour and fame is an illusion today, but in its glory days, such as the 1920s and the 1950s, Broadway was considered "the Great White Way" (because of all of its outdoor lights) and the highest form of show business in America. (Both *You Can't Take It with You* and *A Raisin in the Sun* premiered on Broadway in that golden age.) This is no longer true, but Broadway is still the goal of many artists working in theatre.

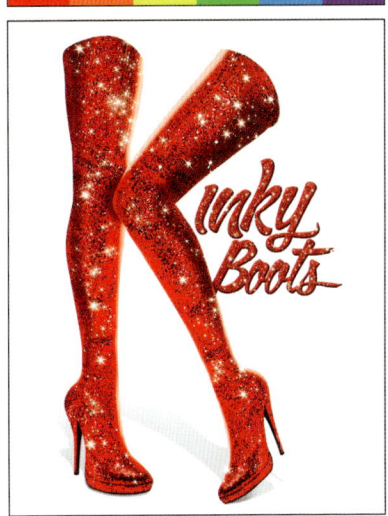

BROADWAY The offerings on Broadway are more diverse today than at any time in the past. A musical like *Kinky Boots*, about a failing boot manufacturing company that finds new life in making footwear for drag queens, would have found a home only Off-Off-Broadway a few decades ago. *Photofest*

Broadway houses tend to be large (from approximately six hundred to two thousand seats) and old (only a half dozen of the current theatres were built after 1929), but most of them are superior playhouses with excellent acoustics and elegant decor. The prices are expensive, and, when the show is very successful, tickets are not easy to get. A play or musical runs on Broadway only as long as it makes money at the box office. We have seen that most productions do not turn a profit, but when one is a major hit, like *Hamilton*, it can run for years and make millions of dollars. Broadway used to be the place to see the newest plays and musicals, but today half of the productions running are usually revivals. It has become too expensive to experiment with untried works, so even the new plays that arrive on Broadway have probably been produced somewhere else first, be it London or in regional theatres. *Hamilton*, as you may recall, was first tried out at Vassar College and then Off Broadway before arriving on Broadway.

Who is the audience at Broadway productions? Nearly half of them are tourists. Broadway is more a tourist attraction today than at any time during its long history. Theatregoing in New York used to be a regular habit for the locals from the New York–New Jersey area, like going to the movies. But as theatre ticket prices rose, going to a Broadway show became a special event, something not done casually or as a matter of habit. For many people, going to a Broadway production is something done on vacation or as a special treat. While Broadway may bring in millions of dollars each year, this is not a healthy sign for the future. A theatre event should be special but not something that is a holiday from real life. It is difficult for serious dramas to compete with spectacular musicals or star vehicles when the theatregoer is only looking for holiday-like entertainment. On the positive side, Broadway offerings are more diverse today than perhaps at any time in its history, so the selection can be quite varied. Rock musicals, family shows, African American works, classic revivals, escapist musicals, one-person plays, and even new works are presented side by side in the Theatre District. Like any good tourist attraction, there seems to be something for everyone—provided one can afford it. Efforts over the past decades to make Broadway more affordable have met with mixed success. Discount coupons are sent to schools; group rates are sometimes available; and, like any business, there are specials and sales on occasion. The most successful project has been the TKTS booth in Times Square, a nonprofit service run by the Theatre Development Fund, which sells discounted tickets for New York theatre productions that are not sold out. But even with such incentives, Broadway remains expensive. It may no longer be the heart of the American theatre, but it remains a shining example of talent, showmanship, and sometimes even art.

The Road

Most Broadway hits, particularly musical successes, will go on tour within a year of opening in New York. These professional, for-profit productions are replicas of the originals on Broadway, though the scenery might be simplified for touring and the cast may not have the same or similarly notable stars. The first tour to go out—called the *national* or *first-class* company—is usually very high quality and accurately brings the Broadway experience to places far from Times Square. National tours play only in major cities, though, and sometimes in houses that are considerably larger than the Broadway playhouse where the show originated. Tickets for these productions tend to be high, and, again, going to see these productions often becomes a special event; but in most places the production is offered as part of a season of events, and prices are reduced somewhat if one buys the whole package (usually five shows). Second-class tours will go to moderate-sized cities, and the third-class tour, called a "bus and truck" tour because of the way the actors and scenery travel, might play in college towns or small cities with a suitable theatre. Regardless of the level, touring companies are for-profit, and if business "on the road" is poor, the tour will be canceled or cut short. All the same, tours are valuable theatregoing experiences, and much of America knows Broadway only from these traveling versions of the Great White Way.

The Tony Awards

You may have heard of the Tony Awards, Broadway's equivalent to Hollywood's Oscars, television's Emmys, and the music industry's Grammys. These prizes are officially named the Antoinette Perry Awards after the director-producer Antoinette "Toni" Perry (1888–1946). They are given each spring by the American Theatre Wing, a nonprofit organization that supports theatre in New York and regionally. The awards were first given in 1947 for "distinguished achievement" in the theatre and over the years have grown to become very celebrated, translating to big money for plays or musicals that win in major categories. Productions, authors, actors, directors, choreographers, and designers are nominated for Tonys, with the winners being announced on a live television broadcast. As prestigious as the Tonys can be, there is a certain amount of politicking involved, and sometimes the awards seem to be more a popularity contest than a true measure of quality. Also, since only productions on Broadway can qualify for the Tonys, the awards hardly represent the full range of theatre in New York, not to mention outside of the city. All the same, there is much glamour and notoriety connected with the Tony Awards, and they do serve as a glitzy advertisement for live theatre.

Off Broadway

In the late 1940s, theatre artists and audiences who felt that Broadway was no longer the place for new and experimental work looked elsewhere in the city, and Off Broadway was born. There had been non-Broadway theatre in New York City as early as the 1910s with some ambitious theatre groups who performed demanding plays in small houses. It was called the "little theatre movement," and it introduced important American playwrights, most notably Eugene O'Neill. The Depression put these nonprofit companies out of business, and it was not until the 1950s that there was a thriving series of theatres not interested in capturing the glamour of the Great White Way. Off Broadway has no specific location like the Broadway Theatre District does, though many of the playhouses are located in the Greenwich Village area in lower Manhattan. These theatres are smaller in size (about 150 to 450 seats), less elegant, and much more intimate than Broadway houses. Some are home to nonprofit theatre companies while others are for-profit; all are professional and can rival Broadway productions in talent and creativity, if not expense. Tickets to Off-Broadway productions are priced lower than the Broadway ones, though they are far from cheap. Actors and other artists working in an Off-Broadway house sign union contracts that pay less than Broadway, and production expenses are lower as well.

The audience for Off Broadway is more varied than the Broadway audience, though many people attend both. Fewer tourists and more local residents patronize Off Broadway. They know that the offerings might be a bit more demanding, but they are usually guaranteed quality professional theatre. Today Off Broadway is highly regarded, and noted playwrights and well-known actors often participate in these playhouses; in fact, some prefer it to Broadway (though the money is never as good) because of the more intimate nature of the venues. Most of the offerings Off Broadway are new works, though revivals are not uncommon. Sometimes an Off-Broadway production will be so well received by the press and the public that it will move to a Broadway house, where new contracts are signed, prices are increased, and everyone enjoys success on a larger scale. Such was the case with

OFF BROADWAY The popular musical *Avenue Q* used both puppets and live actors to portray its wacky yet oddly truthful characters, who, regardless of their construction, had to deal with the modern world. The quirky but touching show was a hit first Off Broadway early in 2003, then transferred to Broadway later that year for a long run, then returned to Off Broadway in 2009. Director: Jason Moore. *Photofest*

Hamilton. Yet many popular Off-Broadway productions were more than happy to stay there and run for years, such as the musicals *The Fantasticks* and *Little Shop of Horrors* and the plays *Steel Magnolias* and *Driving Miss Daisy*.

Off-Off-Broadway

By the 1970s many felt that Off Broadway had gotten too popular and expensive and that it was turning into a small-size version of Broadway with little experimentation and too few daring productions. So a group of very small and very ambitious theatres sprung up around the city, and they were soon dubbed *Off-Off-Broadway*. Many of these theatre companies do not operate out of a formal theatre; instead, they perform in converted storefronts or restaurants, church basements, community centers, or any other "found space." Off-Off-Broadway theatres are even smaller than those of Off Broadway (ranging from fifty to 250 seats); ticket prices are considerably lower; and the personnel earns little or nothing for their services. Several companies are professional, but most sign special, low-paying contracts with the theatre unions in order to keep expenses down. The offerings are mostly new works, and experimentation is the goal of most of the theatre groups. Special interest plays, such as feminist works, Asian American scripts, and others to be discussed later in the chapter, are very common Off-Off-Broadway. The productions can afford to be risky, disturbing, and even offensive; it is part of Off-Off-Broadway's credo and reputation.

Sometimes Off-Off-Broadway is used to test new scripts with the hope that they will move on to other venues. These low-cost productions are called *showcases*

OFF-OFF-BROADWAY The New York Theatre Workshop in the Greenwich Village section of Manhattan strives to find new talent and offer new works. Their most famous production was Jonathan Larson's rock musical *Rent* (1996), about young bohemian artists in the East Village of the 1990s who are dealing with relationships, art, and AIDS. *Rent* soon transferred from Off-Off-Broadway to Broadway, where it ran for twelve years. Director: Michael Greif. *Photofest*

or *workshops* and are valuable testing grounds not only for plays but for undiscovered actors, playwrights, directors, and designers. It is difficult to accurately determine how many Off-Off-Broadway productions are done each year (some estimate over three hundred each season) because most cannot afford traditional advertising costs and thus depend on posters and word of mouth. On the other hand, some Off-Off-Broadway companies have strong reputations and are regularly noticed. The New York Theatre Workshop is one of these, and it was here that the popular musical *Rent* premiered, before the same cast and production were transferred to Broadway.

The audience for Off-Off-Broadway is as diverse as the nature of the movement itself. Spectators of all ethnic, social, and economic types can be found here, though one will see few tourists and not many conservative theatregoers who are most comfortable on Broadway. Economically, Off-Off-Broadway is both affordable and accessible; prices are sometimes as low as a donation at the door, and the performance spaces are close to the neighborhoods where many of the spectators live.

Regional or Resident Theatre

At about the same time that Off Broadway was being developed in New York, the regional or resident theatre movement started. The first two notable regional theatres were the Alley Theatre in Houston and the Arena Stage in Washington, D.C.; by the late 1960s there were over forty such theatres, and they were linked together by an organization called the League of Resident Theatres (familiarly called LORT). The goal of all these LORT theatres is to provide professional, stimulating productions in a local theatre for a local audience. The actors, directors, and designers are often from New York, so the quality at these theatres is often as high as that of Off Broadway or even Broadway. Such theatres are sometimes called *resident companies* since many of them used to hire their actors for the whole season (September to May), allowing audiences to see the same performers in a variety of roles. Because of the expense of keeping a whole company of actors on the payroll for eight months, most LORT theatres have abandoned this policy, but the ambitious ideas behind the regional theatre movement are still alive. Just about every regional theatre is located in a large city (some cities have more than one such theatre) so that there is a population sizable enough to support it. The companies are nonprofit, and tickets, which are more reasonably priced than those of national tours, do not cover all the expenses of the productions, so the theatres depend on fund-raising and grants from business and government.

The typical LORT season consists of five productions, ranging from small musicals to classic revivals to an occasional new work, and each production runs about a month. Regional theatres are ideal testing grounds for new plays because the expense is so much less than in New York. Many original works have transferred from regional theatres to Broadway with success, sometimes taking the same actors, director, and designers with them. Just as with a series of touring shows, audiences can buy a subscription to all five plays in the regional theatre's season; this helps the theatregoers save money and gives the theatre a guaranteed audience for all of its performances. Whether the play is popular or not does not affect the schedule; productions in regional theatre continue their designated run, and a season of varied theatre experiences is guaranteed. Released from many of the risks of for-profit enterprises, LORT theatres can sometimes afford to experiment, offer revivals not

REGIONAL THEATRE One of the nation's oldest and most acclaimed regional theatres is the Arena Stage in Washington, D.C., cofounded in 1950, by director-producer Zelda Fichandler. Shown here is Suzzanne Douglas (center) heading the cast of the 2004 production of the musical *Hallelujah, Baby! Matthew Cavanaugh/New York Times/Redux*

likely to be seen in a commercial playhouse, and keep the variety of American theatre alive. Every regional company has to struggle to stay in operation because money is always short and the cost of maintaining quality productions keeps increasing. A few such theatres have even had to close because they lacked the support to survive. Yet for the most part the regional theatre movement is healthy and doing what it set out to do more than seven decades ago.

The audience for regional theatre is more varied than the Broadway audience. Some theatre companies are justly famous and draw tourists to their productions, but the majority of the spectators are local citizens. Some attend in order to support the culture of the city, while others are looking for quality theatre at a reasonable price. Because LORT theatres offer all kinds of discounts for students, senior citizens, and special interest groups, they are much more accessible than for-profit theatres. Several companies have outreach programs that bring live theatre to schools, senior centers, and even prisons. Also, many of these theatres have grown so that they now occupy an arts center that has two or three performance spaces. This allows for even greater experimentation, trying out new works in the smaller theatre and presenting the more familiar titles in the larger one. This also helps broaden the audience base for the company, making the LORT theatregoers possibly the most diverse audience in the United States.

Theatregoing in Great Britain

Since so many of our theatre and stage traditions originated in Great Britain, it is useful to look at the way professional theatre operates in London and throughout the United Kingdom. London's equivalent to Broadway is the West End, a group of playhouses scattered around the Leicester Square area in West London. These productions tend to be big musicals and plays with stars, and, like Broadway, production costs and tickets are very expensive. But there is a discount ticket booth in Leicester Square that operates much like the TKTS booth in Times Square. Just as major British hits, such as *Oliver!*, *Evita*, *Cats*, *Phantom of the Opera*, *Billy Elliot*, and *Matilda*, played successfully on Broadway, American works like *The Lion King*, *Chicago*, *Wicked*, *The Book of Mormon*, and *Hamilton* can be found in the West End.

What London has that Broadway doesn't are renowned subsidized theatre companies such as the Royal National Theatre and the Royal Shakespeare Company. Such productions receive substantial financing from the British government and can operate without the burden of coming up with box office hits. The subsidized theatres in London offer everything from big musicals to obscure classical works at ticket prices far less than those found in commercial West End playhouses. These theatre companies can also afford to offer new works by both established and promising British playwrights. (In New York, there are a handful of *nonprofit* theatres, such as Lincoln Center Theatre and the Roundabout Theatre, which get some government funding, but they greatly rely on other sources and their ticket prices are as high as commercial Broadway shows.)

London's version of Off Broadway and Off-Off-Broadway is called Fringe theatre, suggesting that these smaller, more experimental theatre groups are on the fringe of the West End. In reality, Fringe theatres can be found throughout London and take place in venues ranging from small but traditional playhouses to pub theatres and "found" spaces. The most experimental and cutting-edge theatre in London takes place in the Fringe theatres. Great Britain also has a strong network of regional theatres that operate in a similar manner as American regional theatres. These highly professional theatre companies can be found in large cities, such as

Edinburgh and Manchester, as well as in small communities, such as Stratford-on-Avon and Chichester. There is a great deal of theatre throughout the British Isles, and it is both encompassing and diverse.

America's National Theatre?

Several countries around the world have a theatre company and playhouse in the capital city that are officially designated as the nation's representative theatre. These national theatres are usually subsidized, at least in part, by the government, and the company aims to preserve the country's theatrical heritage by producing classic works as well as new plays. The first national theatre was the Comédie-Français in Paris, which was founded in 1680, followed by such distinguished companies as the Moscow Art Theatre for Russia, Dublin's Abbey Theatre for Ireland, and London's Royal National Theatre for Great Britain. Although some attempts have been made over the years, there is no official national theatre for the United States, and it seems unlikely that there will ever be one. There are various reasons for this situation. American artists generally do not like the government running the arts. It has been attempted in the past (there was an ambitious Federal Theatre Project during the Depression that failed to survive), but most theatre companies prefer to receive grants from government funds rather than let the state determine how a theatre should be run and what it should produce. There is also a problem of location. Would such a national theatre be located in Washington, D.C., like other capital-city theatres, or in New York City or elsewhere? Finally, the United States has become such a diverse nation that it seems impossible for any one theatre organization to represent all of the many cultural groups across the country.

Yet some commentators have noted that, in a way, we already have a national theatre. It is the network of professional resident theatres located in major cities from coast to coast. Although these theatres are not run as one large operation, they are connected in philosophy and management practices, keeping in touch with each other through organizations such as the League of Resident Theatres (LORT) and the Theatre Communications Group (TCG). Each theatre revives American classics on a regular basis, and most also premiere new works by American playwrights. As similar as they might seem, each regional theatre company also reflects the region in which it is located: Asian American theatres can be found in Hawaii and California, Latinx theatres in Florida and the Southwest, and so on. These theatres are representatives of the different aspects of American culture. While no one theatre can ever hope to encompass the American character, a series of regional theatres comes very close to doing so.

Summer Theatre

Although the heyday of summer theatre, once called *summer stock*, is long gone, there are still many companies that operate in the warm months of the year. They provide both professional and amateur theatre entertainment to playgoers who seldom see other kinds of theatre. The idea of summer stock was born in the early 1900s when great numbers of city dwellers took refuge in rural resorts or vacation communities in order to avoid the heat and crowds of urban life. Any place where Americans vacationed, from seaside towns to lakes in the mountains, was ideal for summer theatre, and hundreds were operating by the 1930s. Some groups performed in tents or outdoors, others in rustic lodges or converted barns. The companies were often semi-professional, sometimes mixing star performers with student apprentices who worked for the experience. Since there was usually a "stock" company of these amateur players who stayed for the whole season, the business was referred to as summer stock.

Today summer theatre can take several forms. Some are fully professional with an ambitious repertory of plays; others mix professionals and students and offer lighter fare, usually comedies and musicals. Many summer theatres are connected with a college, and most are nonprofit. A particular kind of summer theatre is outdoor historical dramas performed near some popular tourist destination and dramatizing a piece of history that happened there. One of the most famous and long-running of such outdoor pageants is *The Lost Colony*, a drama about early settlers in North Carolina, which has been playing every summer (with few interruptions) since 1937. Regardless of the wide variety of summer theatre today, they all share two things in common: they provide a theatre event in a unique setting, and they are still a valuable training ground for would-be professionals, particularly actors.

Theatre Festivals

Also operating in the summer, but with a different agenda, are festival theatres. These are less common but very popular with audiences looking for classic revivals and more demanding theatregoing than what summer stock might offer. The most prevalent kind of festival theatre is that devoted primarily to the works of Shakespeare. Places such as the Colorado Shakespeare Festival, the Stratford Festival in Canada, the Utah Shakespeare Festival, and others offer a summer season of Elizabethan plays, other classics, and even some new works. The most famous such festival in America is the New York Shakespeare Festival, which was begun by Joseph Papp in 1957 as a way of presenting free Shakespeare productions in the city's Central Park. That organization has grown to include the year-round Public Theatre, one of the most renowned nonprofit theatres Off-Broadway, but it still presents free Shakespeare productions at the outdoor Delacorte Theatre in the park. Some festival theatres, such as the Shaw Festival in Canada, concentrate on classical non-Shakespeare offerings. Like summer stock, these companies depend greatly on tourists for their audience. A majority of festival theatres are nonprofit, and most operate with a repertory system, offering different plays on a rotating basis in the same theatre so that a visitor staying in town for four days can see four different plays. Festival theatres present some of the highest-quality theatregoing in North America, and many rank them with Broadway for professionalism and creativity. There are numerous such festivals in Great Britain as well, including renowned events like the Edinburgh International Festival, the Brighton Festival, the Manchester International Festival, and the Chichester Festival.

Dinner Theatre

Another form of theatre that is past its heyday but far from gone is dinner theatre. These for-profit organizations sprang up outside of major cities in the 1960s and offered dinner and a play in the same location. Because many large American cities at the time were deemed unsafe and uninviting at night, suburban dwellers abandoned the downtown theatres and instead drove further out of town to structures where free parking, a buffet dinner, and lighthearted entertainment awaited. Some cities had three or four dinner theatres by the 1970s, but, as many metropolises redeveloped their urban centers and residents and tourists returned to the downtown areas, the dinner theatres were less profitable and most went out of business. Today some still survive in urban areas (Washington, D.C., for example, has over a half dozen in operation) and still appeal to theatregoers looking for convenient and nonthreatening entertainment. Many of the dinner theatres of the past had a bad reputation for doing weak plays and doing them cheaply; the term "dinner theatre production" was sometimes used to describe a feeble comedy done poorly for undiscriminating playgoers. A few of the current operations might still fall under that category, but many dinner theatres today are highly professional and offer quality revivals and sometimes even new plays and musicals.

Community Theatre

Before the rise of the regional theatre network in the 1950s, most cities and towns had a community theatre or two. These were amateur productions that used local community members to act, build, and run the show. The director and some other administrative positions were sometimes paid, but mostly it was a volunteer operation, allowing the community to see its fellow residents onstage. The quality of the productions varied greatly: some were haphazardly thrown together; others were so accomplished that they went to Broadway for brief engagements. As professional theatre came to cities in the form of LORT theatres, many of these community theatres faded away; but hundreds still exist, and in some places a high-quality community theatre production is the favorite show in town. These nonprofit, mostly amateur companies usually present revivals, though in large cities there are ambitious groups who concentrate on new works and offer exciting drama that is on the cutting edge. Most people do not even refer to "community theatre" anymore because of its old-fashioned associations. Still, theatre events created by nonprofessional adults for fellow citizens are good examples of community theatre today. The network of such theatre is unified by the American Association of Community Theatre (AACT), which sponsors play competitions and conventions, and shares news and events within its large organization.

Children's Theatre

Perhaps your first exposure to live theatre was attending a children's theatre production when you were young. For many, this was their first theatrical experience. Children's theatre in the United States is relatively new. One hundred years ago, theatre was rarely intended for children except for the rare musical fantasy or fairy tale done by traditional theatre companies. During the Depression, the short-lived but potent Federal Theatre Project included children's theatre among its many programs, and the idea of a theatre company dedicated primarily to plays for young audiences caught on. This is different from theatre activities or productions presented with child actors in schools, as we will discuss in the section on educational theatre.

As we define it, children's theatre is performed by adults, either professional or amateur, for audiences composed mostly of children. Good children's theatre should entertain adults as well, but the focus is on the young theatregoers; if it speaks to them, the production is successful. Unfortunately, there are many weak and ineffective children's theatre productions throughout the nation because some misguided artists believe that the scripts, acting, direction, costumes, sets, and so on for children's productions need not be of high quality, that kids would not notice them or care. This is simply not true. Children are very observant theatregoers and are not easily fooled. If a production is uninteresting, they will not politely endure it, but, instead, will get restless and bored. The best children's theatre companies today realize this and strive for quality in all the theatrical elements.

Many major cities have excellent children's theatre companies, some with a professional staff and a long history of performing for young audiences. Also, many regional theatres have a children's theatre component in their season. Today children's theatre can be very adventurous, getting young theatregoers directly involved in the production, breaking down actor–audience barriers, and even letting children determine the direction of the story.

Drama Therapy

A fairly recent development in the field of mental health is drama therapy. This is not an art form, but a way of using theatre techniques to aid people with psychiatric problems. We have already seen how people use role-playing in their daily lives. Drama therapy goes beyond that, encouraging patients to act out their fears and emotions, improvise situations to try to deal with them, and participate in group dynamics that range from theatre games to interpersonal interactions. While the creative arts have long been a manner of therapeutics, only within the last five decades or so has drama therapy been developed, taught, examined, and used on a wide scale in hospitals, schools, mental health centers, and even prisons. As the use of drama therapy has grown, so too have the different methods. Today puppetry, psychodramas, improv performances, mime troupes, and performance art are among the many forms used. The North American Drama Therapy Association is the most prominent organization in this field, offering workshops and conferences, providing information through publications, and highlighting colleges and universities where one can train to become a drama therapist.

Educational Theatre

The most prevalent kind of theatre today is that presented in schools. Just about every school in America has some form of theatre event, from a holiday pageant in an elementary school to a complex Shakespeare production at a college or university. For many Americans, their school play in an auditorium or gym was their first and only experience with theatre. Thousands of educational theatre productions occur each week across the country, and one cannot dismiss the impact this has on theatregoing. Just about any theatre professional, from actor to producer, started pursuing theatre while in school. Some school districts have flourishing theatre programs with productions on every grade level, and a high school graduate there may have seen dozens of theatre events by the time he or she goes to college. Other districts offer the minimum, which often means that the quality is poor because theatre productions are not highly regarded by the administration. Regardless, the school play is an important part of American culture, and the majority of theatre events that take place in this country are happening in educational institutions.

Some colleges and universities offer programs that allow students to major in theatre and even prepare them for a career as a professional. But even the places of higher education that can only offer a handful of theatre courses and an occasional production provide a valuable service to the college community and to the city or town where it is located. Because educational theatre is nonprofit and amateur, it has few of the financial constraints of professional for-profit theatres, and one is often able to risk new works, classic revivals, and experimental projects, in addition to the usual repertory of musical and play favorites. Educational theatre is a learning and growing experience for both the performers and the audience. Whether it be a third-grade version of *Tom Sawyer*, a high school production of *Grease*, or a college presentation of a David Mamet drama, the rich and varied life of educational theatre continues to amaze. It is more popular now than at any other time in our history and should not be underestimated.

It should be pointed out at this point that the above locations for theatregoing apply to the American theatre today. In other countries and cultures, the places for a theatre event can be very different. For example, a popular location for theatre in some Asian countries is the tea house, a cultural phenomenon that has no equivalent in the States. In Indonesia, shadow puppet presentations are very popular and are often done outside on the street or in a marketplace. Even in English-speaking nations like Great Britain and Australia, there are theatre traditions that differ from our own. At Christmastime, for example, it is traditional to bring the whole family to a pantomime (or panto, as it is commonly called) which is a unique combination of children's theatre and a Las Vegas spectacular. Again, there is no American equivalent. So as diverse as American theatre is today, world theatre is even more varied.

ALTERNATIVE THEATRE

All of these forms of theatregoing, from Broadway to educational theatre, might be considered mainstream events. They are traditional kinds of performances that are familiar to the general public. But there are alternative forms that have a very specific audience in mind and are not created to appeal to the average theatregoer. The likelihood of your seeing any of this alternative theatre is slim unless you go and seek them out. Yet there is something basic about these forms that make them true theatre events, even if the guidelines are bent a bit. One should be aware of such alternatives in order to understand the full range of the theatre experience.

Experimental Theatre

Every once in a while an artist or theatre group emerges that questions the traditional idea of theatre and finds startlingly different ways of creating a theatre event. In the 1960s, the Polish director Jerzy Grotowski and his "poor theatre" reduced the playwright's script to a mere outline and let the actor become the creative force in

EXPERIMENTAL THEATRE Theatre, dance, mime, and video are among the techniques used in the experimental performance piece titled *Dismorphia*, seen here at the Aberystwyth Arts Centre in Scotland in 2011. Such experimental pieces rarely restrict themselves to one medium or art form. *redsnapper/Alamy Stock Photo*

theatre. In the same decade, the controversial American group called the Living Theatre used ritual, nudity, and audience participation to break the boundary between actor and spectator. Today many such artists and groups continue to offer similarly alternative kinds of theatregoing. Sometimes they are called *avant-garde*, the French expression meaning to be ahead of one's time. A better adjective might be *experimental* because the purpose of such theatre is to try things that mainstream theatre is not willing to risk. A vivid example would be director-designer Robert Wilson. A Wilson production might last twelve hours, will feature video and recorded conversation alongside live actors, and explore a theme through a series of images and phrases rather than traditional plot or dialogue. Although these pieces are visually stunning (Wilson started out as an artist), it is sometimes difficult for the average theatregoer to find satisfaction in such montage-like productions. This is as it should be in experimental theatre: the audience might be composed of artists, intellectuals, and other very specific groups, and the theatre event is developed especially for them.

Street and Guerrilla Theatre

Sometimes new kinds of theatre have distant roots. Street theatre is a presentation by a troupe of players who perform on a portable stage outdoors in a particular kind of neighborhood. This kind of theatre goes back to the wagon stages of the Middle Ages, but in the 1960s it came back as a way to reach people who had never been inside a playhouse. Street theatre may not literally take place on a street, but it is *of* the streets: the actors speak the language and the cultural idioms of the streets. Spanish-language productions in Latinx neighborhoods, African American vernacular in the black sections of town, and politically potent plays in the blue-collar areas speak directly to the people by going to them rather than having spectators seek out a theatre building. Some of these street performances of the past were so potent and so aroused the citizens on certain issues that they were labeled *guerrilla theatre*. These politically aggressive productions hoped to inform and persuade the audience regarding controversial topics of the day. While they were most frequent in the 1960s and 1970s, guerrilla theatre still exists today, and many indoor theatres have utilized some of its bold techniques.

Performance Art

A form of experimental theatre that is very popular today is performance art; it is also the most difficult to describe. Because there are performers (though not necessarily actors), an audience, and some kind of script (though not a traditional play), and because they gather in one place, it is a theatre event. But performance art often celebrates the creation of something rather than the finished product. For example, an artist may sculpt a figure onstage while two dancers interpret a recited text read by an actor. Or a group of actors might form a series of static scenes, or *tableau*, as atonal music is performed by a solo musician. Recently there have been many one-person performance pieces with the authors playing themselves and the scripts being about their own lives. There are no rules in performance art as long as an artist expresses an idea before a live audience. Music, dance, poetry, visual art, video, film, and songs are all common elements in this intriguing kind of theatregoing. Although there are many celebrated performance artists who appear in cities across the country, performance art is not mainstream theatre and can also be described as experimental.

THEATRE OF DIVERSITY

In the first chapter we spoke of the diversity of theatre and the way that all peoples around the world have developed their own version of a theatre event. It is just as important to look at the diversity within the American theatre today and to see how specific plays are written for particular audiences. Theatre of diversity sometimes makes no attempt to include mainstream audiences and seeks to appeal only to a specific group, such as a particular race, gender, or culture. Yet often these productions find a wider audience and become part of the American theatre in general. Because this nation is so diverse in its cultural makeup, theatre often transcends one group and includes many others.

At one time, the American theatre used to classify certain works as "Irish plays" or "Jewish plays." These two prominent groups of immigrants made quite an impact on the theatre in the nineteenth century, and many plays were written and produced with these specific audiences in mind. By the middle of the twentieth century many of these immigrants were assimilated into the population, and a play about a Jewish family or a musical with American Irish characters was considered part of mainstream theatregoing. A playwright such as Eugene O'Neill and Clifford Odets was no longer labeled an Irish or a Jewish writer but simply a playwright. Today there are African American writers and feminist authors whose work has become so interwoven with the American theatre that the labels have fallen away. The difference between contemporary groups and the old Irish and Jewish immigrants lies in modern attitudes. While those foreign-born Americans wanted to be assimilated and Americanized in the "melting pot," many groups today fight to retain the individuality of their culture. For example, the Latinx population wishes to keep the Spanish language and not become swallowed up in mainstream America. Asian actors want to play Asian American characters, just as a gay or lesbian playwright wants to keep sexuality at the center of drama. Theatre of diversity survives and grows, becoming more commonplace even as it retains the qualities that make it unique.

African American Theatre

Although black characters have appeared in American plays since colonial times, they were often portrayed as stereotypes and were usually played by white actors in blackface. Not until the 1920s did African Americans start to appear as serious subjects in American plays. More important, black playwrights and directors eventually emerged, and there were finally African American plays in the true sense of the word. During the 1960s and the civil rights movement, many new black talents entered the scene, and hundreds of plays and musicals about the black experience in America were performed in venues from churches to Broadway. Many of these plays were intended for black audiences only; others were meant to force white audiences to consider the plight of African Americans; still others celebrated the culture and informed both white and black audiences about events and African Americans in the past. The central issue in these plays was racial injustice, and it was not until later in the century that a "black play" could go beyond this and explore characters who were much more than racial symbols.

Today there are African American musicals, serious dramas, and comedies, and many have a wide appeal for all kinds of audience. The most prolific and successful of black playwrights, August Wilson, is a fine example of a writer who deals with ethnic culture but also creates vivid characters (black and white) who come alive for all audiences. On the other hand, the 1960s black playwright Imamu Amiri Baraka (born LeRoi Jones) sought to make white audiences uncomfortable in the theatre and pointed out the differences between the two races. For some African American writers, diversity became a weapon rather than a plea for understanding. These volatile works were very potent, though few have remained popular; they were a product of their time. We are getting closer to the day when a play will not be labeled an "African American drama" but simply a play that happens to be about black Americans.

It was not until black directors and producers emerged in the 1960s that the voice of African Americans was heard clearly. Theatre companies such as the Negro Ensemble Company, which lasted for forty years, were dedicated to black plays and used African American directors, producers, and designers. Today other companies have taken its place, and most major cities have at least one theatre dedicated to African American works. There are also black artists running regional theatres that offer a variety of productions during a season, not just black plays. Today the presence of African American plays is very strong in many regional theatres. The only way an American theatre can be truly American is to consider all the ethnic cultures of the land. In the case of African Americans, that ethnic presence is perhaps more prominent in mainstream theatre than any other group.

AFRICAN AMERICAN THEATRE Playwright August Wilson's ten-play cycle about African Americans in the twentieth century is one of the most ambitious of all theatre projects. Representing the 1980s, *King Hedley II* (2001) is about the ex-con King (Brian Stokes Mitchell), who returns to his old neighborhood in Pittsburgh to try and give his life a new start. Also in the cast was Leslie Uggams as King's mother Ruby. Director: Marion McClinton. *Photofest*

Latinx Theatre

Spanish-language plays in the New World go back to the late 1500s, when European theatre companies toured the Spanish colonies across North and South America. During the 1920s, Latin American theatres flourished in major U.S. cities with large Spanish-language populations. Because of the language barrier, these works were intended for Spanish-speaking audiences only and made no attempt to appeal to outsiders. After a fallow period, Latinx theatre rose again in the 1960s, and several of these works were in English and were attended by wider audiences. One influential play, *Zoot Suit* (1978) by Luis Valdez, was performed on Broadway. Valdez's company El Teatro Campesino was one of many troupes that sprung up in New York, Miami, Los Angeles, and other cities with large Spanish American populations. Performing both in English and Spanish, they made their presence known, producing plays about their cultural past and their current situation.

Today Latinx theatre can be roughly divided into three forms: Chicano theatre, which is interested in political and social dramas, such as *Zoot Suit*; Cuban American theatre, found mostly in Florida, which deals with Cuban Americans' native home in comedies and drama; and Puerto Rican theatre, also called Nuyorican theatre, which is about the Puerto Rican culture in New York City. This last kind of Latinx theatre is especially noted for bringing live theatre to Spanish-speaking neighborhoods by such companies as the Puerto Rican Traveling Company. Sometimes these productions are in Spanish, but there are some groups, such as the Repertorio Español in New York, that offer bilingual theatre, with some productions having sections in both English and the various dialects of Spanish. Some Latinx plays in English, such as the prison drama *Short Eyes* by Miguel Pinero, and the Pulitzer Prize–winning *Anna in*

LATINX THEATRE Although *West Side Story* (1957) features several Puerto Rican characters, the first Broadway musical about Latinx written by Latinx was *In the Heights* (2008). Quiara Alegria Hudes wrote the book, and Lin-Manuel Miranda (center) wrote the music and lyrics, which were in both English and Spanish. Director: Thomas Kail. *Sara Krulwich/New York Times/Redux*

the *Tropics* by Nilo Cruz, have found mainstream audiences, the first finding success Off Broadway and the second being produced on Broadway. In reality, there is so much diversity among Spanish-speaking Americans that no one theatre or one play can hope to represent all Latinx Americans. It is only through individual theatre companies that they can be a vital part of the American theatre.

Asian American Theatre

Americans first became aware of theatre in Asia when visiting theatre companies from China and Japan came to the United States in the early 1900s and toured their colorful, very foreign performance pieces. Later Asian theatre techniques were adopted and used in American works about the Orient, such as in the comedy *The Teahouse of the August Moon* and the musical *Pacific Overtures*. Plays by and about Asian Americans were not much seen until the 1970s, although the Rodgers and Hammerstein musical *Flower Drum Song* (1959) was an early effort. Some of these works concentrated on the countries where the Asian immigrants came from, but most were more interested in how Asian Americans today try to fit into American society and still retain their Asian heritage. The most successful of the Asian American playwrights is David Henry Hwang, who, in works such as *F.O.B.* (meaning "fresh off the boat") and *M. Butterfly*, explores the differences between Eastern and Western culture. Not only were these plays hits on Broadway and Off Broadway, but they have been revived across the nation in places where few Asian Americans live.

In cities with large Chinese, Japanese, Korean, and Indian populations, theatre groups have been formed that explore the Asian American experience, such as the East West Players in Los Angeles and the Pan Asian Repertory Theatre in New York

City. Since fewer and fewer Asian Americans speak their ancestors' language, most productions are in English and are meant for all kinds of audiences. Also, Asian American actors can now be found in many non-Asian musicals and plays, something that did not happen until long after African Americans were integrated into mainstream theatre productions. Most Americans still continue to see Asians only in such hits as *Miss Saigon*, but the presence of Asian American theatre is continually growing.

Native American Theatre

Over the past three hundred years, Native Americans have been portrayed onstage and on the screen in one of two widely different ways. American plays going back to the colonial days often saw them as "noble savages," a primitive people with high regard for nature and a peace-loving, humanistic culture. But for the first half of the twentieth century (particularly on film), Native Americans were more frequently seen as ignoble savages, a warlike people, and a threat to American expansion. Not until the 1960s did some plays emerge that sought to view history through the Native American's point of view, such as in the powerful chronicle play *Indians* by Arthur Kopit. Some of these works were belligerent plays that aggressively blamed the white man and the U.S. government for the inhuman treatment of Native Americans in the past and even the present; other plays celebrated the Native American culture and sought to heal through understanding.

Native Americans had their own forms of theatre long before Europeans arrived in the New World, and only recently have thorough studies been made of these ritualistic performances. These plays were built around legends and the history of the community, so the art form died out when these communities were broken up by white settlers. In the 1970s attempts were made by contemporary Native Americans to revive this early form of theatre. The Red Earth Theatre in Seattle and the Native American Ensemble Theatre in New York were two early groups, later joined by others, but a revived Native American theatre still is experiencing growing pains. Recently a series of films about contemporary Native Americans has managed to find a wide audience, and it is hoped that this will help pave the way for a stronger Native American theatre.

Feminist Theatre

Although there have been women actors, managers, and playwrights since the 1700s, plays by and about women and their role in society are relatively recent. Late in the twentieth century, women directors, composers, and designers entered the mainstream American theatre as well, influencing the theatre in new ways. But feminist theatre is about more than women participating in theatre. The form grew out of the women's movement of the 1970s, when the National Organization for Women (NOW) was established and efforts were made to pass an equal rights amendment to the Constitution. Theatre groups such as It's Alright to Be a Woman, Omaha Magic Theatre, Women's

FEMINIST THEATRE American actress and political activist Eve Ensler started performing her one-woman show *The Vagina Monologues* in small clubs and cafes in Greenwich Village in 1996. The serio-comic piece looks at a variety of women's issues with humor and brutal honesty. Today on V-Day (February 14) every year, thousands of performances of *The Vagina Monologues* take place throughout the world. Pictured is Ensler when she performed her feminist play Off Broadway in 1996. *HBO/Photofest © HBO*

Experimental Theatre, and Spiderwoman Theatre were formed to explore the political aspects of women's rights. Outspoken playwrights such as Megan Terry and Maria Irene Fornes used expressionistic techniques in their works to raise political and social consciousness. The movement was too often confused with lesbian theatre (discussed next) because many of the issues were the same. Equal pay, the right to abortion, women empowerment, and other controversial topics sometimes made for potent theatregoing and other times lapsed into speechifying. It seemed that any issue could be turned into a feminist one when looked at from a radical point of view.

Feminist theatre still exists today, but it has mostly been assimilated into other forms. Performance art, for example, is often feminist, as solo performers use humor and anger to look at the role of women today. Some feminist theatre companies, such as the Split Britches troupe, can more accurately be described as lesbian theatre. Yet unlike other forms of diversity, feminist theatre usually seeks to be heard by audiences outside the special interest group. A feminist performance with no men in the audience can be a narrow experience. Some plays, such as Eve Ensler's popular *The Vagina Monologues*, have a greater impact with an audience of both sexes. A feminist play that enters the mainstream of theatre is no longer considered feminist; it is now a play that takes a feminist point of view. Playwrights Beth Henley, Marsha Norman, Paula Vogel, and Wendy Wasserstein were labeled feminist writers early in their careers because their work had such a strong women's point of view. Yet as each of these playwrights offered more plays to the theatregoing public, audiences simply accepted them as talented writers, ignoring the concept that male and female playwrights should be judged differently.

Gay and Lesbian Theatre

Of all the special interest groups, none remained as invisible for so long as did gays and lesbians. There have been homosexual characters in plays over the last one hundred years, but they were so ambiguously portrayed that audiences did not see them unless they wanted to. For example, Lillian Hellman's drama *The Children's Hour* (1934) hinted at a possible lesbian affair between two teachers, but it was more about a vicious rumor than an insightful look into homosexuality. The first play about gays to become a mainstream hit was Mart Crowley's Off-Broadway comedy-drama *The Boys in the Band* (1968), about a group of homosexuals gathered for a birthday party. Today it might seem rather tame, but at the time it was both a shocking and a fascinating look into a counterculture that most theatregoers had never seen before. Many Off-Off-Broadway groups in the 1970s and 1980s catered to gay audiences, and some of them, such as Charles Ludlam's the Ridiculous Theatrical Company, found wider audiences than previously seen. The first major gay play to become a hit on Broadway was Harvey Fierstein's *Torch Song Trilogy* (1982), three one-act plays about love and sex in the gay world, which had been produced earlier Off-Off-Broadway. *La Cage aux Folles* (1983) and William Finn's *Falsettos* (1992) were the first gay musicals to find mainstream acceptance on Broadway, and soon they were seen in theatres across the country.

GAY AND LESBIAN THEATRE The theme of homosexuality is present in so many dramas and musicals today that most audiences do not even consider them "gay" plays. A case in point is Richard Greenberg's comedy-drama *Take Me Out* (2003), in which a popular professional baseball player, played by Daniel Sunjata, casually mentions to the press his homosexual preferences and his world is turned upside down. *Photofest*

By the 1990s, gay characters were evident in dozens of new works, only a few of which could be classified as gay plays. Tony Kushner's epic drama *Angels in America* (1993) had some gay characters but was about so much more than sexuality that it defied mere labeling. The same can be said about the musicals *Rent* and *Kinky Boots*. Today there are fewer and fewer plays that can be considered specifically gay theatre; most are plays that include homosexual characters and issues within a much more complex piece of playwriting. And while gay theatre companies are still active in cities across the country, gay theatre is being assimilated into the culture just as Irish and Jewish works once were.

FOREIGN INFLUENCES

Very little in American culture is purely American. We are a country forged from many different peoples from varied places, and everything from our language to our food has been influenced by others. The same is true of the arts, and theatre is no different. Our plays, playhouses, and artists have been affected by foreign ideas and practices since the colonies were founded, and that influence continues today. One cannot look at the American theatre and not point out some of the ways in which we are still a melting pot.

The country that has had the most obvious influence on American theatre is the United Kingdom. The first plays produced in the colonies were British works acted and produced by English men and women. When Americans started writing their own plays and building their first theatres, they were both in the English manner. Throughout the centuries British plays have held an important place on Broadway and across the nation. This was still the case during the 1980s, when a sort of British invasion brought *Cats*, *The Phantom of the Opera*, and other megamusicals to Broadway. French plays have been also a favorite in the American theatre since the beginning, though often they were translated into English with American settings and names. France, too, would be part of the 1980s foreign invasion, with musicals such as *Les Misérables* and *Miss Saigon*. At the same time, American works (particularly musicals) have long been popular in both Britain and France, and one can argue that we have been a major foreign influence on those countries as well.

Less obviously, Asian theatre has affected the American theatre since the late nineteenth century. Americans and Europeans were fascinated by the "Orient" in the Victorian era, and everything from Japanese gardens to Chinese furniture became the rage. Because Asian theatre was so different from Western culture, many artists borrowed Eastern techniques as a way to find fresh approaches to performance. The two most influential kinds of Asian theatre are the Peking Opera from China and the Kabuki theatre from Japan. Both are highly stylized,

FOREIGN INFLUENCES In telling the story of a French diplomat who falls in love with a Chinese spy in David Henry Hwang's *M. Butterfly* (1988), director John Dexter used many techniques from the Asian theatre, ranging from scenic devices to stylized stage movement. *M. Butterfly* was the first Asian American play to be presented on Broadway. Costume designer: Eiko Ishioka. *Sara Krulwich/New York Times/Redux*

involve singing and dancing in ways not seen on Western stages, and present unique ideas about storytelling. The German playwright-director Bertolt Brecht was strongly influenced by both, and his adaptation of Asian models filtered to America. Plays from Far Eastern countries were adapted into American works, sometimes keeping the Asian setting and other times retelling the same tale in American terms. We are still using Eastern ideas today, particularly in our musicals. *Pacific Overtures* (1976) attempts to show the opening of Japan to Westerners in 1853 through the Asian point of view; it is an American Broadway musical that uses Kabuki and other styles, blending the two cultures on one stage. The popular *The Lion King* borrows from a handful of cultures, from Japanese makeup to African masks to Indonesian shadow puppets. Other foreign influences range from Spanish theatre and Hindu pageantry to Russian acting and directing styles and Arabic performance pieces; each culture that comes in contact with America leaves something that affects us and our theatre.

Sometimes these influences come in the shape of a person. We saw in the chapters on acting and directing how the Russian artist Stanislavsky changed the Western world's ideas about performance, and in the chapter on directing how Brecht's form of expressionism steered the style of theatre away from realism. There have been other foreign artists who have affected the American theatre during the last half of the twentieth century. The French director Ariane Mnouchkine, for example, has been a major force in street theatre and theatre in "found" spaces. Her company, Theatre du Soleil, has performed in garages and factories around the world, and her ideas helped establish Off-Off-Broadway. The German director Peter Schumann came to the United States in 1961 and founded the renowned Bread and Puppet Theatre, which explored storytelling and political themes through the use of jugglers, acrobats, and giant expressionistic puppets. (The company's name came from the admission charge: patrons paid with loaves of bread, which were later given to the poor.) Perhaps the most influential of all is British director Peter Brook, who has—through his writings, theatre productions, and films—found innovative ways to interpret both classic and new works. For many decades, Brook experimented with different theatre groups, from the Royal Shakespeare Company in England to the International Centre for Theatre Research in Paris, redefining how theatre space is used and how theatre pieces might be developed by performers rather than writers. Among his famous productions was a radically fresh version of Shakespeare's *A Midsummer Night's Dream*, which toured the world in the 1970s. Artists such as Brook, Schumann, and Mnouchkine are truly international theatre practitioners. Technology and communication have helped shrink our world, and the idea of a global theatre is not so far-fetched. Yet live theatre does not travel as quickly as movies, music, and television, so there is still a long way to go before theatre can become as international as other, more technical media.

Before leaving the subject, let us look at our four sample plays and see how they were influenced by non-American forces. Of the four, three are American works. *You Can't Take It with You* and *A Raisin in the Sun* might seem to be thoroughly American, yet even they follow the French idea of the well-made play with everything logically set out. In *You Can't Take It with You*, exposition about giving Grandpa's name to a stranger who died prepares the audience for the ending when the U. S. government thinks Grandpa is dead. In *A Raisin in the Sun*, we hear about the insurance check; we see the check arrive; we learn what occurs because of the check. This solid French play construction is used by many American dramas, and George S. Kaufman, Moss Hart, and Lorraine Hansberry mastered the technique in their plays. Finally, *Hamilton* looks like German or Russian expressionism, with its wooden galleries for scenery and all the lighting instruments and microphones in full view. The musical is sung through with little dialogue—a trend borrowed from the British and French musicals of the 1980s—and the open use of space harkens back to innovative directors such as Brook. Here are three uniquely American works yet each was influenced from beyond our borders.

TOPICS FOR GROUP DISCUSSION

1. Discuss the places, from Broadway to educational theatre, where you might find productions of the sample plays *Macbeth*, *You Can't Take It with You*, and *A Raisin in the Sun*.
2. Watch scenes from *Hamilton* online and list the different forms of diversity one encounters.
3. Discuss any plays and musicals that you have seen on Broadway or on tour in terms of the type of audience most likely to attend.

POSSIBLE RESEARCH PROJECTS

1. Using the *Variety* or *Playbill* website, determine which productions are currently playing on Broadway, then determine which are new works and which are revivals.
2. Go to the websites of two regional theatres that are members of LORT and compare and contrast the kinds of plays and musicals each is presenting this season.
3. View some examples of performance art on YouTube and note the different forms of diversity that you find.
4. Using playbill.com, broadway.com, or another website, look up a listing of theatre offerings on Broadway and in London's West End, and chart how many productions in each city come from across the Atlantic.

FURTHER READING

Aston, Elaine. *Feminist Theatre Practice.* New York: Routledge, 1999.
Atkinson, Brooks. *Broadway.* New York: Macmillan, 1974.
Blau, Herbert. *The Audience.* Baltimore: Johns Hopkins University Press, 1990.
Bloom, Ken. *Broadway: An Encyclopedia.* New York: Routledge, 2003.
———. *Routledge Guide to Broadway.* New York: Routledge, 2006.
Botto, Louis. *At This Theatre: 100 Years of Broadway Shows, Stories, and Stars.* New York: Applause Books, 2010.
Bradwell, Mike. *The Reluctant Escapologist: Adventures in Alternative Theatre.* London: Nick Hern Books, 2011.
Canning, Charlotte. *Feminist Theatres in the USA.* New York: Routledge, 1995.
Chach, Maryann, ed. *The Shuberts Present 100 Years of American Theatre.* New York: Harry N. Abrams, 2001.
Chinoy, Helen K., and Linda W Jenkins, eds. *Women in American Theatre.* New York: Theatre Communications Group, 1987.
Chorpenning, Charlotte Barrows. *Twenty-One Years with Children's Theatre.* Louisville, KY: Children's Theatre Press, 1954.

Crespy, David A. *Off-Off-Broadway Explosion*. New York: Back Stage Books, 2003.
Dunlap, David W. *On Broadway: A Journey Uptown over Time*. New York: Rizzoli International, 1990.
Eliot, Marc. *Down 42nd Street: Sex, Money, Culture, and Politics at the Crossroads of the World*. New York: Warner, 2001.
Frommer, Myrna Katz, and Harvey Frommer. *It Happened on Broadway: An Oral History of the Great White Way*. New York: Harcourt, 1998.
Geiogamah, Hanay, and Jaye T. Darby, eds. *American Indian Theatre in Performance*. Los Angeles: University of California Los Angeles American Indians Studies, 2000.
Goldberg, Rosalee. *Performance: Live Art Since the 60s*. London: Thames and Hudson, 2004.
———. *Performance Art: From Futurism to the Present*. New York: Harry N. Abrams, 2011.
Grainger, Robert. *Drama and Healing: The Roots of Drama Therapy*. London: Jessica Kingsley Publishers, 1995.
Hay, Samuel A. *African American Theatre*. New York: Cambridge University Press, 1994.
Hill, Errol, and James V. Hatch. *The Theatre of Black Americans*. New York: Applause Books, 2005.
Hischak, Thomas S. *Off Broadway Musicals since 1919*. Lanham, MD: Scarecrow, 2011.
Holdsworth, Nadine. *Theatre and Nation*. New York: Palgrave Macmillan, 2010.
Johnson, David Read. *Current Approaches in Drama Therapy*. Springfield, IL: Charles C Thomas, 2009.
Kanellos, Nicolas. *A History of Hispanic Theatre in the United States*. Houston: Arte Publico, 2014.
Lane, Stewart F. *Black Broadway: African Americans on the Great White Way*. Garden City Park, NY: Square One, 2015.
Lee, Esther Kim. *A History of Asian American Theatre*. New York: Cambridge University Press, 2011.
Lee, Josephine. *Performing Asian America*. Philadelphia: Temple University Press, 1998.
LoMonaco, Martha Schmoyer. *Summer Stock: An American Theatrical Phenomenon*. New York: Palgrave Macmillan, 2004.
Marsolais, Ken, Rodger McFarlane, and Tom Viola. *Broadway Day and Night: Backstage and Behind the Scenes*. New York: Simon and Schuster, 1992.
Mason, Bim. *Street Theatre and Other Outdoor Performance*. New York: Routledge, 1992.
Moore, J. Paul. *Guerrilla Theatre for Fairies and Festivals*. New York: Ion Drive, 2009.
Morrow, Lee Alan. *The Tony Award Book*. New York: Abbeville, 1990.
Natalle, Elizabeth J. *Feminist Theatre: A Study in Persuasion*. Metuchen, NJ: Scarecrow, 1985.
Olsen, Christopher. *Off-Off Broadway: The Second Wave, 1968–1980*. N.p.: n.p., printed by Amazon/CreateSpace, 2011.
Richardson, Michael. *Youth Theatre: Drama for Life*. Abingdon-on-Thames, UK: Routledge, 2015.
Roose-Evans, James. *Experimental Theatre from Stanislavski to Peter Brook*. London: Routledge and Kegan Paul, 1996.
Sagalyn, Lynne B. *Times Square Roulette: Remaking the City Icon*. Cambridge, MA: MIT Press, 2001.

Sanders, Leslie C. *The Development of Black Theatre in America.* Baton Rouge: Louisiana State University Press, 1988.

Schechner, Richard. *Environmental Theatre.* New York: Applause Books, 1994.

Shank, Theodore. *Beyond the Boundaries: American Alternative Theatre.* New York: St. Martin's, 2002.

Siks, Geraldine B., and Hazel B. Dunnington. *Children's Theatre and Creative Dramatics.* Seattle: University of Washington Press, 1974.

Sinfield, Alan. *Out on Stage: Lesbian and Gay Theatre in the Twentieth Century.* New Haven, CT: Yale University Press, 1999.

Stanlake, Christy. *Native American Drama.* New York: Cambridge University Press, 2010.

Stone, Wendell C. *Caffe Cino: The Birthplace of Off-Off-Broadway.* Carbondale: Southern Illinois University Press, 2005.

Svich, Caridad, and Maria Teresa Marrero. *Out of the Fringe: Contemporary Latina/Latino Theatre and Performance.* New York: Theatre Communications Group, 1999.

Woll, Allen L. *Black Musical Theatre: From* Coontown *to* Dreamgirls. Baton Rouge: Louisiana State University Press, 1989.

Wood, David, and Janet Grant. *Theatre for Children: A Guide to Writing, Adapting, Directing, and Acting.* Lanham, MD: Rowman & Littlefield, 1999.

Yordan, Judy E. *Experimental Theatre: Creating and Staging Texts.* Long Grove, IL: Waveland, 2005.

Young, Harvey. *The Cambridge Companion to African American Theatre.* New York: Cambridge University Press, 2014.

10

THE PLAYGOERS II: THE CRITIC

THEATRE CRITICISM

Discussion about the theatre audience naturally leads to a consideration of criticism. Following every theatre event is some form of criticism, be it as informal as casual conversation between spectators leaving the playhouse or as weighty as an all-important review in the *New York Times*. One reacts to a theatre performance twice: during the event and afterward. During the performance audience members may laugh, yawn, applaud, listen attentively, get restless, even daydream. Obviously, some audiences are more vocal than others. During a performance on the street, the spectators might shout out comments (approving or disapproving) to the actors. Yet most playgoers tend to let the theatre event proceed uninterrupted and wait to express their feelings later. This postperformance reaction, no matter what form it takes, is *theatre criticism*. It is different from *dramatic criticism*, which comprises written essays or books about theatre literature and the "drama" aspect of theatregoing. Theatre criticism is about the event, and, while it certainly includes commentary on the script, it must take in the whole experience, from the theatre space to the actors and designers to the reactions of the audience in general.

Theatre criticism can be divided into formal and informal. A printed review in a newspaper or journal, a planned panel discussion on the subject of a recent production, or a critical book written about a series of theatre events—these are all very formal. A classroom discussion among students who saw the same production, friends casually talking about the play in a bar after the performance, or an arts chat line on the internet would be examples of informal criticism. One kind is not superior to the other; in fact, many theatregoers pay much more attention to the opinions of friends and colleagues than they do to "professional" critics. The concept of favorable "word of mouth" is still a strong one, and there have been many plays that were dismissed by formal critics but found positive support from informal criticism and ran despite the press's "thumbs down." This is particularly true outside of New York City. In Manhattan, formal theatre criticism is more powerful than it is anywhere else, and sometimes damning reviews close a play before informal reactions can be solidified. Yet in regional and educational theatre, newspaper reviews carry much less weight, and criticism becomes more an exercise in evaluation than a decree of success or failure. Formal or informal, opinions about a theatre event are bound to be varied, and theatre criticism can be a very delicate and complicated aspect of the modern theatre.

THEATRE CRITICISM When Jack Kirkland's melodrama *Tobacco Road*, about a low-life family of Georgia "crackers" with no redeeming values, opened on Broadway in 1933, theatre critics universally agreed that the play was worthless. Yet audiences were curious and came anyway, keeping *Tobacco Road* running for a record-breaking eight years. Pictured is Will Geer, who played the decrepit patriarch Jeeter Lester for a period of time during the long run. *Photofest*

Critics and Reviews

A professional theatre critic is someone who is paid by a media company to see a play and to publicly express an opinion about it. It is supposedly a service that the newspaper, television or radio station, or website is offering its readers or viewers, and the purpose is to inform the public whether it should attend a certain theatre event. This formal expression of opinion is called a *review*, and it is printed or broadcast as a guide to potential audiences. In theory, that is what happens. In reality,

---

Censorship in the American Theatre

The history of world theatre is filled with periods of heavy censorship. All the playhouses in England, for example, were closed by the Puritans for a time in the seventeenth century. Later in that same century, Moliere's French classic *Tartuffe* was banned by the Catholic Church as being immoral. Censorship comes in many forms, stemming from political to moral reasons, and it has occurred in America over the years. Yet because of the U.S. Constitution's free speech amendment, there has actually been less censorship here than in nations abroad. (In Great Britain, for example, all new plays had to be approved by the office of the Lord Chamberlain until 1968.) Hollywood movies were carefully censored beginning in the 1930s, and later television producers were also very fearful of offending sponsors; yet, theatre was left alone most of the time. In the World War I drama *What Price Glory* (1924), for instance, colorful language and expletives were used that were not heard in a movie until forty years later. Nudity was onstage by the 1960s, and gay plays were produced before the subject was openly portrayed on film and the tube. Many writers valued the theatre because it had fewer constraints than had the other media.

Yet there have also been numerous examples of plays or musicals that went too far, even for theatre audiences and critics, and were thus met with censorship. When George Bernard Shaw's play *Mrs. Warren's Profession* (1905) was first presented in New York, the subject of prostitution was so blatantly handled that the police closed the production and arrested the cast. The same thing happened to actress-playwright Mae West when her scandalous play *Sex* (1926) arrived on Broadway. The issues that have brought on censorship in the American theatre have ranged from incest and religion to abortion and homosexuality. By the 1970s it seemed there were few taboos left in the theatre, although isolated instances have arisen on occasion. When Terrence McNally's play *Corpus Christie* opened Off-Broadway in 1998, the public heard that it depicted Jesus Christ and his followers as homosexuals, and death threats were sent to the playwright and cast. The *New York Times* would not allow the plays *Shopping and Fucking* (1998) and *Fucking A* (2003) to advertise in the newspaper unless the offensive title was censored. In both events, the plays were produced without government interference. But public opinion is a strong force in America, and it might be said that censorship in the American theatre is usually in the hands of the public; what is acceptable in one community may not be in another. The harmless musical comedy *The Best Little Whorehouse in Texas* (1978) was not as accepted on the road as it was in New York, just as decades earlier plays from the North about African Americans were not embraced in the South. In the 1970s, the Supreme Court handed down some decisions that confirmed that local authorities had the right to determine if an art event was deemed offensive to their communities. This has led to some controversial decisions when New York plays were presented regionally. Theatre continues on with the unsettling knowledge that there are always some who would, for a number of reasons, still rejoice in censorship.

some critics have become so powerful that the purpose of theatre seems to be to please the professionals so that the play can run long enough to make money. Critics are read or heard by the public, but far from everyone takes their advice, especially if the reviewer has a reputation for being unusually condescending or nasty in his or her criticism. Yet even a sour critic should not be able to do too much damage to a production if there are plenty of critics and the public can get a consensus of opinion from the group. Before World War II, New York City had dozens of newspapers, many of them daily publications. But as different papers folded and the city was left with only a few by the 1960s, the remaining critics carried much more weight than before. During much of the last decades of the twentieth century, the major *New York Times* critic was the most powerful person in the American theatre. The critic's word outranked that of any playwright, producer, or star. Fortunately, with the rise of theatre websites, chat rooms, and even scenes from plays on YouTube, the power of the New York critic has been somewhat diluted. Many shows on Broadway today did not get the approval of critics but have been enthusiastically endorsed by the public so they continue to run. The number of Broadway productions that have survived critical dismissal has risen over the years; it seems that in some cases the audiences decide for themselves what to see, regardless of the reviews. Equally encouraging is the number of theatres across the country that are not under the thumb of professional critics. Regional theatres sell subscriptions, and most of the seats are filled before any review can praise or condemn a particular production. Festival and summer theatres have built-in audiences, and their patrons make plans to attend with little regard to critical reactions to the plays. Educational theatre, the largest component across the nation, has never depended on or feared formal criticism.

Theatre artists in the United States have complained about critics for more than two hundred years, and the love–hate relationship between producers and critics continues on. How can it be a love relationship? When critics praise a production, producers are the first to plaster those rave notices in newspaper ads, on buses, and on billboards. The hate part of the relationship should be pretty self-evident, but if a critic can destroy a show, he or she can also make a production a hit. So the strange interaction between presenting theatre and criticizing theatre continues on.

CENSORSHIP Nudity was first seen on Broadway in the musical *Hair* (1968), and although it was brief and in low light, it caused a sensation. Many cities refused to book the touring company of *Hair*, and nudity is still not accepted in some communities. On Broadway, many plays since *Hair* have included nudity, such as the 2008 revival of Peter Shaffer's drama *Equus*, starring film actor Daniel Radcliffe, pictured here with Anna Camp. Director: Thea Sharrock. *Gielgud Theatre/Photofest © Gielgud Theatre*

> **What to Expect When Viewing a Play**
>
> 1. Every play is different. Go to the theatre with an open mind. *Romeo and Juliet* cannot be viewed in the same way as *Mamma Mia!* Each play asks that you approach it in its own unique way.
> 2. This is live theatre. Your reactions to the play and the live actors are an immediate and vital part of theatregoing. The actors are much more aware of your presence than you think. Laugh, applaud, enjoy!
> 3. Theatre productions come on many different levels. One cannot have the same expectations viewing a high school production as with a professional regional theatre or Broadway production.
> 4. Theatregoing requires more concentration than other entertainment forms. Be prepared to listen, observe thoroughly, and take in as much as possible.
> 5. Be patient. Most plays are longer than most movies or television programs. Also, most theatre events have an intermission. Theatregoing is not a rushed experience. Allow and appreciate the time that the event takes.

THE STUDENT AS CRITIC

Leaving the cutthroat business of for-profit theatre and critics, let us concentrate on the kind of theatre criticism that a student can have about a production. Having learned something about each of the major areas of theatre, you are in a very good position to express an opinion about any play or musical that you attend. While this might be said of any audience member, there is much to be said for the informed theatregoer. You should see much more than others do when you watch and listen to a play because, hopefully, you have been made aware of so much more. When you are asked to discuss or write about a theatre event, your opinions ought to carry with them an understanding of both the theoretical and the practical aspects of playwriting, acting, directing, and designing. One does not need to be a writer of fiction to form an opinion about a novel, but it certainly helps if the person has read and studied the novel form and has had the life experiences that can contribute to the evaluation. With your own life experiences and with what we have covered throughout this book, you are ready to engage in formal as well as informal theatre criticism.

There are two rather obvious steps in theatre criticism: watching the performance and then evaluating it. What is not so obvious is that much of the work can be done during the first step. An alert, observant theatregoer is in a much better position to critique a theatre production afterward than one who is not engaged during the performance. Seeing and hearing everything that goes on is not difficult; the play was meant to be grasped by an audience unfamiliar with the playwright, plot, or style of production. Some theatre events are much more challenging than others, but no play should be viewed as casually as watching a television program or glancing at something on your laptop while texting or conversing with friends. Theatre seeks to captivate, but even the most gripping production demands that the spectator give full attention and focus to the event. Active and conscientious theatregoing leads to more solid theatre evaluation.

The process of criticizing any artwork can go back to a standard trio of questions that critics have used for ages: What was the artist trying to do? How successful was the artist in achieving this idea? Was it worth doing? Using that first basic question, one can look at any human-made creation and begin to understand it. If you view a production of *Macbeth* in which most of the male characters are dressed in Nazi uniforms, your emotional reaction might be very strong. Asking yourself what the director and designer intended by such an approach will allow you to rationally consider the production rather than simply praise it or dismiss it. The question of how well the artist succeeded can also be answered with clarity, though it can hardly be an objective answer. You might agree that the use of those German uniforms made one think of Macbeth's rise to power in a way you had not considered before. Or you might come to the conclusion that the idea hurt the play at every turn and only confused the issues at hand. The third question, regarding the worth of the concept, can be a rather emotional one. You can rationalize the uniforms, agree that they were effective, but still come to the conclusion that it was an idea that did not work for you. No theatre criticism can be completely objective and scientifically rational. Neither should the criticism be prejudiced or small-minded. We insist that theatre is human action, and judging this human behavior, either real or fictional, has never been a simple task.

What Is Expected of You When You View a Play

1. Be on time. Leave yourself plenty of time to arrive at the theatre, buy your ticket at the box office, and be seated in the theatre. Get your ticket ahead of time online if possible. Arriving late for a play is much different than walking in on a movie that has already started.
2. Enjoy the play but avoid talking, texting, popping gum, opening noisy candy wrappers, taking pictures or video, and moving about unnecessarily. This is annoying to other patrons and distracting to the actors as well. Such activity is perfectly acceptable for some forms of entertainment, such as a rock concert, but it is extremely detrimental during a theatre event.
3. Watch the play. Do not take notes or read your program during the play. Watch the show as a member of the audience. Keep your program for reference later, and make any notes you want at intermission or after the play.
4. Listen to the play. Plays demand that you listen to words much more than with film and television, which are visual media. Theatre is both visual and aural. What is said, whether it be in a Shakespeare play or a musical, is essential.
5. Keep a sharp eye. Notice everything onstage. Let your eyes wander and take in the scenery, lighting, costumes, makeup, and props, as well as the actors and their gestures and movements.

One of the most common mistakes made in criticizing theatre is to overwhelmingly praise the production or to wholeheartedly dismiss the play. Very few productions are flawless, and even fewer are not without some merit. Student criticism, both spoken and written, sometimes tends to be a vote of approval or rejection. No one need make such a sweeping and final conclusion about a theatre event. Because one did not think the script worth doing, does it mean that all the acting, direction, and designs were worthless as well? Even though another spectator thoroughly enjoyed the script, does it follow that all aspects of the production were therefore commendable? In the professional theatre, a review that registers as much praise as it finds fault is termed a *mixed notice*. This can sometimes just be a matter of hedging one's opinions by not coming out and saying what one really thinks. But in most cases a critique has both positive and negative things to say about a theatre event. An uninformed spectator may laugh at a comedy and conclude that everyone and everything about the production must be first-rate. We have seen that it is not so simple. Theatre mirrors life, and life is rarely so uncomplicated.

If you are asked to write about a production that you have seen, chances are you have not been requested to write a review. In education, one usually writes a *critique* of a theatre event, though it may not be specifically called that. A review, we have seen, is for the public to read and advises the potential theatregoer to either see or not see a production. A critique is written as a class assignment for an instructor who has already seen the play and is not interested in decisions about theatregoing. The purpose, rather, is to analyze and evaluate the production, using what you have learned about the theatre and applying it to this criticism. Reviews often explain the plot of the play so that readers will get an idea of what it is about. Critiques need not convey plot; the reader/instructor already knows the story well. It is more important to express an opinion *about* that plot, as well as all the other elements of the production. Do not think that a theatre critique is like those "book reports" you wrote for teachers years ago, proving that you read the book by providing enough information to fill in the blanks. Critiques prove that you experienced the production, thought about it, and have now organized those thoughts into a coherent written evaluation.

Throughout this book, most chapters have ended with a section about evaluating the work of the playwright or designer or other theatre artist. So how does one evaluate the work of a critic, be it a professional or a student? The best way is to look for qualities in the writing that suggest a person whose opinions are worth reading. Does the critic seem informed? It is not necessary to be a Shakespeare scholar and to know everything about *Macbeth* before going into the theatre. Yet familiarity with the playwright, the period of theatre history, and the long literary traditions about the tragedy certainly makes for a richer analysis. More important,

VIEWING A PLAY One experiences a stage production differently than other media. The eye and ear have so much more to take in and absorb, be it the acting and dancing or the scenery and the costumes. Consider everything there is to see and hear while viewing the choreographed rumble between the rival gangs in *West Side Story* (1957). Director-choreographer: Jerome Robbins. *Photofest*

does the evaluator seem to know enough about the different elements of theatre to have knowledgeable opinions about the acting or the lighting? An informed critic is always more reliable than one who simply has instinctual reactions to everything onstage. One should also question how observant the evaluator is. Did he or she notice everything, from the theme of the play to the makeup style used? Or was the entire production discussed and judged by only a handful of the many elements at work in live theatre?

> **Guidelines for Writing a Critique**
> 1. Cover everything. Most people just mention the actors because they are the easiest to notice. Cover the entire production: sets, lighting, costumes, props, sound, etc. In a musical, discuss the choreography and singing as well.
> 2. Notice the direction. Since no one sees the director, few write about his or her contribution. Notice where people were placed and how they moved (blocking), what the pace of the show was, how consistent the various elements were, and what the mood or atmosphere of the play was. These are part of the director's job.
> 3. This is just one production. Since all productions are different, do not judge this production in terms of another you have seen. The play is never the same as the movie. An educational theatre production cannot be like the Broadway version, nor should it be like your high school one. You may compare but realize the different situations.
> 4. Express an opinion. Write honestly what you thought and felt about the play. Be critical but not narrow-minded or mean-spirited. Give reasons or examples for your opinions. Ask yourself, What were they trying to do in this production? Then answer how successful they were in doing it.

An effective critic should be demanding enough to expect quality in all areas of the production but reasonable enough to understand the level of theatre being produced and the shortcomings of that level. One can complain that the actors playing Grandpa and Mr. Kirby in a Broadway revival of *You Can't Take It with You* were too young and seemed too inexperienced; to level the same criticism at a high school or even a college production of the play might be considered a foolish observation. Understanding that each theatre works under particular circumstances is essential in order to appreciate both an amateur community theatre mounting of *A Raisin in the Sun* and a professional regional theatre production of the same script. The theatres are different, and so must be the expectations. Yet one should not go to the extreme and believe that any amateur production is superb because everyone is doing one's best or that all professional plays are impressive because they have more money and talent. A reasonable critic considers all the circumstances surrounding the theatre event and evaluates it with those circumstances in mind.

Finally, theatre criticism should be written with a clear and engaging style. Ideas must be expressed in a simple, succinct manner, not a grandiose and flowery kind of writing that seeks to impress the reader. On the other hand, criticism that is dry, humorless, and uninvolved is also to be avoided. Someone writing theatre criticism ought to have some passion for theatregoing, and that should come out in the writing. After all, one is discussing the ways in which a group of artists has attempted to re-create the human experience on a stage. That is an exciting and ambitious thing to do on any level of professionalism. How can you evaluate such a bold and exciting adventure without some of that excitement rubbing off on each audience member?

TOPICS FOR GROUP DISCUSSION

1. Discuss which forms of criticism, from printed reviews to opinions of friends, affect your decision to attend a movie or a play.
2. Take a printed theatre review from the *New York Times* or other newspaper and discuss how the critic did or did not fully cover the many elements of a theatre event.
3. Select a current Broadway play or musical and see how many formal and informal reviews of it you can find online.

POSSIBLE RESEARCH PROJECTS

1. Look up the critics' reviews of the 2004 or the 2014 Broadway revival of *A Raisin in the Sun* in various New York newspapers and national magazines and compare and contrast the notices it received.
2. *Wicked* is the most successful new musical of the twenty-first century, yet it was not greeted with rave reviews when it opened in 2003. Look up the original reviews and comment on how they did or did not write accurately about the production.

FURTHER READING

Brustein, Robert. *Who Needs Theatre?* New York: Atlantic Monthly, 1987.
Clurman, Harold. *Lies Like Truth: Theatre Reviews and Essays.* New York: Macmillan, 1958.
Dolan, Jill. *The Feminist Spectator as Critic.* Ann Arbor: University of Michigan Press, 2012.
Fisher, Mark. *How to Write about Theatre.* London: Bloomsbury Methuen Drama, 2015.
Fortier, Mark. *Theory/Theatre: An Introduction.* Abingdon-on-Thames, UK: Routledge, 2016.
Gerould, Daniel. *Theatre—Theory—Theatre.* Milwaukee, WI: Applause Theatre Books, 2003.
Gussow, Mel. *Theatre on the Edge: New Visions, New Voices.* Milwaukee, WI: Applause Theatre and Cinema Books, 2000.
Kaufmann, Stanley. *Theatre Criticisms.* New York: Performing Arts Journal, 1984.
Kerr, Walter. *Journey to the Center of the Theatre.* New York: Knopf, 1979.
Nathan, George Jean. *The Critic and the Drama.* New York: Knopf, 1922.
Palmer, Richard. *The Critics' Canon: Standards of Theatrical Reviewing in America.* New York: Praeger, 1988.
Rich, Frank. *Hot Seat: Theatre Criticism for the New York Times, 1980–1995.* New York: Random House, 1998.
Simon, John. *On Theatre: Criticism, 1974–2003.* Milwaukee, WI: Applause Books, 2006.
Suskin, Steven. *More Opening Nights on Broadway.* New York: Schirmer Books, 1997.
———. *Opening Nights on Broadway.* New York: Schirmer Books, 1990.
Tynan, Kenneth. *Curtains: Selections from the Drama Criticism and Related Writings.* New York: Atheneum, 1971.
Wardle, Irving. *Theatre Criticism.* London: Faber, 2013.
Windman, Matt. *The Critics Say: 57 Theatre Reviewers in New York and Beyond Discuss Their Craft and Its Future.* Jefferson, NC: McFarland, 2016.

PARTING THOUGHTS

You are no longer an average, ordinary theatregoer. Having explored the concepts in these ten chapters, you now know more about the ideas behind a theatre event and the workings of a theatre production than the average spectator does. Other audience members may have seen many more productions than you have, but, unless they have pursued a study of theatre as basic as this, they are still spectators who mostly see only what is placed before them. When you see an actress step onstage or the costume she is wearing, you should now understand some of what went into that simple entrance and that stage costume. When you encounter something in the theatre that is strange or unexpected or even upsetting, you are better able to consider what is being attempted. You should no longer take any aspect of the theatre event for granted.

Does this make you a better theatregoer than the average one? Not necessarily. Are you able to enjoy a production more than someone unaware of what you know about this art form? Probably not. Theatre has always existed for a popular audience, an unenlightened and even illiterate audience. Your recently gained knowledge does not make you a member of an exclusive club or part of a select few who are "in the know." Theatre for such a narrow audience is probably questionable at best. You are still just one individual in a line of so many others over so many centuries who might be caught up in the mysterious hold that theatre has always had over humans. Perhaps you understand that mystery a little better than others, but you cannot explain it away. No one can. We are all mesmerized by this very simple, very intricate human phenomenon known as theatre.

GLOSSARY

absurdism A style of theatre originating in France in the 1950s that sees the world as illogical and nonsensical and argues that the arts should be just as meaningless.

acoustics The science of how sound travels in an interior space. A playhouse in which the actor's voice carries well without muffling the sounds or echoing is considered to have good acoustics.

actor-manager A starring actor who also runs his or her own theatre company. Seldom seen today, actor-managers were major forces in eighteenth- and nineteenth-century theatre.

Actors' Equity Association (AEA) The union for professional stage actors. Although a majority of its members are unemployed at any one time, the union negotiates and monitors actors' wages, benefits, and working conditions.

alienation A theatrical concept developed by German playwright-director Bertolt Brecht in which the audience is emotionally distanced from the play and characters in order to have an intellectual experience rather than an emotional one.

arena stage An architectural arrangement in a theatre in which the audience completely surrounds the actors in their playing space. Although it is also called *theatre-in-the-round*, the stage itself is often rectangular rather than circular.

aside A theatre convention in which an actor may deliver a line to the audience or to a specific actor onstage and it is understood that the other characters do not hear it.

asymmetrical balance A principle of scenic design in which the stage is balanced even though the two opposite sides of the set are not identical.

audition The process by which most actors are hired for theatre productions today. The actor performs a prepared or impromptu reading for the director to demonstrate one's acting abilities.

auteur A French term for "author" that, in theatre, implies that a director becomes the creator of a theatre event as much as the playwright.

backdrop A large, flat piece of scenery made of cloth that covers the entire width and height of the proscenium opening. Backdrops can be painted to depict scenes or colorless and used for projections or back lighting.

backers Those who invest money into a for-profit theatre production with the hopes of sharing in the profits if it is financially successful. They are also called *investors* or *angels*.

black box An interior space usually consisting of four black walls in which the audience seating arrangement and the acting area can be changed for each production.

blocking The movement of an actor onstage. Blocking is usually given to the actors by the director during a blocking rehearsal and recorded in the prompt book by the stage manager.

body mic A small microphone hidden in an actor's hair or costume, used to amplify the performer's voice onstage, particularly in musicals.

Broadway The most expensive and famous kind of professional, for-profit theatre in America. Most Broadway playhouses are located in New York City's Times Square area, known as the Theatre District.

character A person in a play, whether fictional or based on a real figure, as portrayed by an actor onstage. Character is also the element of drama that Aristotle placed second to plot in importance.

character makeup Theatrical makeup that attempts to change the actor's face, such as by aging it, adding facial hair, or exaggerating features such as the nose or chin.

choregus In ancient Greece, the person who paid the expenses to put a play on. It is the first form of theatrical producer. The name comes from the fact that the choregus pays the chorus members.

choreographer The person who devises the dances for a musical and teaches it to the dancers.

climax The point in which a theatre production reaches its highest emotional peak. In a tragedy it might be the moment of greatest tension, while in a comedy it may be the most exciting and comic point of the play.

cold reading An audition in which an actor is asked to read a speech or scene from a play for which he or she has had little or no time to prepare.

color-blind casting Casting the best actor in a role, even if, racially, the performer may not be what the playwright describes in the script.

comedy A type of play in which the humor is derived from the characters and/or the language used in the script.

comedy of manners A comic play that satirizes the social behavior of a particular class or type of people.

community theatre Theatre productions that are presented by members of a community to be enjoyed by others in the community. Community theatre is usually nonprofit and amateur, though directors and other administrative staff might be paid.

complication In the plotting of a play, any moment when something goes wrong for a major character and the story line is propelled in a new direction.

composer The person who writes the music for the songs and dances in a musical theatre production.

conclusion The final section of a play when the confusions or conflicts of the plot are resolved and a new balance is established. It is also called the *denouement*.

confidant A character in a play—usually a friend, relative, or servant—to whom the hero or heroine can speak and express ideas that might otherwise be heard in a soliloquy in a less-realistic play.

convention An unwritten and unspoken understanding between the audience and the actors to accept certain theatrical activities onstage. A character singing her or his thoughts in a musical, an aside from one actor to the audience, and the audience's belief in a character dying onstage are among the many theatre conventions used all the time.

costume plot A chart devised by the costume designer that indicates which costumes are worn by the characters in each scene of a play.

critic A person who is paid to view a theatre production and then write a review of it for some form of media.

critique A written analysis of a theatre production, evaluating the many elements of the theatre event and expressing an opinion as to how effective they were.

cue A line or action that signals an actor to speak or move onstage.

designer An artist who creates, on paper and with charts, the scenery, costumes, lighting, props, makeup, or sound for a theatre production.

dialogue The conversations between characters in a play, as written by the playwright. Dialogue may be realistic and lifelike or poetic and romanticized.

diction The language and manner of speech in a play, according to Aristotle. Today the term also refers to the ability of the actor to speak clearly and articulately.

dimmer board A mechanism through which all of the lighting instruments in a theatre are wired and controlled, allowing the operator to select which lights to use and at which intensity.

dinner theatre A form of theatregoing in which the audience has a meal then views a production in the same location.

director The person who unifies a theatre production by selecting the style and concept for the play and then works with actors and designers to achieve that concept.

dramatic criticism Written evaluation of drama, as opposed to critiquing a theatre event.

dramatic elements The six major aspects of a theatre production, as defined by Aristotle: plot, character, theme, diction, music, and spectacle.

Dramatists Guild An organization for professional playwrights, composers, and lyricists. Although not technically a union, the guild does negotiate contracts and helps secure royalties for writers in the theatre.

dress rehearsal A series of final technical rehearsals in which the cast is in full costume and the play is performed as if before an audience.

educational theatre Any form of theatre in a school, with students as the actors, from elementary school skits to university theatre productions.

emotion memory An acting technique devised by the Russian actor-director Konstantin Stanislavsky in which an actor recalls an experience in his or her own life and uses it to re-create the emotions needed for a role onstage.

empathy The audience's understanding of a character's state of mind. Unlike sympathy, in which the spectators feel sorry for a character, empathy implies a deep and even personal apprehension of what a character is going through.

Equity An abbreviated term for Actors' Equity Association, the union for professional actors.

experimental theatre Any form of theatre production that does not conform to the traditional methods of the day. Plays that were considered experimental at one time might be looked on as mainstream in another era.

exposition In the structure of a play, information given to the audience about past events in the plot or actions that occur offstage. Exposition can be accomplished through dialogue, announcements, a soliloquy, song, or other forms.

expressionism A style of theatre presentation in which the world is looked at psychologically rather than realistically. The play, the acting, the designs, and the direction can be described as expressionistic when this style is used.

fantasy Any play that creates its own reality and presents a world that contains fantastical logic.

farce A comic play in which the humor arises out of situation, broad action, and familiar stock characters.

flat A piece of stage scenery, usually rectangular in shape, made from stretching cloth over a frame. Flats can be painted and combined in ways to create walls and other structures.

foreshadowing Any information given in a play that hints at or clearly points to some event that occurs later in the plot.

for-profit theatre A theatre venture that must make a profit at the box office in order to continue operation.

gel A transparent piece of plastic or glass that is tinted with a color. When placed in front of a lighting instrument, the gel gives color to the beam of light.

genre A French word used to indicate what type of play is being produced: tragedy, comedy, farce, and so on.

germinal idea The initial idea that a playwright has that leads to the creation of a script. Germinal ideas can be a person, place, theme, setting, and so forth.

ground plan The layout of walls, doors, furniture, trees, and other scenic pieces on a chart that shows the acting space from above. Also called a *floor plan*, it is similar to blueprints for the interior of a house.

guerrilla theatre An activist form of theatre production, usually performed in nontraditional spaces, that has an aggressive political agenda and seeks to incite the audience for social change.

hand prop Any property that is manually handled by the actors, from a handkerchief to a rifle.

house The section of the theatre building where the audience sits.

inciting incident In play structure, a past event that probably occurred before the curtain rose that affects the actions of the characters and plot.

interp Short for *interpretation*, the process in which the actors and director discuss and experiment with the script in order to develop the characters. A rehearsal dedicated to this might be called an *interp* or *character rehearsal*.

League of Resident Theatres (LORT) An organization of professional nonprofit regional theatres across the United States.

librettist The person who writes the "book" for a musical play: plot, characters, dialogue.

light plot A chart devised by the lighting designer that indicates where each lighting instrument is to be hung, wired, and focused and which color light it will cast.

lyricist The person who writes the lyrics (or words) to the songs in a musical theatre production.

mask Something that covers part or all of the face, either hiding the actor's identity or indicating that the performer is someone or something other than the real self. In ancient times, masks told audiences what character an actor was portraying. Today masks usually represent animals and other nonhuman characters or are used to exaggerate the physical features of a character.

melodrama A serious play that does not attain the heights of tragedy. The slangy expression "mellerdrama" today means a hokey and sentimental melodrama to be laughed at.

Method An American form of acting adapted from the Russian system that places emphasis on the performer's ability to develop characters emotionally rather than intellectually.

music One of Aristotle's elements of drama, it refers not only to the use of chanting and musical instruments in the theatre but also to the rhythm and harmony in the language of the play.

musical A play that uses songs and usually dance in telling its story.

musical director The person who teaches the cast of a musical the songs and often conducts the orchestra during the performances.

naturalism A style of theatre presentation that is an extreme form of realism, emphasizing details and relying on the senses to re-create real life onstage.

nonprofit theatre A theatre venture that cannot support itself through box office income and relies on fund-raising, grants, and other means to finance the operation.

nontraditional casting The use of actors onstage not traditionally considered for a particular role. The performers might be a different sex or race or may have some other physical uniqueness that differs with the script, but they are cast nonetheless because of their talent.

Off Broadway A group of professional theatres scattered throughout Manhattan that offer an alternative to Broadway.

Off-Off-Broadway A collection of small performing groups throughout New York City that present original and often experimental productions, usually in non-traditional spaces.

option Money paid to a playwright by the producer to retain exclusive rights to produce a script.

performance art A nontraditional theatre event that utilizes many arts, from painting to dance, to express ideas outside of the linear structure of a play. Some performance pieces are more concerned with the process of creating art rather than presenting it, but these events are performed before an audience and are considered theatre.

perspective The art of creating the illusion of depth on a flat surface. Perspective greatly affected theatre scenery beginning in the Italian Renaissance.

playwright One who writes the script to be used in a theatre production.

plot The story line of a play. It is the dramatic element that Aristotle considered the most important.

point of attack A moment in a play, usually early on, in which the audience's interest is aroused. It is often the beginning of the action of a theatre event.

preview A performance for a paying audience before the production has officially opened to the press and public.

producer The person who raises the money for a theatre production, hires the personnel, and oversees the management of the play's performances.

prompt book A copy of the script that includes all of the actors' blocking, notes on performance, and technical notations.

prop An object used onstage, from something as small as a pencil to one as large as a sofa. The word is a shortened version of "properties."

property A producer's term for a play that he or she has secured rights to and hopes to find the finances to produce. Not to be confused with a stage property or prop.

proscenium An arch that separates the audience from the acting space in a proscenium-style theatre. In such a configuration, the spectators watch the actors through the proscenium arch.

public domain A play that was written before copyright laws were established and can be produced without paying a royalty.

publicist A person hired by a producer to handle the advertising and other publicity for a theatre production.

read-through An early rehearsal in which the cast reads the play aloud, with everyone playing the specific roles in which they were cast.

realism A style of theatre production that attempts to re-create events onstage as they appear in real life.

regional theatre A professional nonprofit theatre company located in an American city outside of New York that presents a series of productions during a designated theatre season.

rehearsal A general term for any gathering of actors with a director to prepare for a public theatre production.

rendering A sketch by a designer, usually in color, that illustrates what the scenery or the costumes for a production will look like.

resident theatre A regional theatre that hires a company of actors who play a variety of roles in a series of plays during a season.

retrace A rehearsal in which the actors review the blocking given to them by the director and retrace their steps to see if the movements work effectively.

review A published or broadcast criticism of a play written by a critic and used to encourage or discourage the public to attend a particular theatre production.

revival A play or musical that is not being produced for the first time; it is being "revived" in a new and different production.

the road Slang for the business of touring professional for-profit theatre productions to different cities.

romanticism A style of theatre that presents a heightened and poetic version of reality, using poetry, music, and other romanticized elements.

royalty The money paid to a playwright (or to his or her estate) every time a script is produced, either professionally or by amateur theatre groups.

run-through A rehearsal in which the entire script is "run" in the manner in which it will later be presented before a live audience.

satire A form of comedy that ridicules the ideals and beliefs of a certain type of person or people.

set prop A stage prop that is part of the scenery, such as furniture or a fountain.

showcase A semiprofessional theatre production done Off-Off-Broadway that tests a new script and hopes to interest producers in presenting it elsewhere. A showcase is similar in intent to a "workshop" production.

sight lines The lines of vision from every seat in the house to the stage. Both theatre architects and scenic designers must be aware of sight lines if all of the audience is going to see the stage clearly.

soliloquy A speech delivered by a character in a play when he or she is alone onstage. Soliloquies can be delivered directly to the audience or can be the character's thoughts expressed aloud.

spectacle The visual aspects of a theatre production, from the scenery and costumes to dancing and stage combat. Aristotle placed spectacle as the least important element of theatre, but over the centuries many productions have emphasized such visuals.

spine According to Stanislavsky's system of acting, the central goal or drive that is the clue to understanding a character.

stage manager The person who runs the production during technical rehearsals and performances, calling cues and seeing that the director's work is carried out at each public showing of the play.

straight makeup Stage makeup that does not attempt to change the facial characteristics of the actors but instead attempts to highlight them so that they look natural under theatre lights.

street theatre Performances done in neighborhoods for audiences who might not attend traditional theatre productions. Most street theatre is focused specifically on the inhabitants of the neighborhood, even using their language and cultural idioms.

style The manner or form in which a production is presented. The director usually decides on the style of presentation, and all of the other aspects of the production, from the actors to the designs, should support this style.

subsidiary rights Income that a playwright and a producer receive from non-royalty income, such as movie rights, cast albums, T-shirts, and other merchandise.

summer stock Seasonal theatre companies located in places that enjoy an influx of tourists and provide entertainment for them. Summer theatres range from fully professional for-profit to semiprofessional nonprofit, and the offerings can range from escapist to ambitious.

symmetrical balance An element of scenic design in which both halves of the stage are balanced because they are identical to each other.

System A theory of acting introduced by Stanislavsky that is the basis for all modern acting. The System is based on observation, research, concentration, and using personal recollections to create a character and achieve truthful acting.

technical director The person who supervises the crew who builds the scenery and props from the renderings and construction drawings provided by the designer. TDs, as they are often called, are also in charge of the movement of scenery and other matters during technical rehearsals.

theatre criticism Written or oral evaluation of a theatre production, as opposed to the criticism of a piece of dramatic literature.

theatre festival A theatre company that offers a selection of classic plays during a season, usually in the summer. Several such festivals concentrate on Shakespeare, but there are others that feature vintage musicals, American favorites, and even new works.

theatre-in-the-round Another name for an arena-style stage or theatre.

theatre of diversity Plays or theatre companies that concentrate on special interest groups, from ethnic and cultural identification to political or sexual-preference issues.

theme The major idea that a play is about. One of Aristotle's six elements, theme is rarely a moral or judgment but rather an exploration of ideas or issues that are not easily resolved.

thespians An archaic term for actors, named after the legendary Greek figure Thespis, who is considered the first actor.

three-quarter stage Another name for a thrust stage, in which the audience surrounds the actors on three of four sides.

thrust stage A playhouse structure in which the stage extends or thrusts out into the audience and the actors are surrounded on three sides by the spectators. Also called a *three-quarter stage*.

tragedy A serious play in which the hero or heroine is a great and good figure who has a flaw and is punished because of that flaw.

tragicomedy A play that mixes tragic elements of life with comic ones.

unit set A scenic design for one basic nondescript set that allows for a variety of playing areas and is ideal for plays with many locations, each of which can be suggested by a few pieces of scenery or furniture.

United Scenic Artists (USA) The union for professional scenic designers, lighting designers, and costume designers.

well-made play A play in which all of the elements of the plot are carefully and logically presented, making for a linear and rational story line.

workshop A public performance, usually Off-Off-Broadway, in which actors, directors, and designers work on a new script for little or no pay, hoping that the piece will develop into a full production.

WEBSITES

Actors' Equity Association: www.actorsequity.org
The website for the union for professional actors contains news, casting notices, information on the union, a documents library, and ticket discounts for members.

American Alliance for Theatre Education: www.aate.com
This organization of theatre educators and artists sponsors conferences and programs that are described on the site, as well as a guide to resources and publications.

American Association of Community Theatres: www.aact.org
Particular community theatres are featured on the site along with a list of productions across the country, a resource directory, and news on conferences.

American Federation of Television and Radio Artists (AFTRA): www.aftra.org
The union for professional radio and television actors operates this site, which offers news, articles, reports, and a directory of its members.

American Theatre Critics Association: www.americantheatrecritics.org
This organization sponsors awards, fellowships, and conferences, all of which are described, as well as news and a calendar of events.

Arts Lynx: www.artslynx.org
This research site has links to libraries and other resources with information on theatre, dance, music, and film.

Broadway.com: www.broadway.com
Covering mostly New York and London theatre, the site offers feature articles, reviews, and links to theatres to buy tickets.

Broadway Direct: www.broadwaydirect.com
In addition to articles about theatre past and present, this site offers lotteries in which one can buy theatre tickets at reduced prices.

Broadway World: www.broadwayworld.com
Although this website concentrates on news, charts, and features about Broadway, it also looks at international theatre with links to theatres to buy tickets.

Dramatist Guild: www.dramaguild.com
The organization for professional playwrights, composers, and lyricists maintains this site, which offers information on playwriting contests and conferences, fellowships, and a directory of theatres across the nation that accept manuscripts.

Educational Theatre Association: www.edta.org
Covering all kinds of theatre education, from high school to university, this organization sponsors conferences and puts out several publications, all described on the site.

Internet Broadway Database: www.ibdb.com
Facts and figures about people, plays, and theatre organizations are among the information in this site, which is difficult to browse but easy to use to look up specific items.

Internet Theatre Database: www.theatredb.com
With a wider range than the Internet Broadway Database, this site includes much on theatre history as well as current names and plays.

Musical Heaven: www.musicalheaven.com
Broadway, London, and movie musicals are the subject of this reference site, which also reviews recorded scores and has links to purchase CDs.

Musicals 101: www.musicals101.com
Concentrating on film and stage musicals, this site not only covers current shows but has much information about musical theatre history, including biographies, reviews, articles, and facts and figures.

Playbill: www.playbill.com
This website, for the magazine-like program given to patrons for most Broadway theatres, covers New York, regional, and London theatre with news stories, feature articles, facts and figures, and links to theatres to buy tickets.

Screen Actors Guild (SAG): www.sag.org
This site is provided by the union for film actors and includes news, a calendar of events, and a directory of members.

Show Tickets: www.ShowTickets.com
Articles about theatre past and present are the highlight of this site, which also has news and offers ways to get discounted tickets to professional theatre throughout the country.

Shubert Archive: www.shubertarchive.org
Theatre memorabilia, photos, programs, and other artifacts are stored in this collection, with much of the contents available for viewing.

Telecharge: www.telecharge.com
Primarily a tool to purchase theatre, sports, and concert tickets, this site also offers information on the shows currently playing across the country, with links to individual websites.

Theatre Communications Group: www.tcg.org
The organization that assists and promotes professional nonprofit theatre in America operates this site, with articles, news, job listings, and publications.

Theatre Development Fund: www.tdf.org
This nonprofit organization promotes theatre by offering ticket discounts and special events for members.

Theatre History: www.theatrehistory.com
International theatre history is the subject of this site, with articles and facts on people and plays.

Theatre Mania: www.theatremania.com
Theatre in New York and other major cities is highlighted in this site, with articles, news, and links to sites to buy tickets.

Ticketmaster: www.ticketmaster.com
Along with Telecharge, the company that seems to have the monopoly on buying tickets to Broadway plays and musicals. It provides information on the shows for which it sells tickets.

Tickets Now: www.ticketsnow.com
A smaller and alternative source for buying tickets for all kinds of events, including those of theatres across the country.

United Scenic Artists: www.usa829.org
The website for the union for professional scenic, lighting, and costume designers contains news, information on the union, a designer's showcase, and articles on new technology.

Variety: **www.variety.com**
The website for this "show business bible" includes news and reviews, including a section on "legit" theatre.

FILM AND VIDEO VERSIONS OF THE PLAYS

All four of the plays discussed throughout the textbook have been filmed, some of them several times. The following is a selective and annotated list. There are many resources for purchasing these films on video and DVD. The production information given here will help identify the versions that you may wish to rent or purchase.

MACBETH

There are over forty different film and television versions of *Macbeth*, including foreign-language productions and animated versions. Some of the most accessible or recommended ones include the following:

(Republic Pictures 1948). Featuring Orson Welles, Jeanette Nolan, Dan O'Herlihy, Edgar Barrier, Roddy McDowell. Directed by Orson Welles. This very atmospheric piece, filled with theatrical images and symbols, is one of the few versions in which Scottish accents are used. B&W. 89 minutes, though a restored version runs 105 minutes.

Throne of Blood (Toho Company 1957). Featuring Toshiro Mifune, Isuzu Yamada, Takashi Shimura, Minoru Chiaki. Directed by Akira Kurosawa. A cinema classic, this bloody but engrossing Japanese film tells Shakespeare's story as a samurai tale, using an Asian perspective that sheds light on the English original. B&W. 108 minutes.

(TV 1960). Featuring Maurice Evans, Judith Anderson, Michael Hordern, Ian Bannen. Directed by George Schaefer. A British television production that was shown briefly in American movie houses in 1963, this very poetic version featured a renowned cast. It is not easy to locate but worth the effort. Color. 108 minutes.

(Columbia 1971). Featuring Jon Finch, Francesca Annis, Martin Shaw, Nicholas Selby. Directed by Roman Polanski. Very bloody and graphic British film (killings only spoken of in the play are shown with grisly detail) but effective on many levels. Color. 140 minutes.

(TV 1979). Featuring Ian McKellen, Judi Dench, John Woodvine, Bob Peck. Directed by Philip Casson. Based on a British stage production directed by Trevor Nunn, this version takes a very theatrical and unconventional approach to the play. Color. Approx. 125 minutes.

(TV 1981). Featuring Jeremy Brett, Piper Laurie, Barry Primus, Simon MacCorkindale. Directed by Arthur Allan Seidelman. This is a simple, rather stagy production but boasts some fine performances. Color. 132 minutes.

(TV 1983). Featuring Nicol Williamson, Jane Lapotaire, Ian Hogg, Tony Doyle. Directed by Jack Gold. This British television version is perhaps the most complete and most traditional of all screen adaptations. Color. 148 minutes.

(TV 1998). Featuring Sean Pertwee, Greta Scacchi, Lorcan Cranitch, Michael Maloney. Directed by Michael Bogdanov. A short, concise British television version with a modern setting that was made to be broadcast to high schools. Color. 88 minutes.

(Film Victoria/Mushroom Pictures 2006). Featuring Sam Worthington, Victoria Hill, Lachy Hulme, Steve Bastoni. Directed by Geoffrey Wright. A visually exciting version of the tragedy set in the contemporary ganglands of Melbourne, Australia. Color. 109 minutes.

(See-Saw Films 2015). Featuring Michael Fassbender, Marion Cotillard, Sean Harris, Paddy Considine. Directed by Justin Kurzel. This Great Britain–France production directed by the Australian Kurzel is realistic, fast moving, and far from stagy. Color. 113 minutes.

YOU CAN'T TAKE IT WITH YOU

(Columbia Pictures 1938). Featuring Lionel Barrymore, Jean Arthur, James Stewart, Edward Arnold, Spring Byington, Ann Miller, Mischa Auer, Eddie Anderson. Directed by Frank Capra. Although the stage script is very altered, turning the focus from Grandpa (Barrymore) to the uptight Mr. Kirby (Arnold), there are still some delightful performances. B&W. 126 minutes.

(TV 1979). Featuring Art Carney, Jean Stapleton, Blythe Danner, Barry Bostwick, Beth Howland, Harry Morgan, Eugene Roche, Paul Sand, Marla Gibbs. Directed by Paul Bogart. A very faithful adaptation, this slightly shortened version has a top-notch cast of television stars with plenty of stage experience. Color. 97 minutes.

(TV 1984). Featuring Jason Robards, Elizabeth Wilson, Maureen Anderman, Nicolas Surovy, Bill McCutcheon, Rosetta LeNoire, Carole Androsky, George Rose. Directed by Kirk Browning, Ellis Rabb. The superb 1983 Broadway revival was taped for *Great Performances* on PBS-TV, providing a wonderful archive of an outstanding production. Color. 116 minutes.

A RAISIN IN THE SUN

(Columbia Pictures 1961). Featuring Claudia McNeil, Sidney Poitier, Ruby Dee, Diana Sands, Ivan Dixon, Louis Gossett, John Fiedler. Directed by Daniel Petrie. This very faithful and beautifully filmed screen adaptation features some members of the Broadway cast re-creating their stage performances. B&W. 128 minutes.

(TV 1989). Featuring Esther Rolle, Danny Glover, Starletta DuPois, Kim Yancey, Lou Ferguson, John Fiedler. Directed by Bill Duke. This television version is even more complete than the 1961 movie; while it is slow at times, it is saved by some vibrant performances. Color. 171 minutes.

(TV 2008). Featuring Phylicia Rashad, Sean Combs, Audra McDonald, Sanaa Lathan, John Stamos. The cast of the acclaimed 2004 Broadway revival was reassembled for this TV movie that opened up the play somewhat but retains the essence of the original. Color. 131 minutes.

HAMILTON

Although a film or television adaptation of *Hamilton* has not yet been made, there is an excellent 2016 documentary about Alexander Hamilton and the creation of the musical called *Hamilton's America*. The ninety-minute television film, directed by Alan Horwitz for PBS-TV, includes interviews with politicians, historians, actors, and other people involved in the making of the musical. There is also a 2017 ninety-minute British documentary titled *Hamilton: One Shot to Broadway*, written and directed by Elio Espana, about the making of the musical.

INDEX

Note: Page numbers in bold indicate photographs or illustrations.

Abbey Theatre (Dublin), 166
absurdism, 98-99, 193
acoustics, 146-47, 193
acting, 73-90; analysis of, 81; art and craft of 74-75; auditions for, 84-85; business of, 84; convention of, 11-12; evaluation of, 87-88; external approach to, 79; first actor, 76; history of, 75-77; internal approach to, 79-80; process of, 81-83; superstitions of, 89; sustaining a performance, 83; theories of, 79-80; terms of, 86-87; tools of, 80; union for, 85; vs. character, 88; vs. role playing, 73
actor-manager, 193
Actors' Equity Association (AEA), 85-86, 193
Actors Studio, 78
ad-libbing, 86
African American theatre, 172-73
After the Fall, 64
Ah, Wilderness!, 61
aislesitter, 117
Albee, Edward, 65
Alexander technique, 86
alienation, 98, 193
All My Sons, 64
Alley Theatre (Houston), 163
alternative theatre, 170-71
Amadeus, 64, **65**
amateur theatre, 158-59
American Association of Community Theatre (AACT), 168
American Buffalo, 69
An American Daughter, 70
The American Dream, 65
American Theatre Wing, 161
amplification (sound), 147
And Baby Makes Seven, 70
Androcles and the Lion, 60
angel, 117
Angels in America, **1**, 36, 177
Animal Crackers, 45
Anna in the Tropics, 173-74

apprentice, 86
apron, 150
Arcadia, 67
arena stage, 123, **126**, 193
Arena Stage (Washington, D.C.), 126, 163-64
Aronson, Boris, 128, 130
Aristotle, 28-32, 34, 46-47, 48, 56, 76
Arms and the Man, 60
articulation, 86
As Thousands Cheer, 45
As You Like It, 44
Asian American theatre, 174-75
aside, 12, 193
Assassins, 66
asymmetrical scenery/balance, 130-31, 193
at liberty, 86
Auburn, David, 29
auditions, 84-85, 102-3, 193
auteur, 110, 193
Avenue Q, **162**

The Bacchae, **77**
backdrop, 129, 193
backers, 115, 193
backlighting, 144
Baker, Andy, 126
The Baltimore Waltz, 70
The Band Wagon, 45
Baraka, Amiri (LeRoi Jones), 172-73
Barefoot in the Park, 64
Beckett, Samuel, 98-99
Beggar on Horseback, 44
Bennett, Alan, 66-67
Bennett, Michael, 84, 100-101
The Best Little Whorehouse in Texas, 184
Beyond the Fringe, 66
Big Fish, 94
Billy Elliot, 165
Biloxi Blues, 65
Bitter Sweet, 63
Björnson, Maria, 31

black box, 124, **126**, 193
Black Comedy, 64
Blakemore, Michael, 33
Blithe Spirit, 63
blocking, 104, 193
body mic, 147, 150, 193
Bonnie and Clyde, **3**
The Book of Mormon, **106**, 165
border, 150
Born Yesterday, 46
box set, 126, 129
Boyd, Chad, **3**
The Boys in the Band, 176
Bramble, Mark, 108
Brando, Marlon, 78, **79**
Bread and Puppet Theatre, 178
break a leg, 89
break-even point, 117
Brecht, Bertolt, 39, 98, 178
The Bridge of San Luis Rey, 62
The Bridges of Madison County, 69
Brightman, Sarah, **31**
Brighton Beach Memoirs, 65, 128
Brighton Festival (Great Britain), 167
Bring It On, 46
British theatre: Fringe theatre, 165; influence on American theatre, 177-79; subsidized theatre, 165; theatregoing today, 165-66; West End, 165
Brittan, Robert, 37
Broadway, 157-58, 159-60, 193
Broadway Bound, 65
Brook, Peter, 178-79
Buckley, Jessie, **65**
Burbage, Richard, 114
Buried Child, 68
bus and truck tour, 160

The Cabala, 62
cabling (lighting), 145
Caesar and Cleopatra, 60
Caldwell, Zoe, **75**
Camelot, 45
Camp, Anna, **185**
Candida, 60
Carell, Candace, 11
Cariou, Len, **56**, **66**
Carlisle, Greg, 126
Carney, Art, **33**
Carousel, 62

casting, 102-3
Cat on a Hot Tin Roof, 64, **96**
Cats, **11**, 56, 165, 177
cattle call audition, 85
Cavalcade, 63
censorship in the theatre, 184
Champion, Gower, 100-101, 108
Chapter Two, 65
character, 28-29, 54, 57, 193
character makeup, 149-50, 194
character rehearsals, 104
cheat (acting), 86
Chekhov, Anton, 55
Chenoweth, Kristin, **149**
Chernow, Ron, 47
chew the scenery, 86
Chicago, 110, 165
Chicano theatre, 173
Chichester Festival, 167
The Children's Hour, 63, 176
children's theatre, 168
choregus, 113, 194
choreographer/choreography, 93, 106-7, 194; business of, 107-9, evaluation of, 110
A Chorus Line, 56, **84**
Christie, Agatha, 117
Chronicles of England, Scotland and Ireland, 48
Church, Jonathan, 65
Churchill, Caryl, 67-68
Circus Valentine, 69
climax, 39, 194
Cloud Nine, 67
Clybourne Park, 26
The Coast of Utopia, 67
Cobb, Lee J., **35**
The Cocoanuts, 45
cold reading, 85, 194
Colins, Ashlee, 126
The Color Purple, **69**
Colorado Shakespeare Festival, 167
color-blind casting, 103, 194
Comédie Français (Paris), 166
comedy, 33-34, 194
The Comedy of Errors, 44
comedy of manners, 34, 194
community theatre, 168, 194
comp ticket, 117
Company, 66
complications, 38, 194
composer, 56, 194

computer technology, 151–53
computer-aided design (CAD), 152
computer-aided manufacture (CAM), 152
concept drawing, 131–32
conclusion, 39, 194
confidant, 194
Congreve, William, 34
Connelly, Marc, 44
conventions (theatre), 10–14, 194; acting, 11–12 of place, 11; of time, 11
Conversation Piece, 63
Conway, Kevin, **75**
Cook, Peter, 66
Corpus Christie, 184
costume design, 137–41; business of, 153–54; evaluation of, 154–55; functions of, 137–38; process of, 139, 141; quick changes of, 141
costume plot, 139, 194
counter (acting), 86
counterweight, 150
Coward, Noel, 63
Crawford, Cheryl, 114
Crawford, Michael, **31**
critic, 184–86, 194
critique, 188–89, 194
Cromer, David, 25
Crowley, Mart, 176
The Crucible, **53**, 64
Cruz, Nilo, 174
Cuban American theatre, 173
cue (acting), 82, 194
curtain call, 89
cyclorama, 150

Daldry, Stephen, 146
Daniele, Graciela, 74
Davison, Bruce, **47**
A Day at the Races, 45
de Lacois, Choderlos, 140
De Niro, Robert, 78
Dean, James, 78
Dear Ruth, 45
Death of a Salesman, 32, **35**, 64
Dee, Ruby, 19
A Delicate Balance, 65
Delsarte, François, 77
Deneyer, Paul, 2, 126
denouement, 39
Desdemona—A Play about a Handkerchief, 70
Design for Living, 63

designer, 127–55, 194; costume, 137–41, 153–54; lighting, 141–46, 153–54, 155; makeup, 148–50; props, 148; scenic, 127–34, 153–54; sound, 146–48
Desire under the Elms, 61
Dewhurst, Colleen, **25**
Dexter, John, 47, 177
dialogue, 48–52, 57, 194
diction, 30, 57, 194
Diderot, Denis, 77
Diggs, Daveed, **27**
dimmer board, 144, 195
Dinner at Eight, 44
dinner theatre, 167, 195
directing/director, 195; analysis of, 102; art of, 94–95; business of, 107; concepts of, 94; definition of, 94; evaluation of, 109–10; first director, 100; history of, 99–100; process of, 101–7; styles of, 96–99; tools of, 93; women in, 114
directorial concept, 94
Dismorphia, **170**
distribution (lighting), 144
diversity, theatre of, 172–77, 199
Dixon, Ivan, 19
The Doctor's Dilemma, 60
Dodd, Jeff, 3
Don Juan Comes Home from Iraq, 70
Doubt, **58**
Douglas, Suzzanne, **164**
downlighting, 144
downstage, 86
drama, 1–2, 23–39; definition of, 2; elements of, 27–32; types of, 32–36; vs. theatre, 1–2
drama therapy, 169
dramatic criticism, 183, 195
dramatic elements, 27–32, 195
dramatic structure, 37–39
Dramatists Guild, 59, 116, 195
draper, 139
Dreamgirls, **101**
dress form, 139
dress parade, 139
dress rehearsal, 83, 139, 141, 195
dress the house, 117
Drew, Mrs. John, 114
Driving Miss Daisy, 162
Dulcy, 44
Dulude, Joseph, II, 149

East West Players (Los Angeles), 174
Edinburgh International Festival (Scotland), 167
educational theatre, 169, 195
El Teatro Campesino, 173
elevation drawings, 132
Elliott, Marianne, 1
Ellis, Scott, 103
emotion memory, 78, 195
empathy, 29, 195
Endgame, 99
Ensler, Eve, **175**, 176
environmental staging, 124
Epidaurus Festival (Greece), 6
Equity. *See* Actors Equity Association (AEA)
Equus, 64, **185**
Euripides, 77
Everett, Rupert, **65**
Evita, 165
experimental theatre, 170–71, 195
exposition, 38, 195
expressionism, 97, 195
exterior set, 129
Eyre, Richard, 53

F.O.B., 174
Face the Music, 45
Falsettos, 176
The Fantasticks, 162
fantasy, 36, 195
farce, 33–34, 195
Fattizzi, Dani, **140**
Fearon, Ray, 24
Federal Theatre Project, 168
feminist theatre, 175–76
Fences, **68**
Ferber, Edna, 44
Fichandler, Zelda, 164
Fiddler on the Roof, 100, **128**
Fierstein, Harvey, 176
Finn, William, 176
first hand, 139
first-class tour, 160
Fisher, Rick, 146
Fitzgerald, Tara, 24
Five Finger Exercise, 64
flat, 130, 195
flexible space, 124, **126**
floor plan, 132
Flower Drum Song, 174
fly loft, 129, 150

Follies, 66, **116**
Fonda, Jane, 78
Fool for Love, 68
foreign influences on American theatre, 177–79
foreshadowing, 38, 195
Fornes, Maria Irene, 176
for-profit theatre, 158, 195
42nd Street, **108**
Forty Years On, 67
Fosse, Bob, 100, 110
found space, 126, 162, 165
Fox, Ben, **63**
Frayn, Michael, 33
Fringe Theatre (Great Britain), 165
front of house, 117
The Front Page, 45
Fucking A, 184
A Funny Thing Happened on the Way to the Forum, 66

Garfield, Andrew, **1**
gay and lesbian theatre, 176–77
Geer, Will, **183**
gel, 144–45, 195
Gem of the Ocean, 69
genre, 32–36, 195
Gentleman's Agreement, 45
Georg II, Duke of Saxe-Meiningen, 100
George Washington Slept Here, 45
germinal idea, 46–48, 196
Getting Out, 69
The Glass Menagerie, 46, **47**, 63–64
Glengarry Glen Ross, 69
Globe Theatre (Elizabethan), 16, 23, 54, 124 **125**, 131, 142
Globe Theatre (new), **16**, **24**, 125
Glomboski, Simone, **3**
The Goat, or Who Is Sylvia?, 65
gobo, 150
Gossett, Louis, 19
Grease, 138, 169
greasepaint, 151
Great Britain (theatregoing in), 165–66
green room, 86
Greenberg, Richard, 176
Greif, Michael, 163
Grotowski, Jerzy, 170
ground plan, 132, 196
guerrilla theatre, 171, 196
guidelines for writing a critique, 189

Guthrie, Tyrone, 124
Guthrie Theatre (Minneapolis), **124**
Guys and Dolls, 13, 45, **133**
Gwinne, Matthew, 48
Gypsy, 66

Habeas Corpus, 67
The Habit of Art, 67
Hair, 185
Hairspray, 150, **152**
Hall, Peter, 77
Hallelujah, Baby!, **164**
ham (acting), 86
hamartia, 32
Hamilton, 2, 10, 12, **19**, 26, **27**, 29, 30, 31, 35, 36, 38, 51-52, 56-57, 59, 75, 82-83, 87, 89, 95-96, 99, 126-27, 129, 130-31, **132**, 137-38, 144, 147, 153, 158-59, 162, 165, 178; dialogue in, 51–52; directorial concept for, 95–96; germinal idea for, 47; original production of, 19; performance space for, 129; plot description of, 26–27
Hamlet, 44
Hammerstein, Oscar, 35-36, 61-62, 65, 174
Hampton, Christopher, 140
hand props, 148, 196
Hans Christian Andersen, 45
Hansberry, Lorraine, 1, 18, 23, 25, 29-30, 37, 38, 43, **45**, 46-47, 58, 95, 128, 178
The Hard Problem, 67
Hart, Moss, 1, 17, 23, 25, 44, **45**, 59, 178
Hay Fever, 63
Heard, John, **47**
Hedda Gabler, **81**
The Heidi Chronicles, 70
Hellman, Lillian, 63, 176
Hello, Dolly!, 62, 113
Henley, Beth, 176
Henry, Lenny, **68**
Hilferty, Susan, 149
Hispanic theatre. *See* Latinx theatre
The History Boys, 67
Hoffman, Philip Seymour, **68**
Holder, Donald, 143
Holinshed, Raphael, 48
Holliday, Jennifer, **101**
The Hot L Baltimore, 47
Hot 'n Throbbing, 70
house, 121, 196
house manager, 121
How I Learned to Drive, 70

Hudes, Quiara Alegria, 46, 174
Hughes, Doug, 58
Huntley, Paul, 152
Hwang, David Henry, 174, 177

Ibsen, Henrik, 81
ice (producing), 117
The Iceman Cometh, **61**
I'd Rather Be Right, 45
improvisation, 86
In the Heights, 46, **174**
inciting incident, 37, 196
Indecent, **70**
Indian (Hindu) theatre, 13
Indians, 175
An Inspector Calls, **146**
intensity (lighting), 144
interior set, 129
International Centre for Theatre Research, 178
interpretation (interp) rehearsals, 104, 196
Into the Woods, 66
The Invention of Love, 67
Irwin, Bill, **65**
Ishioka, Eiko, 177
Isn't It Romantic, 70
It's Alright to Be a Woman (theatre group), 175

Jitney, 69
Joe Turner's Come and Gone, 69
Johns, Glynis, **66**
Jones, Bill T., 98
Jones, Cherry, **58**
Jones, James Earl, **103**
Jones, LeRoi, 173
Judd, Ashley, **96**
Jumpers, 67
June Moon, 45
Junior Miss, 45

Kabuki theatre (Japan), 13, **14**, 32, 177-78
Kail, Thomas, 95, 174
Kanin, Garson, 46
Kathakali, 13
Kaufman, George S., 1, 17, 25, 43, 44, **45**, 59, 133, 178
Kaufman, Moisés, 126
Kazan, Elia, 35, 100, 110
Keene, Laura, 114
Kern, Jerome, 35, 61
Khan, Iqbal, 24

The King and I, 62
King Hedley II, 69, **173**
King Lear, 44
Kinky Boots, **159**, 177
Kirkland, Jack, 183
Klotz, Florence, 116
Kopit, Arthur, 175
Korins, David, 131-32
Kushner, Tony, 1, 177

La Cage aux Folles, 176
La Chiusa, Michael John, 74
Lacey, Maggie, **63**
Lady in the Dark, 45
The Lady in the Van, 67
Lansbury, Angela, **56**
The Laramie Project, **126**
Larson, Jonathan, 163
Last Dance, 69
The Late George Apley, 45
Latinx theatre, 173-74
Lawrence, Amanda, **1**
Le Gallienne, Eva, **81**, 114
League of Resident Theatres (LORT), 163-65, 166, 168, 196
Lee, Eugene, 62
Leigh, Vivien, **78**
Les Blancs, 46
Les Liaisons Dangereuses, **140**
Les Misérables, **36**, 177
Lettice and Lovage, 64
Leveaux, David, 67
librettist, 56, 196
A Lie of the Mind, 68
light cues, 145
light plot, 145, 196
Light Shining in Buckinghamshire, 67
Light Up the Sky, 45
lighting: 141-46; business of, 153-54; color of, 144-45; computerized, 151; design of, 141, 143; distribution of, 144; evaluation of, 155; function of and elements of, 142-45; history of, 142; intensity in, 144; process of, 145
limelight, 151
limited partnership agreement, 116
Lincoln Center, 165
Linden, Hal, **4**
Linney, Laura, **53**
The Lion King, **13**, **143**, 165, 178
The Little Foxes, 63

A Little Night Music, **66**
Little Shop of Horrors, 162
Living Theatre, 171
Long, William Ivey, 138, 152
The Long Christmas Ride Home, 70
Long Day's Journey into Night, 61, **75**
LORT. *See* League of Resident Theatres
The Lost Colony, 167
Lost in Yonkers, 65
Love and Information, 68
Ludlam, Charles, 176
lyricist, 56, 196

M. Butterfly, 174, **177**
Ma Rainey's Black Bottom, 68
Macbeth, 1-2, 6, **7**, 10-11, 23, **24**, 28, 29-30, 31, 32, 36, 43, 48, 54, 56-57, 59, 73, 83, 89, 99, 103, 124, 126-27, 129, 148, 150, 153-54, 158, 186, 188; dialogue in, 48-49; directorial concept for, 94-95; film and video versions of, 205-6; germinal idea for, 48; in the present tense, 7-9; original production of, 16; performance space for, 129; plot description of, 24; superstitions about, 89
MacNeil, Ian, 146
Mad Forest, 68
The Madness of George III, 67
magic if, 78
makeup, 148-50
Mackintosh, Joan, **4**
Major Barbara, 60
Mamet, David, 49, 69, 169
Man and Superman, 60
The Man Who Came to Dinner, 45
Manchester International Festival, 167
Mantello, Joe, 149
Marie Christine, 74
mask, 12-13, 196
The Master Butchers Singing Club, 69
The Matchmaker, 62
Matilda, 165
Matthau, Walter, **33**
Mattias, Sean, 99
Mayer, Michael, 98
McClinton, Marion, 173
McCook, Andrea, 140
McDonald, Audra, **74**
McGuire, Joshua, **67**
McKellen, Ian, **99**
McNally, Terrence, 184

McNeil, Claudia, **18**
melodrama, 34–35, 196
Menzel, Idina, **149**
Mercer, Randy Houston, 152
Merrily We Roll Along, 45
Merton of the Movies, 44
Method acting, 78, 196
A Midsummer Night's Dream, 44, 127, 178
Midler, Bette, 113
Mielziner, Jo, 133
Miller, Arthur, 32–33, 35, 53, 64, 100
Miller, Jonathan, 66
Miller, Lawrence, 138
mimic instinct, 74
The Mineloa Twins, 70
Miranda, Lin-Manuel, 2, **19**, **27**, 29, 38, 43, 46, 53, 56, 59, **174**
Miranda, Luis A., 46
Miss Saigon, 175, 177
Mister Roberts, 138
Mitchell, Brian Stokes, **173**
Mnouchkine, Ariane, 178
Moiseiwitsch, Tanya, 124
Moliere, 184
Monroe, Marilyn, 64
A Moon for the Misbegotten, 61
Moore, Dudley, 66
Moore, Jason, 162
Moriarty, Michael, **75**
Moscow Art Theatre, 100, 166
The Mousetrap, **117**
Mrs. Warren's Profession, 60, 184
Murray, Brian, **53**
music (Aristotle's element of), 30, 196
musical director, 106–7, 196
musicals, 35–36, 196
muslin, 130
My Fair Lady, 45
My Sister Eileen, 45

Napier, John, 11
National Theatre (Great Britain), 165
national tour, 160
Native American Ensemble Theatre, 175
Native American theatre, 175
naturalism, 98, 196
Naughton, James, 63
Neeson, Liam, **53**
Negro Ensemble Company, 173
Nemiroff, Robert, 37, 46

New York Shakespeare Festival, 167
New York Theatre Workshop, 163
Newman, Paul, **63**, 78
Nicholaw, Casey, 106
Nichols, Mike, 33
'night, Mother, 69
A Night at the Opera, 45
Night of the Iguana, 64
Nine, **138**
Noises Off, **33**
nonprofit theatre, 158, 165, 196
nontraditional casting, 103, 196
Norman, Marsha, 69, 176
Norris, Bruce, 26
North American Drama Therapy Association, 169
Nothing Sacred, 45
Nunn, Trevor, 11, 36
nut (producing), 117
Nuyorican theatre, 173

objective, 78
O'Brien, Jack, 152
O'Byrne, Brian F., **58**
The Odd Couple, **33**, 64
Odets, Clifford, 172
Oedipus the King, 32
Of Thee I Sing, 45, 59
Off Broadway, 158, 161–62, 165, 197
Off Off Broadway, 126, 162–63, 165, 197
Oklahoma!, 13, 36, 56, 62, 158
Oleanna, 69
Oliver!, 165
Olivier, Laurence, **78**, 79
Omaha Magic Theatre, 175
Once in a Lifetime, 17, 45
O'Neill, Eugene, 49, 60–61, 75, 161, 172
O'Neill, James, 60
option, 58, 115, 197
Our American Cousin, 114
Our Town, 62, **63**, 127

Pacific Overtures, 174, 178
Pacino, Al, 78
Page, Anthony, 65, 96
Pan Asian Repertory Theatre, 174
paper the house, 117
Papp, Joseph, 167
The Paradox of the Actor, 77
Parker, Mary-Louise, **29**
Parker, Trey, 106

Patric, Jason, **96**
Peking Opera (China), 177
performance art, 14, 171, 176, 197
periaktoi, 151
Perry, Antoinette, 161
perspective, 122, 197
Peter Pan, 36
The Phantom of the Opera, **31**, 150, 165, 177
The Piano Lesson, 69
Pinero, Miguel, 173
pitch, 87
play analysis, 102
play doctor, 117
play selection, 101–2
playwright, 43–71, 197; business of the, 58–60; as creator of the blueprint, 43; definition of the, 43; evaluation of the, 55–58; origin of the word, 43; process of the, 48–55
plot, 28, 53, 56–57, 197
Plummer, Amanda, **47**
pluralism, 14
Poetics, 28, 32
point of attack, 37–38, 197
Poitier, Sidney, **18**
polish rehearsal, 104
Present Laughter, 63
preview performance, 105–6, 197
Priestley, J. B., 146
Prince, Harold, 31, 56, 62, 66, 116
Prince of Players, 45
The Private Ear, 64
Private Lives, 63
producer, 113–18, 197; business of, 115–18; definition of, 113–14; overlap with director, 93; terms of, 117; women as, 114
professional theatre, 158–59
projection (acting), 87
prompt book, 102, 197
Proof, **29**
property (producing), 58, 115, 197
props (theatre properties), 148, 197
proscenium stage, 121, **122**, 197
protagonist, 32
public domain, 59, 197
The Public Eye, 64
Public Theatre (New York), 19, 167
publicist, 14, 197
Puerto Rican theatre, 173
Puerto Rican Traveling Company, 173
Pulitzer, Joseph, 59

Pulitzer Prize, 59
Pygmalion, 60

quick changes (costumes), 141

Rabb, Ellis, 25
Radcliffe, Daniel, **67**, **185**
Radio Golf, 69
Ragtime, 74
Raisin, 37
Raisin in the Sun, 1, 10–12, **18**, 19, **25**, 26, 28, 29–30, 31, 34, 36, 37–38, 43, 45, 50–51, 54, 56–57, 58, 59, 68, 74, 80–81, 89, 95, 99, 103, 126–27, 128, 129, 137–38, 148, 153–54, 158, 159, 178, 189; dialogue in, 51; directorial concept for, 95; film and video version of, 206; germinal idea for, 47–48; musical version of, 37; original production of, 18; performance space for, 129; plot description of, 25–26; scenic approach to, 128
Randall, Paulette, 68
rate (acting), 87
read-through (rehearsal), 103–4, 197
The Real Thing, 67
realism, 96–97, 197
Red Earth Theatre (Seattle), 175
The Red Shoes, 69
regional theatre, 163–65, 197
Register, Justin, **140**
rehearsal schedule, 104–5
rehearsals, 82–83, 103–5, 197
renderings, 130, 132, 139, 140, 197
Rent, **163**, 177
Repertorio Español, 173
resident theatre, 163–65, 197
resolution, 39
resonance, 87
retrace, 104, 197
review, 184–85, 188, 198
revival, 158, 198
Richard III, 44
Richards, Lloyd, 95
Ridiculous Theatrical Company, 176
Riley, John C., **68**
ritual, 9
road (touring), 160, 198
Robards, Jason, **25**, **75**
Robbins, Jerome, 100–101, 110, 128, 188
Rock 'n' Roll, 67
Rodgers, Richard, 36, 62, 174

role-playing, 73-74
romanticism, 97, 198
Romeo and Juliet, 44, **78**
Rose, George, **25**
The Rose Tattoo, **130**
Rosencrantz and Guildenstern Are Dead, **67**
Rosenthal, Jean, 128
Roundabout Theatre, 165
The Royal Family, 44
The Royal Hunt of the Sun, 64
Royal National Theatre (Great Britain), 165, 166
Royal Shakespeare Company (Great Britain), 165, 178
royalty, 59, 116, 198
run-through rehearsal, 104, 198
Ryskind, Morrie, 44

Saint Joan, 60
The Sandbox, 65
Sands, Diana, 19
Sarah and Abraham, 69
Sater, Steven, 98
satire, 34, 198
scalper, 117
scenic design, 122-34: business of, 153; evaluation of, 154; functions of, 127-29; implementation of, 134; kinds of, 127; process of, 131-34
Schumann, Peter, 178
scrim, 151
The Sea Gull, 55
The Secret Garden, 69
Serious Money, 68
set props, 148, 198
Seven Guitars, 69
Sex, 184
Sexual Perversity in Chicago, 69
Shaffer, Peter, 64-65, 185
Shakespeare, William, 1, 8, 43, **44**, 48-49, 53-54, 59, 67, 89, 97, 114, 123, 125, 131
Shanley, John Patrick, 58
Sharrock, Thea, 185
Shaw, George Bernard, 60, 67, 184
Shaw Festival (Canada), 167
Sheik, Duncan, 98
Shepard, Sam, 68
Sheridan, Richard B., 34
Shopping and Fucking, 184
Short Eyes, 173
shotgun mic, 151
Show Boat, 35, 61, **62**

showcase, 162, 198
Shubert Brothers, 113
sight lines, 121, 198
The Sign in Sidney Brustein's Window, 45
Silk Stockings, 45
Simon, Neil, 33, 34, 64-65, 128
The Sisters Rosensweig, 70
The Skin of Our Teeth, 62
Skinner, Randy, 108
The Skriker, 68
sleeper, 117
Society of Stage Directors and Choreographers (SSDC), 109
The Solid Gold Cadillac, 45
soliloquy, 12, 198
Sondheim, Stephen, 56, 65-66
Sophocles, 32
sound design, 146-48; acoustics, 146-47; amplification, 147; effects, 147-48
sound effects, 147-48
The Sound of Music, 62
South Pacific, 62, 138
Spa Theatre (Yorkshire), **122**
spectacle, 31, 198
Spelvin, George, 86
Spiderwoman Theatre, 176
spine, 78, 198
The Spitfire Grill, **2**
Split Britches (theatre group), 176
Spring Awakening, **98**
SRO. *See* standing room only
Stage Door, 44
stage manager, 107, 198
standby, 87
standing room only (SRO), 117
Stanislavsky, Konstantin, 77-79, 100, 102, 178
A Star Is Born, 45
Steel Magnolias, 162
Stewart, Patrick, **99**
Stoppard, Tom, 67
straight makeup, 149-50, 198
Strasberg, Lee, 79
Stratford Shakespeare Festival (Canada), **115**, 167
Streep, Meryl, 78
street theatre, 171, 198
A Streetcar Named Desire, 63, **79**
Strike Up the Band, 45
Stroman, Susan, **94**
style (directing), 96-99, 198
subsidiary rights, 59, 198

success d'estime, 117
Sullivan, Daniel, 29
Summer and Smoke, 63
summer stock (summer theatre), 166–67, 198
Sunday in the Park with George, 66
Sunjata, Daniel, **176**
swatch, 151
Sweeney Todd, the Demon Barber of Fleet Street, **56**, 66
Sweet Charity, 110
swing, 87
symmetrical scenery/balance, 130–31, 198
System (acting), 78, 199

Taichman, Rebecca, 70
Taisey, Kip, 2
Take Me Out, **176**
Talking Heads, 67
Talley's Folly, **4**
The Taming of the Shrew, 44
Tandy, Jessica, **47**, **79**
Tartuffe, 184
Taylor, John, 44
Taymor, Julie, 13, 143
The Teahouse of the August Moon, 174
technical director, 131, 199
technical rehearsals, 104
technical theatre terms, 150–51
The Tempest, 44
Terry, Megan, 176
theatre: ability to change, 9–10; addressed to a group mind, 15; architecture, 121–26; conventions of, 10–14; criticism of, 183, 199; definition of, 2–3; diversity of, 15, 171–77; foreign influences on, 177–79; four basic elements of, 3; as "literature for the illiterate," 6; masks and, 12–13; origins of, 9; in the present tense, 5; pluralism of, 14; spelling of, 5; vs. drama, 1–2
Theatre Communications Group (TCG), 166
Theatre Development Fund (TDF), 160
Theatre du Soleil, 178
theatre festivals, 167, 199
Theatre of Alienation, 98–99
theatre-in-the-round, 123, 199
theme, 29–30, 58, 199
thespians, 76, 199
Thespis, 76
Third, 70
This Year of Grace, 63

Three Tall Women, 65
three-quater stage, 123, **124**, 199
thrust stage, 123, **124**, 199
TKTS booth, 117, **157**, 160, 165
To Be Young, Gifted and Black, 45–46
Tobacco Road, **183**
Tom Sawyer, 169
Tonight at 8:30, 63
Tony Awards, 161
Top Girls, 68
Torch Song Trilogy, 176
Towns, Luz, 46
Toys in the Attic, 63
tragedy, 32–33, 199
tragicomedy, 32, 35, 199
trap, 151
Traveler in the Dark, 69
Travesties, 67
True West, **68**
Tune, Tommy, 138
Turner, Kathleen, **65**
turntable, 151
turkey (producing), 117
Twelfth Night, 44
21 Chump Street, 46

Uggams, Leslie, **173**
Uncommon Women and Others, 70
understudy, 87
unit set, 129, **132**, 199
United Scenic Artists (USA), 154, 199
upstage, 87
Utah Shakespeare Festival, 167

The Vagina Monologues, **175**, 176
Valdez, Luis, 173
Variety, 117
A View from the Bridge, 64
Vogel, Paula, 70, 176
voice quality, 87
The Vortex, 63

Wahl-Temple, Elaina, 2, 140
Waiting for Godot, 98, **99**
Walker, Alice, 69
Warchus, Matthew, 68
Washington, Denzel, 19, **25**
Wasserstein, Wendy, 69–70, 176
Watch on the Rhine, 63
Webber, Andrew Lloyd, 31

Wedekind, Frank, 98
well-made play, 37, 199
West, Mae, 184
West End (London), 177, 165
West Side Story, 14, 66, 100, 174, **188**
What Price Glory, 184
Wheeler, Hugh, 56
White Lies, 64
Who's Afraid of Virginia Woolf?, **65**
Wicked, **6**, 31, **149**, 150, 165
wiggle lights, 151
Wilder, Thornton, 5, 15, 62–63
Williams, Tennessee, 46–47, 63–64, 79, 96, 100, 130
Willis, Jack, **53**
Wilson, August, 49, 68–69, 172–73
Wilson, Elizabeth, **25**
Wilson, Lanford, 4, 47
Wilson, Robert, 171
wings, 151
Woldin, Judd, 37
Wolfe, George C., 61

Women's Experimental Theatre, 175–76
Woodward, Joanne, 78
Words and Music, 63
workshop, 108, 199

Yale Repertory Company, 4
Yoshitsune and the Thousand Cherry Trees, **14**
You Can't Take It with You, 1, 10–11, **17**, **25**, 28–29, 31, 34, 38–39, 43, 45, 50–51, 54, 56–57, 59, 75, 80–81, 83, 88, 99, **103**, 126–27, 129, 137, 139, 148, 150, 153–54, 158, 159, 178, 189; dialogue in, 50; directorial concept for, 95; film and video versions of, 206; original production of, 17; performance space for, 129; plot description of, 25

Zaltzberg, Charlotte, 37
Zhangazha, Ashley, **68**
Zipprodt, Patricia, 128
The Zoo Story, 65
Zoot Suit, 173

SEP 05 2019

HEWLETT-WOODMERE PUBLIC LIBRARY

3 1327 00671 5486

28 DAY LOAN
Hewlett-Woodmere Public Library
Hewlett, New York 11557

Business Phone 516-374-1967
Recorded Announcements 516-374-1667
Website www.hwpl.org